S0-BPO-753

Jewish Remnants in Spain

SIDNEY DAVID MARKMAN

Jewish Remnants in Spain
Wanderings in a Lost World

SCRIBE PUBLISHERS

Mesa, Arizona
2003

Cover figure: Seville. Torre del Oro on the left bank of Guadalquivir River with the cathedral and Giralda in the distance. Torre del Oro was one of the redoubts in the walls of fortification of the city of Seville during the Middle Ages, built by Moslems (1120). Here King Pedro el Cruel had his once trusted official, Samuel ha Levi of Toledo, tortured and put to death.

Published by Scribe Publishers

2048 S Beverly St.
Mesa, AZ 85210

Copyright © 2003 – Scribe Publishers

All rights reserved. No part of this publication may be reproduced or transmitted in any form or by any means, electronic or mechanical, including photocopy, recording, or any information storage or retrieval system, without permission in writing from the publisher, except in the case of brief quotations employed in reviews and similar critical works.

Published in the United States of America.

LaTeX technical consulting and Linux support by Sebastian J. Bronner.
Editing, book design, typesetting, and graphic art by Evelyn E. Smith.
Printing by Access Laserpress, Inc.

Publication Data

Jewish Remnants in Spain: Wanderings in a Lost World
Markman, Sidney David, 1911-
267 pages, 186 illustrations
Includes bibliographical references and index
ISBN 0-9727237-0-6
Library of Congress Control Number 2003111412

May the chapters that follow be
Kaddish
for those who died in fire and in flame for
Kiddush ha Shem

Contents

List of Figures ix

Acknowledgment xxx

Preface xxxi

1 Introduction 1

2 History: Some Reflections and Facts 5

3 Astorga 11

4 Bembibre 13

5 Zamora 17

6 Salamanca 29

7 Avila 37

8 Madrid 41

9 Segovia 47

10 Toledo 57
    Santa María La Blanca 61
    Synagogue of Nuestra Señora del Tránsito 65
    The Palace of Samuel ha Levi 73

11 Córdoba 75

12 Ecija 91

13 Carmona 95

14 Alcalá de Guadaira 101

15 Seville 109

16 Jewish Vestiges in Andalucía 139

17 Granada 143

18 Málaga 147

19 Lucena 155

20 Cáceres 159

21 Plasencia 169

22 Béjar 173

23 Burgos 179

24 Vitoria 183

25 Gerona 185

26 Barcelona 193

27 Lérida 203

28 Zaragoza 205

29 Gibraltar 213

Books for Further Reading 223

List of Figures

1.1   Map of Spain. Jewish places described in the text. xxxii

3.1   Astorga. Calle de Matías Rodríguez. Formerly known as Calle del Arco and site of judería. 10

3.2   Astorga. Roman wall at edge of city enclosing former Jewish cemetery, known until recently as Paseo de la Sinagoga. 10

4.1   Bembibre. Church of San Pedro. East end and south side. 12

4.2   Bembibre. Church of San Pedro, formerly a synagogue. West front. 14

4.3   Bembibre. Street leading away from plaza and synagogue-church of San Pedro. Probably part of judería on former outskirts near river. Main part of city lies beyond. 15

5.1   Zamora. Map showing location of three juderías and their synagogues. 17

5.2   Zamora. Calle de Ignacio Gazapo, formerly Plaza de la Judería. Full of houses, this area had been center of judería. The houses were torn down mid-twentieth century to provide access for automobile road now skirting the Duero, thereby opening up a view of medieval bridge over river. 18

5.3   Zamora. House No. 5, Calle de Ignacio Gazapo, formerly known as Plaza de la Judería. This building is on site of synagogue of local judería and is occupied by automobile repair shop. 19

5.4   Zamora. *Calle de los Baños* (Baths Street). View from Calle de Ignacio Gazapo rising to north away from riverbank and Plaza de la Judería. This street was possibly part of judería near river. 20

5.5   Zamora. *Calle de la Manteca* (Lard Street). View to south from Plaza Santa Lucía toward Calle de Ignacio Gazapo and riverbank where main part of judería had once been located. This street was also within perimeter of judería. 21

5.6   Zamora. View of Calle de Cipriano, from Plaza de Santa Lucía, remains of medieval city wall to left or south. Judería located on lower ground near river, may have extended uphill as far as Plaza Santa Lucía, but not beyond or inside city wall on Calle de Cipriano, which continues uphill to city center.   22

5.7   Zamora. The corner intersection of Calle de Ramos Carrión and Calle de Moreno. Doorway to building where men are standing is all that remains of synagogue of second judería of Zamora. Building is now used as warehouse for newsprint and other paper products. This section of street, Calle de Moreno, extremely narrow but widens just beyond building. Narrow bottleneck of Calle de Moreno may be site of gate to judería.   23

5.8   Zamora. Calle de la Vega, location of third judería of Zamora on northern outskirts of city. East wall of synagogue is preserved and appears at corner of second house from right with hooded chimney on roof directly above it. Synagogue building suffered many changes and alterations when converted to church, later used as private dwelling.   24

5.9   Zamora. Remains of Roman wall of fortification opposite former synagogue of judería La Vega.   25

5.10   Zamora. Remains of Roman wall of fortification and medieval castle to south and high above Calle de La Vega and judería.   26

5.11   Zamora. Narrow passageway leading from Calle de La Vega and judería to gate and redoubt in Roman walls.   27

5.12   Zamora. Remains of east wall of former Synagogue of La Vega. .   27

5.13   Zamora. North wall of ruined Synagogue of La Vega.   27

6.1   Salamanca. Map of judería.   28

6.2   Salamanca. Roman bridge over Tormes River. Judería located near entrance to bridge along riverbank, also extended to higher ground on bluff above.   29

6.3   Salamanca. La Gota de Leche building on Plaza de La Merced on site of synagogue.   30

6.4   Salamanca. Tower and dome of cathedral from Plaza de La Merced in judería at intersection of Calle de Moneda on left.   31

6.5   Salamanca. Calle de la Vera Cruz. Principal street of medieval judería from intersection of Calle Libreros toward east. Calle de Tentenecio in background.   32

6.6   Salamanca. East of Calle Libreros from Calle de la Vera Cruz to dome of Church of La Clerecía, Jesuit seminary church, in background. Second synagogue in vicinity of intersection.   32

6.7   Salamanca. Calle de Tentenecio at foot of principal street of medieval judería, Calle de la Vera Cruz, near cathedral tower. Street probably one of entrances to judería.   33

6.8   Salamanca. View to north of Calle de Tentenecio from below near riverbank; Calle de Ribera del Puente, toward Calle de la Vera Cruz, the principal street of judería. Dome of cathedral dominates background.   33

6.9   Salamanca. Ancient Roman bridge over Tormes River from Plaza del Río in medieval judería on riverbank lower down slope from Ribera del Puente.   34

6.10 Salamanca. Mill just east of Plaza del Río in lower section of medieval judería.   35

7.1   Avila. Calle de Esteban Domingo located in northeast part of town, probably street in medieval judería.   37

7.2   Avila. Calle de López Núñez, Puerta de San Vicente, medieval wall fortification, possible entrance judería.   38

8.1   Madrid. Map showing medieval judería.   40

8.2   Madrid. Calle de la Fe, formerly known as Calle de la Sinagoga, possibly main street of judería. View from higher ground in front of Church of San Lorenzo at corner of Calle de Baltasar Bachero looking down to Plaza Lavapies.   41

8.3   Madrid. Calle de la Fe, formerly Calle de la Sinagoga and possibly main street of judería. View from midway down street at intersection of Calle de Zurita, looking toward Church of San Lorenzo on higher ground.   42

8.4   Madrid. The corner of Calle de Argumosa and Calle de Dr. Fourquet, former site of Jewish cemetery, located downhill in southeasterly direction from Calle de la Fe, probably outside walls of judería. Cemetery now occupied by four-story garage.   43

8.5   Madrid. Plaza Mayor. Northwest angle. Place where Inquisition executed sentences of the condemned, usually through *auto da fe*. Spectators watched from many windows in buildings surrounding plaza.   44

8.6   Madrid. Plaza Mayor. North side with Casa de la Panadería. Windows in this section best for viewing spectacles of *autos da fe*. . . .   45

9.1   Segovia. Map of judería.   48

9.2   Segovia. Portal to courtyard of Church of Corpus Christi, formerly synagogue. Gothic arch over entrance probably contemporary with date of synagogue, wall itself subject to alterations and repairs. Located on busy street, not far from main plaza.   50

9.3   Segovia. Entrance to synagogue-church of Corpus Christi. Door located on right side of court as one enters from street, at far end of building. Nave extends to left. Horseshoe-shaped arch spans door. Above, under eaves, a two-bay window also spanned by two horseshoe-shaped arches. Wall with door and twin-arched window repaired in 1902, indicated on inscription to right at bottom of lunette just above door.   50

9.4   Segovia. Plan of synagogue-church of Corpus Christi. Building suffered severe damage in fire (1899). All interior decoration in modeled plaster as well as all Hebrew inscription lost. Only its plan could be restored to original state.   51

9.5   Segovia. Synagogue-church of Corpus Christi. Prayer hall toward East Wall oriented toward Jerusalem. Where Ark of Torah had been located now occupied by main altar of church. Chancel arch is horseshoe shaped as are arches of nave arcades, windows in clerestory to either side of nave, except the five windows at far end. Wall surfaces before fire decorated with designs in modeled plaster and Hebrew inscriptions comparable to those of synagogue-church of El Tránsito in Toledo.   52

9.6   Segovia. Synagogue-church of Corpus Christi. Detail showing nave arcade and clerestory. Each bay spanned by horseshoe-shaped arch of mudéjar style, comparable to arches of nave arcade in synagogue-church of Santa María La Blanca in Toledo.   52

9.7   Segovia. Calle de la Judería Vieja. Synagogue-church of Corpus Christi is located at place where Calle de Juan Bravo changes in name to Calle de la Judería Vieja. Street is irregular and narrow. Houses, modern now, stand on same sites as were occupied by medieval Jewish community.   54

9.8   Segovia. Calle de la Judería Nueva. View from intersection of Calle de los Leones west and Calle de Almuzara. Street center of second or new Jewish quarter and center of area into which Jews were confined after 1412. It descends sharply and borders right side of Plaza de La Merced where Synagogue of Judería Nueva stood.   .   54

9.9   Segovia. Calle de Almuzara, view to northeast. This street is a continuation of Calle de la Judería Vieja. In 1412 another synagogue, located somewhere on Calle de Almuzara, turned over to monastic order of La Merced for use as hospital. High stone wall in background encloses Plaza de La Merced on higher ground where synagogue-hospital once stood.   55

9.10   Segovia. Calle de Almuzara. View southeast with cathedral in background dominating Judería Nueva. Plaza de La Merced to left, behind high retaining wall. Calle de la Judería Nueva intersects at corner. High wall right encloses private houses built on highest section of precipice above Clamores River. On Opposite bank, Cuesta de los Hoyos, Jewish burial ground, location of Jewish refuge when Decree of Expulsion reached Segovia in 1492.   55

10.1   Toledo. Map of judería. Key: 1. Sta. María La Blanca, 2. El Tránsito, 3. Palace of Samuel ha Levi, 4. San Juan de los Reyes . .   58

10.2   Toledo. Main door of Synagogue of Santa María La Blanca. Door has been reconstructed, not preserving original form. Originally, probably spanned with horseshoe-shaped arch similar to Synagogue of Corpus Christi in Segovia. Doorjambs finished with smoothly trowelled white plaster, which must be whitewashed from time to time to cover graffiti inscribed by Jewish visitors.   62

10.3   Toledo. Synagogue of Santa María La Blanca. The central aisle looking toward door. Horseshoe-shaped arches span space between columns. Intricate designs in modeled and carved plaster decorate spandrels (space between arches) and lower section of clerestory wall. Blind arcade of clerestory above probably bricked up after synagogue converted to church. Main door transformed at some unknown date. Not original are door and square window immediately above it as well as pair of windows higher up and the circular window in gable.   62

10.4   Toledo. Plan of synagogue of Santa María La Blanca. This building subjected to radical alterations when converted to church. Neither two short walls nor two long walls parallel to each other. Except for southwest corner where facade and south long wall meet, walls do not meet at right angles. Building divided into five aisles by four rows of seven octagonal columns, except for extreme right-hand row of only six. Seventh column replaced by spur wall that projects from rear cross wall.   63

10.5   Toledo. Synagogue of Santa María La Blanca. Column capital. This capital in mudéjar style of Islamic inspiration and derived from much older Byzantine prototypes. Note profusion of scrolls and interlace of delicately carved bands or ribbons defining space occupied by each scroll.   64

10.6   Toledo. Synagogue of El Tránsito. Main door, located at end of one of long side walls, does not preserve original form and seems out of place when compared to double window opening of mudéjar style above. Two pointed horseshoe-shaped arches share short column in center. Arches enclosed within frame called *alfiz*, mudéjar in style. Main door probably spanned by similar arch. Note masonry, also typical mudéjar. Wall laid up with courses of rough undressed stones of varying sizes separated at intervals by leveling courses of brick. Brickwork of door opening recent construction, different in character from adjoining section of original wall.   65

10.7   Toledo. Synagogue of El Tránsito. Exterior view of clerestory that lights prayer hall inside. Clerestory is above roof of women's gallery that projects along this side of prayer hall. Note mudéjar type of masonry walling of women's gallery and also cornice, a brick corbel table with closely set brackets, under eaves of roof above clerestory.   66

10.8   Toledo. Plan of the Synagogue of El Tránsito. Main prayer hall flanked by section with entrance vestibule and other rooms above which is women's gallery. Rooms on other side, now housing gift shop and museum, probably not part of original construction but added when synagogue converted to church.   67

10.9   Toledo. Synagogue of El Tránsito. Interior, East Wall. Space divided into three panels decorated with intricate overall patterns or arabesques. Effect like that of oriental rugs or tapestries hung on walls. At bottom and center of each of side panels is a tablet with inscription in Hebrew six lines long, forming a single text of twelve lines between two tablets. Inscriptions give details of synagogue furnishings and mention that Samuel ha Levi built it.   68

10.10 Toledo. Synagogue of El Tránsito. East Wall, left-hand panel. Inscription below panel proper also has one in Hebrew, from Book of Psalms. In worse repair than that in right-hand panel.   70

10.11 Toledo. Synagogue of El Tránsito. East wall, right-hand panel. Moldings around panel decorated with Hebrew inscriptions. In bad state of repair, some of text obliterated, large inscription below panel taken from Book of Psalms.   70

10.12 Toledo. Synagogue of El Tránsito. East wall, right-hand panel. Detail of Hebrew inscription below panel containing texts from Book of Psalms interspersed with references praising Samuel ha Levi and King Pedro el Cruel as protectors of Israel.   70

10.13 Toledo. Synagogue of El Tránsito. Clerestory windows north side of prayer hall. Arcade has lobulated pointed arches. Alternate bays of arcade blind. Each open window has delicate lace-like grill, no two alike. Intricate vine with leaves and interspersed blazons entwined on broad continuous band below clerestory. Horizontal moldings above/ below clerestory arcade decorated with Hebrew inscriptions taken from the Psalms.   71

10.14 Toledo. Synagogue of El Tránsito. Interior, West Wall. Three windows lower part of wall. Middle largest with lobulated pointed arch. Other two have simple semicircular arches. All three arches framed by panel, each filled with delicate lace-like grill. Four windows in clerestory above, spanned by lobulated, pointed, horseshoe-shaped arches filled with grills.   71

10.15 Toledo. Synagogue of El Tránsito. Capital from supporting pier in women's gallery. Design worked in carved plaster. Horizontal band above capital has moldings above and below, decorated with Hebrew inscriptions. Medallion immediately above capital has Arabic inscription.   72

10.16 Toledo. The street between Synagogue of El Tránsito on left and palace of Samuel ha Levi on right. In seventeenth century, palace home of renowned Spanish painter of Greek origin, El Greco. . . .   73

10.17 Toledo. Palace of Samuel ha Levi, House of El Greco. Door leading to patio has carved plastic decoration around top in style of carving inside synagogue.   73

11.1   Córdoba. Map of judería.   76

11.2   Córdoba. Puerta del Almodóvar. Gate in ancient city wall giving direct access to judería had been known in Arabic as *Bab al Yahud*, in Spanish as *Puerta de los Judíos*.   79

11.3   Córdoba. Calle de Maimonides, formerly called Calle de Judíos. View to south from intersection of Calle de Fernández Ruano. . .   80

11.4   Córdoba. Calle de Maimonides. East Wall of synagogue on right. Too narrow for automobiles, street displays channels gouged out of house walls to accommodate hubs of wheels of horse-drawn carriages.   80

11.5   Córdoba. Plazuela de Maimonides. Prior to commemoration of eight-hundredth anniversary of death of Maimonides, plaza called Plazas de las Bulas. Site of building of large synagogue in thirteenth century. A Papal Bull issued in 1250 halted construction, thus providing original name, Plaza of the Papal Bulls.   81

11.6   Córdoba. Synagogue patio. Memorial plaque to Maimonides, native son of Córdoba, commemorates eight-hundredth anniversary his death.   83

11.7   Córdoba. Synagogue. Old man in synagogue door with cane in hand awaits visitors to relate history of synagogue.   84

11.8   Córdoba. Synagogue. "This is the Synagogue of Córdoba, the church of the Jews...."   84

11.9   Córdoba. Plan of synagogue. An extremely small building, the prayer hall measures approximately twenty-two by twenty-one feet. Women's gallery directly above vestibule.   85

11.10   Córdoba. Synagogue. Interior, NE corner. Decoration in carved plates executed with arabesques/repeated geometric designs on individual panels. Similar to textile wall hangings.   86

11.11   Córdoba. Synagogue. Niche for Ark of Torah on East Wall. Upper portion over niche extant. Mudéjar style, framed within alfíz covered with carved plaster decoration. Hebrew inscriptions almost obliterated.   86

11.12   Córdoba. Synagogue. Women's gallery. Wall once covered with carved plaster.   86

11.13   Córdoba. Synagogue. East Wall, right-hand panel with Hebrew inscription below, stating that synagogue was built by Isaac Makeb in 1314/1315. "Arise, O Lord, hasten to rebuild Jerusalem."   87

11.14   Córdoba. Synagogue. East Wall, right-hand panel. Overall geometric pattern carved plaster. Pattern simulates that of mudéjar carpentry *alfarje* (wood-paneled ceiling) with carefully joined moldings creating overall geometric pattern. Dedicatory inscription below panel.   88

11.15   Córdoba. Synagogue. Niche center panel of west wall opposite niche for Ark of Torah. Niche spanned by lobulated, pointed arch inset in elongated alfíz, surface covered with interlace of repeated pointed arches containing interior designs. Moldings once decorated with Hebrew inscriptions.   88

12.1   Ecija. Tower, Church of San Juan. Medieval judería possibly located in vicinity. Destroyed during race riots (1391), four hundred years before Church of San Juan with tower was built in eighteenth century.   91

12.2   Ecija. Calle de Garcilópez, probable location of obliterated judería.   93

12.3   Ecija. Calle de Garcilópez and intersection of Calle de Estudio, probable part of judería before destruction of 1391.   93

13.1   Carmona. View to plain, to east from Alcazar, the ruined Arab fortress.   95

13.2   Carmona. Puerta de Sevilla, main gate in wall of fortification. Romans built first city wall, later Arabs strengthened it. Semicircular horseshoe-shaped arch spans opening. Ancient judería located inside wall at short distance to left of gate.   96

13.3   Carmona. The west end of Church of San Blas, formerly Synagogue of Carmona. Belfry rising from ridge of roof is from eighteenth century.   97

13.4   Carmona. Synagogue-church of San Blas. Main door, eighteenth-century date, located on south side of building near western end. .   98

13.5   Carmona. Synagogue-church of San Blas. Main door, north side of building, only remnant of synagogue. Located above Calle de San Blas, accessible through second story of house in street below abutting foundation of church above. Door original construction of synagogue 13th/14th centuries.   98

13.6   Carmona. Calle de San Blas, principal street of judería. View to west, section of ancient city wall of fortification with houses abutting. Former synagogue, now Church of San Blas, towers above street to left out of picture.   99

14.1   Alcalá de Guadaira. View to south of Barrio de San Miguel, former judería, from plaza before main entrance to Alcazar. Synagogue, converted to Church of San Miguel, top left of photograph. Olive grove just beyond judería, wheat fields in distance.   102

14.2   Alcalá de Guadaira. View of northern side of *Alcazar* (Arab fortress) on western edge of site as seen from Seville road. Ancient judería lies on sloping ground outside fortress on other side.   103

14.3   Alcalá de Guadaira. Alcazar from south. Barrio de San Miguel, former pre-1392 judería, nestles up against wall between two enormous redoubts.   104

14.4   Alcalá de Guadaira. West front of synagogue-church of San Miguel, principal street in barrio of same name.   105

14.5　Alcalá de Guadaira. Main door of synagogue-church of San Miguel, converted to church after 1391, ceased to function as church at later date. Building restored and converted (ca. 1957) to elementary school for children in neighborhood. 105

14.6　Alcalá de Gua-daira. Puerta Almohade in outer ring of walls of Alcazar, one of entrances from city to judería, which lay west. . . . 106

14.7　Alcalá de Gua-daira. View to east from inside Puerta Almohade. Ancient Roman bridge spanning Guadaira River to right in distance. 106

14.8　Alcalá de Guadaira. Father and son, residents of Barrio of San Miguel. *"¡Ríete, Currito!"* (Smile, little Curro!) 107

14.9　Alcalá de Guadaira. View to east of city from Plaza del Aguila on summit of hill where Alcazar located. Ancient judería, present Barrio de San Miguel, on slope to west. 108

14.10　Alcalá de Guadaira. View from Plaza del Aguila to west of Barrio of San Miguel, built up against walls of Alcazar. Olive groves and wheat fields in distance. 108

15.1　Seville. Map of Barrio de Santa Cruz, location of judería. 110

15.2　Seville. View to southeast of Barrio de Santa Cruz, former judería, from campanile of Giralda. Modern, long after Jews no longer resident, aesthetic ensemble of whitewashed walls, red-tiled roofs, and greenery of patios. Ancient layout of streets, dating from Moslem (Arab) period of Spanish history. 112

15.3　Seville. Plaza del Triunfo at rear of cathedral. Entrance gate in Alcazar wall to left opens on large rectangular courtyard, Patio de las Banderas. At opposite end, covered passageway leads to Calle de la Judería. 113

15.4　Seville. View of Patio de las Banderas from Calle de la Judería looking back to Alcazar walls, Plaza del Triunfo, and Giralda of cathedral. Giralda, cathedral tower, looms above Alcazar walls. Topmost stories above main shaft of Giralda added in seventeenth century long after Jewish community of Seville extinguished, true, also, of present Gothic cathedral, largely of fifteenth and sixteenth century date. Original cathedral dating from Moorish times, replaced mosque that had been converted to Christian use after Reconquest in 1253. 114

15.5　Seville. Entrance passageway of Calle de la Judería from Patio de las Banderas. Entrance street cuts through walls of Alcazar. 115

15.6 Seville. Calle de la Judería. View to arched entrance passageway leading back to Patio de las Banderas. Alcazar walls of fortification and redoubt rise high above street. Calle de la Judería runs under private residence abutting against wall, continues through redoubt. 115

15.7 Seville. Calle de la Vida in judería. View from Plazuela de la Vida toward Plaza de la Doña Elvira. Old man and his cat walk slowly up street. 116

15.8 Seville. Plazuela de la Vida from intersection of Callejón del Agua. Redoubt in Alcazar wall through which Calle de la Judería cuts in background. Wall with arched opening on opposite side of street leads back to Calle de la Judería. 117

15.9 Seville. Callejón del Agua from corner of Calle de la Pimienta. Street marks southern boundary of medieval judería. City wall to right. 117

15.10 Seville. Calle de Santa María La Blanca, formerly principal street in medieval judería. It continues to city gate now known as Puerta de la Carne, formerly Puerta de la Judería. Main facade of Church of Santa María la Blanca with pointed arch on left. Church converted from synagogue after 1391. Jewish cemetery lay outside Puerta de la Judería, no trace visible, area has been developed. 118

15.11 Seville. The Giralda from Calle de Mateos Gago one of boundaries of judería, reduced in size after 1391. Giralda continued to dominate reduced judería although not as tall as now. Arcaded section on top crowned with weather vane, *giralda*, added in seventeenth century. 118

15.12 Seville. Plaza de los Curtidores (Plaza of the Tanners) in former judería. Tower of Church of San Bartolomé in background occupies site of one of three synagogues left standing after riots of 1391. . . . 119

15.13 Seville. Calle de Santa Marta opening from foot of Calle de Mateos Gago near Plaza de la Virgen de los Reyes at apsidal end of cathedral. Tiny passageway leads to Plazuela de Santa Marta. 120

15.14 Seville. Calle de los Levies. View at intersection of Calle de San José, continuation in northerly direction of Calle de Santa María La Blanca. Street bears name of prominent Jewish family who lived there before destruction of judería. 121

15.15 Seville. Calle de San José. View from intersection with Calle del Conde de Ibarra. Convent of Las Dominicans across street probably site of synagogue. 122

15.16 Seville. Calle de la Pimienta from Callejón del Agua. Street in heart of judería where Jewish spice merchants lived. 124

15.17 Seville. Calle de Susona, known popularly as Calle de la Muerte, runs parallel to Calle de la Pimienta. Susona family lived here as marranos. Daughter unwittingly revealed secret to Christian lover; as consequence, father burned at stake. Daughter converted to Christianity, entered nunnery. Years later, she repented betrayal, requested that after death her corpse be hung in front of house where she and family once lived. 124

15.18 Seville. Church of Los Venerables Sacerdotes. Painting with Hebrew inscription over door leads from patio into church. Painting by baroque Spanish painter, Valdés Leal, from early eighteenth century. Letters of ineffable name of *Yaveh* (God) incorrectly written. 125

15.19 Seville. Plaza de la Santa Cruz, site of one important synagogue of pre-1391 judería, originally a mosque assigned by Fernando III to Jewish community (ca. 1248). 126

15.20 Seville. Plaza de la Santa Cruz, site of synagogue-church of Santa Cruz after anti-Jewish riots (1391). Spanish painter, Murillo, a native of Seville, buried in church as noted on commemorative plaque affixed (1858) to building fronting plaza. Synagogue-church with remains of Murillo destroyed during Napoleonic invasion of Spain, early nineteenth century. 127

15.21 Seville. Church of Santa María La Blanca, former synagogue. Church extensively remodeled in seventeenth and eighteenth centuries; original main portal with pointed arch remains. 129

15.22 Seville. Santa María La Blanca. West facade with main portal and southwest corner on Calle de Archeros. Low pointed arch with saw tooth molding typically mudéjar style, probably constructed after building, former mosque, given to Jewish community by Fernando III (1248). Upper parts of facade rebuilt during seventeenth and eighteenth centuries. 129

15.23 Seville. Santa María La Blanca. Side door on Calle de Archeros now bricked up. Columns flanking doorway possibly Visigothic in origin and date before Arab conquest of eighth century. Arab architects often employed used materials from older non-Moslem buildings in construction of mosques. 130

15.24 Seville. Santa María La Blanca. View toward main altar. Interior completely altered in seventeenth and eighteenth centuries, baroque in style. Nothing of medieval Jewish or earlier Moslem origin remains. 130

15.25 Seville. Calle de Verde from corner of Calle de Archeros up the
     street from Santa María La Blanca. Once a typical Jewish street
     near principal synagogue. Because of narrowness, sun rarely reaches
     down to street level except in midsummer. 131

15.26 Seville. Calle de la Virgen de la Alegría from Calle de San Clemente.
     Once in heart of judería, end of street one side of the Church of San
     Bartolomé, site of another important pre-1391 synagogue. 131

15.27 Seville. Main facade of Church of San Bartolomé, which is on site
     of synagogue dating before widespread attacks on Jewish communi-
     ties in 1391. 132

15.28 Seville. Calle de los Levies, small section of street up from Calle de
     San José. Street named for prominent Jewish family that lived there
     before 1391. Street twists and turns, forming a dogleg shape. 133

15.29 Seville. Plaza de Santa Marta on a Sunday morning with stamp
     market in operation. A little plaza, part of post-1391 judería, entered
     from near the foot of Calle de Mateos Gago. 134

15.30 Seville. Torre del Oro on left bank of Guadalquivir River with
     cathedral and Giralda in distance. Torre del Oro one of redoubts
     in walls of fortification of city of Seville during Middle Ages, built
     by Moslems (1120). Here King Pedro el Cruel had his once trusted
     official, Samuel ha Levi of Toledo, tortured and put to death. . . . 135

15.31 Seville. Callejón de la Inquisición, right bank, Guadalquivir River
     in Barrio de Triana. Modern door with iron gate approached by
     short flight of steps. Inquisition inaugurated in Seville (1480). Place
     of judgment/execution probably located here, name *Inquisición* pre-
     served in local toponymy. 136

15.32 Seville. Callejón de la Inquisición. Iron gate in door looks down
     Callejón de la Inquisición. Office of Inquisición probably stood on
     site of private buildings that flank narrow alley, ending on bank of
     river. Dam upstream from Seville cut off Guadalquivir; no water
     fills this narrow alley except when sluice gates open. 137

16.1 Cazalla de la Sierra. Calle de la Virgen del Monte. According to
     informant, until first part of twentieth century this narrow street
     known as Calle de la Judería. Jewish community of Cazalla de la
     Sierra destroyed (1391); its existence lives on in folk memory of
     inhabitants. 140

17.1 Granada. Winter's day in Granada with a view of Acera del Darro. Darro River, once running through this part of town open to sky, now channeled underground. Although no certain evidence exists, the judería possibly located in vicinity of river on medieval outskirts of city. Sierra Nevada hidden behind clouds in distance. 142

18.1 Málaga. Paseo de Reding with Alcazaba in distance. Judería located to right of low stone wall. Area, occupied by Paseo de Reding, nonexistent in medieval times. Part of ancient harbor filled in, creating a new shoreline in twentieth century. Medieval judería possibly located near shore of Mediterranean before configuration of harbor of Málaga altered. 148

18.2 Málaga. Plaza at foot of Subida de la Coracha. Synagogue possibly located on this little plaza, center shaded by wide-branching tree. Paseo de Reding and Plaza de Toros in distance to right. Narrow and steep little street, Callejón de Aragoncillo opens just to left of parked motorbike behind tree. Possibly one entrance to medieval judería. 150

18.3 Málaga. Callejón de Aragoncillo. Narrow bottleneck entrance to street from little plaza behind low stone wall on Paseo de Reding. Narrow sloping passageway laid out with broad steps or short terraces hemmed in between two houses. 151

18.4 Málaga. Callejón de Aragoncillo, possibly part of medieval judería. View from top of bottleneck entrance. Street widens here, paved with pebbles in ancient traditional manner. 151

18.5 Málaga. Subida de la Coracha looking back to little tree-shaded plaza at foot of hill bordering Paseo de Reding. Street possibly part of medieval judería with houses huddled against steep slope of mountain surmounted on summit by Alcazaba at one end and Gibralfaro at other. 152

18.6 Málaga. View from Gibralfaro toward Alcazaba. Walls and ruins of Alcazaba at top of picture. Subida de la Coracha at left. Jewish cemetery located somewhere on slope in area between Alcazaba and Gibralfaro, probably near/in wooded area at bottom of slope. 152

18.7 Málaga. Harbor view from Gibralfaro. Judería at mountain foot to left, out of picture. 153

19.1 Lucena. Plaza with Castillo. Relatively new part of town, dating from long after demise of Jewish community, in 1146. 154

19.2   Lucena. Calle de Jalmín. Typical street in medieval section of town. Whole of town unlike medieval towns of Christian Spain, more in character with Arab towns in Near East/North Africa. . .   156

19.3   Lucena. Calle de Zamora, typical street in medieval section of town. Street plan most irregular, more difficult to find one's way than in majority of medieval towns of northern Europe. Note traditional pebble paving of street.   156

19.4   Lucena. José Burgeño, a potter. Water jug, which he holds, made of porous clay that allows water to seep slowly to outer surface, allowing pot to sweat, thereby cooling water inside. Traditional shape of water jug—a double-handled amphora—harks back to Roman and Moslem eras.   158

20.1   Cáceres. Plan of Church of Espíritu Santo, formerly a synagogue. Building almost square in plan. Roof supported by two rows of columns supporting pointed arches, one horseshoe shaped. Porch and polygonal apse added when synagogue converted to church, probably after 1391.   162

20.2   Cáceres. Church of Espíritu Santo. Porch or portico on south side later style than interior and probably added when converted to church from synagogue. Section to right with roof higher than main body of building forms apse that houses main altar of church, also added after conversion.   164

20.3   Cáceres. Typical house of Barrio of Espíritu Santo, in proximity to Church of Espíritu Santo. No telltale vestiges exist in barrio to indicate characteristics of judería before extinction and conversion of synagogue.   164

20.4   Cáceres. Church of Espírtu Santo. Interior, north side aisle toward west. Side aisle arches lower in conformity with slope of pitched roof. Low or squat, side aisle arch mudéjar version of pointed arch, tending more to horizontal than vertical as in normal Gothic pointed arch.   166

20.5   Cáceres. Church of Espíritu Santo. Interior, view to west. Door to prayer hall on left. Roof supported on two arcades of three pointed arches. Center arches higher than other two in each arcade, horseshoe shaped as well. Each arcade contains four columns with chamfered corners. Only center columns freestanding. Those at end of arcades embedded into walls. Middle arches higher in conformity with slope of pitched roof. Reader's table probably located in middle bay with higher pointed, horseshoe-shaped columns. In style, arches and piers typically mudéjar may date from fourteenth century. 166

20.6   Cáceres. Church of Espíritu Santo. Apse at east end, added after synagogue converted to church. Neighborhood houses appear on right. 167

20.7   Cáceres. Church of Espíritu Santo. West end of building, altered after conversion. 167

21.1   Plasencia. Plazuela de Santa Isabel. View to north from Calle de Santa Isabel. Synagogue, once located on little plaza in heart of medieval judería, converted to church under advocation of Santa Isabel in honor of Queen after Expulsion. Synagogue-church no longer exists; plaza now surrounded by private homes. 169

21.2   Plasencia. Calle de Santa Isabel from Plazuela de Santa Isabel. View downhill to west. One block long and so narrow that sun reaches street level only at midday, this street principal/only one of medieval judería. 170

21.3   Plasencia. Calle de Santa Isabel. View uphill to Plazuela de Santa Isabel to east. Lower sections of walls on left, with semicircular arched openings, contemporary with time of judería. Upper sections house walls recent construction. 170

22.1   Béjar. Calle del 29 de Agosto, formerly Calle de la Antigua and main street of medieval judería. Three houses on left, Nos. 3, 5, and 7, once synagogue. Cantilevered balcony of house in center, No. 5, torn down mid-twentieth century. Main entrance to synagogue, in this section of building, also dismantled. Original interior obliterated during alterations. 172

22.2 Béjar. Calle del 29 de Agosto. Two women stand before destroyed section of medieval synagogue. Young woman with child in her arms related how her carpenter brother remodeled section of synagogue as a home for her and her family in late 1950s. One section of balcony, house No. 7, appears in photograph. Addition to house built on to projecting balcony, at some unknown date, obliterates medieval portions upper story section of synagogue. 172

22.3 Béjar. Calle del 29 de Agosto. Street paving in bad state of repair, similar to condition of most houses in poor neighborhood. House No. 5, with roughly stuccoed front, once midsection of synagogue where main door located. 174

22.4 Béjar. Calle del 29 de Agosto. View to east. Remains of front wall of medieval synagogue, now houses Nos. 3, 5, and 7. House No. 7 supported on the balcony by extension. House No. 5 remodeled, balcony and main door to synagogue destroyed. Last house, No. 3, preserves balcony in original form. 175

22.5 Béjar. Calle del 29 de Agosto. Pebble pavement, laid down hundreds of years ago, in bad state of repair. House fronts, shabby and nondescript, repaired countless times so that patches have been patched. Children, many fair haired, play and run up and down street seeking warmth of sunny side. 175

22.6 Béjar. Calle del 29 de Agosto. Cantilevered beam ends of balcony still extant on house No. 3. Three rows of wooden beams, cantilevered out one above other, support floor of balcony. Balcony once ran across front of synagogue, now divided into three houses, Nos. 3, 5, and 7. Ends of beams decorated with carved designs, some interpreted as rams' heads. Forty beam ends still preserved on two extant sections of balcony. 176

23.1 Burgos. Gate of San Martín with horseshoe-shaped arch of tenth-century date in city wall on western edge of city. Post-1391 judería, including synagogue, in immediate vicinity of gate. No vestige remains. 178

23.2 Burgos. Gate of San Martín. View of west side of gate from outside with circular redoubt, one of many in wall. Synagogue of post-1391 judería just inside gate. 178

23.3 Burgos. City wall with redoubts descends down slope and turns corner to left. It continues in easterly direction along Paseo de los Cubos. Post-1391 judería confined to area just behind part of city wall of fortification. 179

23.4   Burgos. Calle de Santa Agueda to east. Post-1391 judería, occupied by *new Christians* (forcibly converted Jews) on street just inside city walls. Ruined stone wall on left probably contemporary with judería and originally part of Jewish new Christian houses.   180

23.5   Burgos. Calle de Santa Agueda to west. Location of post-1391 judería. Before 1391 massacres, judería located farther up slope of hill to right on summit where ruins of castle of El Cid was discovered. 180

25.1   Gerona. View of medieval part of city along Onyar River. Main street of medieval judería, Calle de la Forza, short distance from river running parallel to it. One spire of cathedral surges above roofs of multi-storied houses. In museum or treasure room of cathedral cloister, some Hebrew inscriptions from synagogue and Jewish cemetery of Gerona found. Medieval judería literally in shadow of cathedral extending in southerly direction, marked on map in *Guide Michelin* as *Ciudad Antigua.*   184

25.2   Gerona. Calle de la Forza, view to south from plaza in front of cathedral. Principal street of medieval judería. Extremely narrow, street prohibits vehicular traffic except for motor bikes that youth of town race up and down. Noise amplified by many decibels as sounds echo and re-echo from walls of many storied tenements to either side.   186

25.3   Gerona. Calle de la Forza, view to north near intersection of Calle de Cervantes. Jewish assembly or meeting hall probably located in open area in foreground.   186

25.4   Gerona. Calle de Cervantes, view to east from Calle de la Forza. Street at southern end of Calle de la Forza, paved with stairway as it ascends hill to main area of former judería. Left turn at top of stairs leads into Calle de Cervantes and then to Travesía de Cervantes, formerly Calle de la Sinagoga.   187

25.5   Gerona. Calle de Cervantes, view to south. Very irregular street with many zigzags once center of judería on slope above Calle de la Forza. Buildings quite medieval in character; massive stone walls pierced by few doors/windows facing street, undoubtedly a means of defense.   187

25.6   Gerona. Calle de Cúndaro, view to east from Calle de la Forza. Street no more than narrow passageway between buildings at either side. It ascends, opening at top on diminutive plaza in vicinity where synagogue stood.   189

25.7　Gerona. *Travesía de Cervantes* (Passageway of Cervantes), view to east from head of Calle de Cúndaro. Little street, really passageway, once known as Calle de la Sinagoga, location of one of synagogues of medieval judería of Gerona. 189

25.8　Gerona. Calle de Cervantes. View to west. One of the sections or zigzags of the street. This section on slope and paved with a stair. Defensive character of houses apparent in very small windows set high above street level. Heavy wooden door in massive semicircular arched doorway opening. 190

26.1　Barcelona. Map of medieval judería of Barcelona, in Barrio Gótico.　192

26.2　Barcelona. Calle del Call, view to east from corner of Calle de Baños Nuevos, principal street of medieval judería. Word *call*, Catalán pronunciation of Hebrew word *kahal* (community). Street of *Kahal* is Street of Jewish Community. Use of word *call* not unique to Barcelona; used to designate former Jewish streets elsewhere in Catalonia. 194

26.3　Barcelona. Calle del Call, view to east at intersection of Calle del Arco de San Ramón del Call. Street principal one of medieval judería, now main commercial street in Barrio Gótico. During work-a-day week, Calle del Call, and others, teem with crowds of shoppers. Photograph taken early one Sunday morning when all business establishments closed. Atmosphere probably not far different from earlier Sabbath mornings when Jewish community existed in Barcelona hundreds of years ago. 195

26.4　Barcelona. Calle del Call, view to west from Calle de San Honoratio and Plaza de San Jaime. Synagogue once stood on plaza in medieval times. 196

26.5　Barcelona. Calle del Call, view to west from Calle de Santo Domingo del Call. Street sign affixed to corner of building on right in sense a memorial to *Kahal*, obliterated six hundred years ago. Name joined to that of Christian saint, Santo Domingo. Young husband and wife and two children on way to outing in country as morning advances and sun begins to penetrate some streets of judería. 197

26.6   Barcelona. Calle de Santo Domingo del Call, view to north from Calle del Call. During time of Jewish community in Barcelona, street known as Calle de la Sinagoga Major. Synagogue probably located at head of street further up from Calle del Call. Two women sit in front of door to tenement house; young woman dressed in Sunday best moves with deliberate, even-stepped paces, her high heeled shoes click-clacking down street.   200

26.7   Barcelona. Calle de Santo Domingo del Call, view to north and Plaza de Manuel Ribé. Tall tenements seem to lean toward one another, almost touching roofs. Main synagogue of Jewish community located up ahead, probably in little Plaza de Manuel Ribé. Sun never enters narrow street, except for short moment at midday in midsummer.   200

26.8   Barcelona. Plaza de Manuel Ribé to right and end of Calle de Santo Domingo del Call in background. Main synagogue of medieval judería located here.   201

28.1   Zaragoza. Map of judería of Zaragoza. Judería occupied southeastern quadrant of area of ancient Roman city on right bank of Ebro River.   206

28.2   Zaragoza. The Church of San Gil. Located in former judería, church typical of architecture of Zaragoza, with stylistic remembrances of Islamic past. Tower, with beautiful surface decoration in brick, really minaret similar to those adjacent to mosque. All synagogues and other Jewish communal buildings disappeared, probably same architectural style as tower of San Gil.   208

28.3   Zaragoza. Calle de la Verónica. Street formerly in medieval judería, of which not a trace remains. In 1960s, area was razed, new buildings under construction.   210

28.4   Zaragoza. Plazuela de la Verónica, center of medieval judería. Unknown if anything of judería extant in area before 1960s; modernization in process at time.   210

29.1   Gibraltar. Synagogue in Engineers Lane also known as Synagogue Shar ha Shamayim. Synagogue actually behind house that fronts street. Arched doorway accesses passage through house to synagogue courtyard in back. Chief rabbi of Gibraltar occupies house in front of synagogue.   218

29.2   Gibraltar. Synagogue in Engineers Lane. Main entrance to prayer hall. Stairway (not in photograph) abuts on building to right, accesses women's gallery inside prayer hall. Building dates from late eighteenth/early nineteenth century.   219

29.3   Gibraltar. Synagogue in Bomb House Lane, main facade behind synagogue courtyard wall. Synagogue also known in Spanish as La Sinagoga de la Muralla; in Hebrew as *Kahal Kadosh Nefutsot Yehudah* (Holy Congregation of dispersed of Judah).   220

Acknowledgment

The subject for this book was first suggested to the author by the late Ephraim Rosenzweig, Hillel Director at the University of North Carolina, Chapel Hill, NC. The late Solomon Grayzel, Editor of the Jewish Publication Society, offered him both encouragement and advice.

Preface

It is fitting that one of the most momentous events in the history of western civilization, the discovery of America by Christopher Columbus in 1492, should not be forgotten. Also meriting remembrance is another event which occurred in the same year half a millennium ago, the forced departure of the Spanish Jews from their homeland. The Catholic kings, Ferdinand and Isabella, who supported the voyage and enterprise of Columbus, also issued the Decree of Expulsion driving their Jewish subjects from Spain. At the moment when Columbus was raising anchor and setting his sails in Palos de Moguer to head west, Jews were embarking on ships heading east to the lands of the Turkish empire.

And it is an irony of fate, that Ferdinand and Isabella did not dream, let alone foretell, that Columbus would find America or that they were unwittingly also supporting the ultimate creation of a *New World* where, in the centuries that followed, Jews and all others who sought a better life, would find a safe haven and create a homeland of their own.

Therefore, it is fitting, indeed, that both the discovery of America and the expulsion of Jews from Spain be remembered as benevolent acts of Divine Providence.

This book is concerned with the physical scant tangible remains of the vanished Jewish communities of Spain. Beginning with a brief history of Spanish Jewry, the chapters that follow deal with the pre-Expulsion Jewish communities in about twenty-eight modern Spanish towns. It is then a history of the Jews of Spain as revealed in "the sticks and stones," the remnants, in the towns and villages where Jews lived for about one thousand years.

Jewish Remnants in Spain may also be viewed as a guide book of some utility to tourists, especially Jewish tourists, who visit Spain. The book is the author's account of his travels in Spain in search of the physical remains of the vanished Jewish communities. The few scant remnants from the Jewish past are, betimes, auguries, portends of what was to transpire in twentieth-century Europe.

The Inquisition and the "final solution," The Expulsion in 1492, are all part of the same institutionalized so-called "legal process" harking back to Visigothic times in the fifth century C.E. when Jews were for the first time forcibly segregated from the pagan and Christian communities in the Iberian Peninsula, the purpose of which was the extermination of the Jewish people.

Fig. 1.1: Map of Spain. Jewish places described in the text.

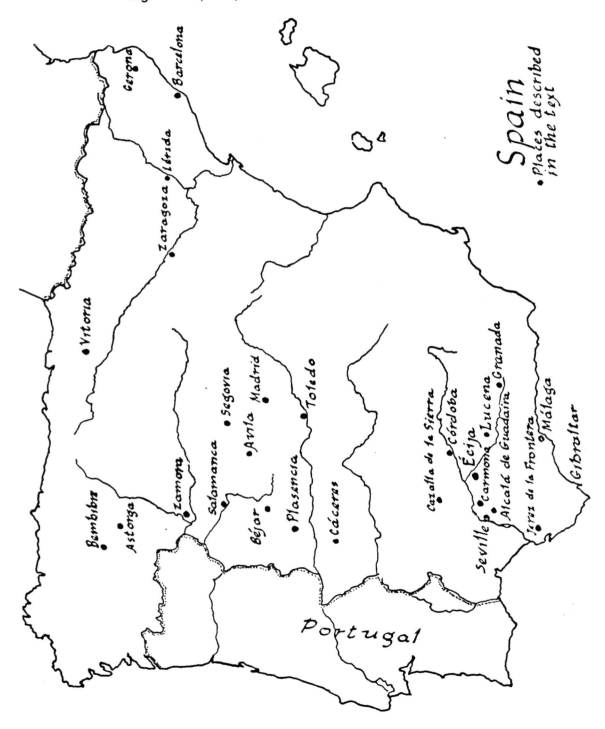

1 Introduction

We know that Christopher Columbus discovered America. We even celebrate Columbus Day each year on October 12. Do we really know the significance of what it means *to discover America* until we discover America ourselves, personally? America was always there, but even Columbus did not know this even after he discovered it. Unaware that he had not reached his intended destination of Asia, he did not lend his name to this New World. Thus, *America* does not refer to Columbus, but rather to a later explorer.

We, all of us, have to discover our own America, too, before we really know America. So it was with me and my discovery of the Jews in Spain—not living Jews, but the sticks and stones the Jews had left behind when they went into exile in 1492. This exile coincided with Columbus' sailing from Palos to the discovery of the New World. I had heard there had once been Jews in Spain, I had even read about them in history books, and I knew of Torquemada and the Inquisition. However, I never imagined there had been Jews in Spain, who, like me, celebrated the Exodus from Egypt and ate matzos. Like Columbus, who discovered America while looking for another continent, I discovered the Jews of Spain while searching for the stylistic connections between the baroque architecture of Spain and that of colonial Central America. I came upon long-forgotten synagogues and Jewish streets in towns and villages—paltry remnants, yet physical, visible, tangible bits of Spanish Jewish history.

The history of the Jews of Spain is not a history of the growth of states, of economic developments, of military feats, nor of political affairs. It is not a history of art monuments, of painters, of sculptors, nor of architects and builders. "How goodly are thy tents, O Jacob," cries the prophet, but he does not mean a Cathedral of Burgos nor an Alhambra of Granada. The Jews of Spain built neither cathedrals nor palaces, and what little they built of brick, stone, and mortar has all but disappeared. Were it not for the written word, little would be known of the Jewish presence. The archaeologist finds few physical vestiges by way of material evidence to piece out the role of the Jews in Spanish history. Hardly discernible spoors come to light now and then: a few tombstones of the Jewish dead, a few bits of shattered Hebrew inscriptions which once graced no longer existing synagogues.

The little that has survived has fallen into oblivion except for a place name here and there. Crooked streets with ramshackle houses of the poor of Spain, a few bits of wall, an arch and a doorway, barely visible traces of synagogues embedded in Christian buildings, altarpieces with statues of Christian saints where once the Ark of the Torah stood. These comprise the few tokens in the record, the physical evidence of the Jewish past in Spain.

How did my discovery of the Jews come about? I had come to Toledo to study the cathedral and other architectural monuments, and passed by a building, marked on my map as *La Sinagoga de Santa María La Blanca* (the Synagogue of Holy Mary the Virgin)! More out of idle curiosity rather than any purposeful intent, I turned and walked through a large gate in the high wall surrounding the yard in front of the main facade. My interest was aroused when I viewed the interior with its horseshoe-shaped arches and fine carving in plaster.

As I was leaving, I noticed some graffiti on the white plastered doorjambs. Visitors with Jewish names had scribbled their autographs, attesting to the fact that they had been there. One item in particular was in Hebrew; it was the opening paean of the Shema prayer proclaiming that there was one God. The incongruity of the name of the synagogue dawned on me. The graffiti on the door constituted underground acts of defiance by the writers, who thereby wishfully reclaimed the building as their own once again.

I walked the few blocks and visited the second synagogue still standing in Toledo. It also had an improbable name, *El Tránsito de Nuestra Señora* (Our Lady of the Transit). Along with Santa María La Blanca and the cathedral, it was one of the chief tourist attractions of Toledo and considered among the finest examples of the *mudéjar* (a blend of Gothic and Islamic elements) architectural style.

At the precise moment when I crossed the threshold, I discovered the Jews of Spain for myself. I realized I, too, had once been in Spain as I also had been in ancient Egypt. The words of Zachariah came to mind, "Not by might nor by power, but by My spirit, saith the Lord of Hosts." The bodily extinct Jews of Spain, with neither power nor might, whose very dust has blown away, still lived on as a reminder of man's inhumanity to man.

After my discovery of the Jews of Spain, I resorted to the works of many who had discovered them before me: Salo Baron, Ytzhak Baer, and others in the reading list at the end of this book, especially Francisco Cantera Burgos, who compiled much of the epigraphical and documentary evidence for the various medieval Jewish communities and their synagogues. His *Sinagogas españoles* (Spanish Synagogues) served as a guide in the location of towns with *juderías* (Jewish quarters or ghettos). I traveled widely throughout the country, a partial itinerary of which follows. Entering from France at Irun and skirting the Pyrenees along the Cantabric coast to Oviedo, I turned south crossing the high mountain pass at Pajares and descended into León. León had once had a flourishing Jewish community, but not a single trace of it exists anymore. As in Oviedo, the stamp of the Visigoths predominates in this sunless, rainy part of Spain.

From León I first went to Astorga, then to Bembibre and back over the same road to Zamora. The next leg of the journey took me to Salamanca. From Salamanca I turned eastward and headed toward Madrid. Once in Madrid I also visited Toledo and Segovia. From Madrid my journey turned southward to the city of Seville. I took up residence there for a year, which allowed countless visits to such places as Córdoba, Ecija, Carmona, and Alcalá de Guadaira, all within a short driving distance. Somewhat further afield were Granada, Málaga, and Lucena; the latter was famous as a *yeshiva* town. During the spring, I drove back to France and stopped betimes in Cáceres, Plasencia, Béjar, Burgos, Gerona, Zaragoza, Lérida, and Vitoria, all with a Jewish past—traces of which I found still there, but in muffled evidence. I spent some time in Granada, Córdoba, Seville, Zaragoza, and Barcelona. I climbed *Montjuich* (Jews' Mount) where the Jews of Barcelona had been buried, but whose graves long have been obliterated. This, in short, is the path I followed into the physical and tangible Jewish past in Spain.

As I wandered about Spain looking for Jewish traces, for physical bits of evidence of the former Jewish presence, I was struck time and time again with the fact that Jews were still there, biologically at least. In speaking with educated Spaniards, I often found them, though reluctantly so, well aware of the Jewish past and the Jewish role in Spanish history. In fact, as far back as the nineteenth century writers such as José Amador de los Ríos and Fidel Fita began a tradition of scholarly interest in the history of the Spanish Jews. From early twentieth century on, Angel Pulido, Julio Caro Baroja, Américo Castro, José María Vallicrosa, Francisco Cantera Burgos, and others have written many articles and books interpreting the Jewish part in the unfolding of Spanish history. The Instituto Arias Montano, devoted to Hebrew and Sephardic studies, has been operating at the University of Madrid since 1940; it publishes the quarterly journal, *Sepharad*.

Probably in imitation of the American Conference of Christians and Jews, a similar organization called the Asociación Judeo-Cristiana was founded in Madrid in 1962. The Asociación purposed to create a closer relationship between Jews and Christians—that is, Spanish Catholics. Dr. Francisco Cantera Burgos, the director of the Instituto Arias Montano, presided. Among the official organizers, a priest and the president of the Jewish community of Madrid also were present.

Jews—that is to say, Sephardic Jews—have obtained special privileges in religious matters from the Spanish authorities. A law, passed in 1965, allowed Jewish congregations to function legally. In general, Spanish citizens consider the Sephardic Jews a stiff-necked people who are, after all, Spaniards and rarely referred to as *judíos* (the Spanish word for Jews). They are called *sefardies* or *Sephardim*. Interestingly, the Sephardim, wherever they are in the world, have maintained their Spanish speech, the Ladino, all these years since the Expulsion of 1492. Spanish writers wishfully have interpreted this language retention as evidence of undying love for Spain, despite the centuries of exile. In fact there was, and probably still is, a law on the books, first promulgated by Primo de Rivera in 1924, stating that Sephardic Jews are Spaniards. This law further states that if they desire to do so they may, under certain conditions, come back to Spain and obtain Spanish passports and Spanish citizenship. Very few have done so, though Jews, both *Sephardim* and *Ashkenazim* (German and East European Jews) began coming to Madrid in the 1920s. By 1931 there were enough families residing there permanently to establish a synagogue, the first in over four hundred years.

Franco and Spain took credit for saving thousands of Jews from falling into Hitler's hands during the Second World War, especially Sephardic Jews whom they classified as Spanish subjects. It is claimed that as soon as the war was over, many *illegal* immigrants found their way to Palestine on Spanish ships or on others sailing from Spanish ports, particularly Algeciras, where the Jewish community of Gibraltar across the bay assisted in this endeavor. Finally Franco went a step beyond that taken by Primo de Rivera, for in 1949 he published a decree giving Spanish citizenship to the Sephardic Jews of Greece and Egypt.

Jews residing in Spain are still a meager handful, with small communities in Madrid, Barcelona, and Seville, as well as Gibraltar, which is really British. Even in Seville, one of the largest cities of Spain with much tangible evidence of the Jewish past, there existed no modern Jewish community until the 1970s.

So the short sketches that follow are descriptions of a sentimental journey in search of Jewish traces, of Jewish remnants, often no more palpable than salt from tears or dust from desiccated bones.

2 History: Some Reflections and Facts

Nondescript though they may often be, there are, nevertheless, many physical remains by means of which one can flesh out the history of the Jews of the Iberian Peninsula. This history extends back to pagan times, long before Christianity became the dominant religion. A synagogue of late Roman date remains discernible in Elche. In very fragmented condition, a single tombstone dated on epigraphic evidence in the third century C.E. exists of a young Jewish child, a girl, who died at the age of one year, three months, and one day. Since the Middle Ages on, the spoors of Jews become clearer and more abundant. The location of *juderías* (the Jewish neighborhoods or quarters) and the Jewish cemeteries are frequently known. The cemetery in Plasencia lies abandoned and still unstudied. Some excavations were carried out in the cemetery of Segovia at the end of the nineteenth century. The Jewish cemeteries of Barcelona, Gerona, and Vitoria still remain in the local toponymy, *Montjuich* in the Catalan language and *Judizmendi* in the Basque. Spanish and foreign scholars have studied the remains of synagogues in Toledo, Córdoba, Segovia, Seville, and in many other towns throughout the Iberian Peninsula. At one time or another, nearly every town in Spain had a Jewish community and a synagogue. Thus, the history of the Jews of Spain is the history of Spain itself.

The Phoenicians and the Carthaginians settled Spain as far back as the eighth century B.C.E. No evidence readily presents itself to the effect that Jews had arrived there as early as that. During the parlous days of the Expulsion in 1492, the Jewish community of Toledo, as evidence of the antiquity of its establishment, presented a letter supposedly written and dated in Toledo the fourteenth day of the month of Nisan, in the "eighteenth year of Caesar and the seventy-first of Augustus Octavian" (in the year 71 C.E.). This letter stated that the Jews of Toledo had been there since the destruction of the First Temple in Jerusalem and could not, therefore, be held responsible for the death of Jesus Christ. Apocryphal, of course, the letter is also a sad comment of how a drowning man will hold on to a straw to save his life.

Whether Jews were there at the time of the destruction of the first temple of Jerusalem is not as pertinent as is the evidence of their certain presence in Spain after the destruction of the Second Temple in 71 C.E. Jewish communities doubtlessly existed in Spain during the Roman domination of the Iberian Peninsula. The archaeological evidence for this conclusion is rather scant. Evidence does suggest that Jews had lived in Spain during Roman times; what their numbers were or where their communities were located can only be conjectured.

Jews and Judaism were the objects of special restrictive legislation at the Council of Illiberis (Granada), also called the Council of Elvira, celebrated at the beginning of the fourth century, either 300 or 303 c.e. This history provides evidence that Jews resided in Spain during the first centuries of the Common Era and even before Constantine had made Christianity the official religion of the Roman Empire in 313 c.e. The nineteen bishops, twenty-four priests, and other clerics felt it necessary to come to the defense of the Church that they believed was being attacked by both paganism and heresy, as well as by Judaism. Apparently Judaism competed strongly with Christianity in gaining adherents among the pagan native population. This religious council promulgated the first piece of legislation that placed limitations on the relations between Jew and Christian. This legislation thereby laid the foundation for a process that culminated in the extinction of Jews and Judaism in Spain more than a millennium later.

By the time of the arrival of the Germanic barbarian hordes from northern and eastern Europe in the fifth century c.e., Jewish communities and the Jewish population were already numerous and influential. The growing strength of the Jews encouraged the Visigoths, who replaced the Romans as the rulers of Spain, to enact social legislation curbing the growing influence of Judaism among both Christians and pagans. The promulgation of the *Lex Romana Visgothorum* (Roman Law of the Visigoths), in 506, forbad Jews to hold public office, intermarry with Christians, build new synagogues, own Christian slaves, or persecute apostates.

The situation for the Jews of Spain really worsened at the end of the sixth century when Reccared, the Visigoth king, became a Roman Catholic after renouncing the Arian form of Christianity, which had been condemned by the Council of Nicea in 325. The Third Council of Toledo in 589 restated in more vigorous form the original restrictions of the Council of Elvira, as well as the Lex Romana Visigothorum. It forbad Jews to take Christian wives or concubines and mandated baptism of children born of such unions. Jews could not have Christian slaves in domestic service. Christian slaves who had been circumcised and converted to Judaism became free and Christians again. Legislation of this sort became progressively more explicit and severe in the later Councils of Toledo. This legislation aimed at the Jews of Visigoth Spain supports the conclusion that they were sufficiently numerous and influential to have represented a threat to Christianity in competition for converts from among the pagan population.

When Sisebut ascended the Visigoth throne in 612, matters became even worse. The new regime accused the Jews of violating the laws of the Third Council of Toledo, especially with regard to proselytizing activity. Based on these and other charges, the king ordered Jews expelled from Spain. As a result of this evil decree, many Jews had no choice but to convert to Christianity. At least they converted outwardly; many clung to their ancestral faith in secret, according to the record.

Many left Spain and settled in those parts of France then under Frankish domination. When Sisebut died in 621, many of the forcibly baptized Jews returned openly to Judaism. In 633, under the impetus of Bishop Isidor of Seville, the authorities enacted new and even harsher legislation against the Jews. This legislation created an even greater and more unbridgeable gulf between Jew and Christian. By 711, the Jews looked upon the Moslem conquerors of Spain as saviors from the harsh punishment rendered by the Christians.

Without the help of the Jews, the Arab conquest probably could not have progressed nor succeeded as rapidly it did. In those newly conquered towns with large Jewish populations, Arab military policy stationed garrisons of Jews under the command of a small Arab detachment while the bulk of the invading army advanced in its sweep across Spain. Jews and Moslems equally guarded Córdoba, Granada, and Seville.

With the Moslem conquest of Spain, there began an epoch, which for good reasons historians have dubbed the Golden Age of Spanish Jewry—a period which lasted until the beginning of the eleventh century. This was especially so under Abd-er-Rahman III, who established an independent caliphate in Córdoba in 928. Córdoba became the most civilized city in the western world, and the intermediary through which ancient Greek philosophy and science were transmitted to Christian Europe. To list the men of learning, both Jewish and Moslem, of the period is to provide a resume of the intellectual history of the early Middle Ages. One alone, *Moses ben Maimon* (Maimonides of Córdoba), 1135-1204, is enough. As the learned said, "From Moses to Moses, there was none like Moses."

In the eleventh century, the caliphate of Córdoba fell apart, and *al-Andalus* (Andalucía) was divided into petty principalities called *taifas*. Weakened and dismembered, the country opened itself to another Moslem incursion, that of the Almoravids. Near the end of the century, these North African Berbers conquered the taifas one by one and reunited al-Andalus. The Almoravid conquest altered the former attitude of tolerance toward Jews and also Christians. Persecution of the Jews eclipsed the splendor and learning of their communities. When in 1146 the Almohads, a fanatical and militant sect of Berbers also from North Africa, replaced the Almoravids as rulers of Moslem Spain, Jewish liabilities increased to an even greater extent than they had under the Visigoths prior to 711. The Almohads caused massacres of the Jews and forced their wholesale conversions to Islam. Nevertheless, the Jews found an avenue of escape—Christian Spain.

Small, scattered Jewish settlements had existed in northern Christian Spain even before the advent of the Almohads in the twelfth century. The Reconquest, a military movement to wrest all of Spain from Moslem domination, caused cities to fall into Christian hands once again; Jews were frequently settled in them. The earliest gains of the Reconquest occurred in the north where many Jews had settled in order to escape Moslem persecution. In that part of the country, under the feudal system, Jews relied on the king or local nobility for protection. They enjoyed relatively good conditions in Christian Spain during the long-drawn-out Reconquest, which gained full momentum in the eleventh century. In fact, in and around the city of León in Asturias, Jews at that time lived on a par with Christians. The Reconquest had begun slowly, almost immediately after the first Arab victories, and continued until 1484, when Granada, the last Moslem kingdom, fell, and with it the last Jewish hopes.

The struggle between the Cross and the Crescent caught the Jews in the middle. Christian Spain, a region which at that time was still undeveloped economically and culturally, welcomed (perhaps not too warmly but at least allowed them entrance) the Jews fleeing their persecutors, when the Almohads invaded Spain in the mid-twelfth century. The Jews came as craftsmen, merchants, scholars, and men of urbane habits who brought the fruits of Moslem culture to the barbarian, serving to illuminate the *Dark Ages* of the medieval Christian Spanish world.

Thus the Jews were inextricably caught between the warring hosts of the Reconquest and were buffeted about in the struggle for political and religious unity of Christian Spain. When it was convenient, the talents of the Jews were utilized and they were given special privileges as a nation apart, as a subject people but with legal and political rights and obligations within their own quasi-independent communities.

Most of the juderías that dot the map of northern Spain date largely from after the end of the eleventh century when Jews fled the Almoravids and accepted specific areas assigned to them within the cities of Christian Spain. For example, when Alfonso VI of León and Castile conquered Toledo in 1085, he granted the Jews a part of the town estimated at between one-fifth and one-fourth its total area. Here the Jewish community flourished and even had a fortress of its own, remaining there until the fateful year of 1391, when the flame and the scourge of hatred and slaughter swept all the juderías, resulting in many forced conversions. The judería of Toledo had been first established soon after the Arab conquest in 711. After the Christian Reconquest of the city, an even larger population than the original settled there. It was here that Alfonso X, *El Sabio* (The Wise), founded his school of translators where so many Jewish scholars produced works that benefited the whole of medieval European civilization.

Soon after taking Seville in 1248, the father of Alfonso X, Ferdinand III, allowed the Jews he found living there to remain in their old quarter near the principal mosque, which was subsequently converted to a cathedral. He assigned that part of the town now known as the Barrio de Santa Cruz to the Jewish community. Jews from Christian Spain, whom he had invited to settle in Seville, considerably augmented its size. Alfonso X treated the Jews far better than he did the Moslems. He gave his Jewish officials houses, vineyards, olive groves, and fields around Seville, all granted in perpetuity for services rendered.

As the Reconquest proceeded, the Jews received decent treatment in many other towns as well. The twelfth and thirteenth centuries provided a zenith for Spanish Jewry similar to the period from the eighth to the eleventh centuries under the caliphate of Córdoba. Jewish officials assumed prominent positions in the Spanish court, where they wielded great authority and influence. One need but recall Samuel ha Levi of Toledo and to see the magnificent synagogue he built in order to gain an idea of the height to which Jewish communal life had risen.

Beginning in the fourteenth century, because of religious fanaticism and the supposed need for uniformity of religion in order to achieve political unity, the Jews became the object of hate and envy of the Christian populace on the one hand, and of special restrictive legislation by the crown and church on the other, both of which resulted in the placing of insurmountable obstacles and punitive liabilities on the Jews, their religion, and their communal life. Pogroms and forced baptisms became more and more common. The change in official policy toward Jews may be explained in terms of realpolitik. Within the philosophy of the Reconquest, Spain necessarily had to impose uniformity in all phases of life, political and social as well as religious.

Giving the matter a simpler though no less rational explanation, the change for the worse in the Jewish position also may have been a blind fanaticism and religious fervor on the part of the populace, raised time and time again to fever heat by the clergy. That group kept alive the libel of deicide, holding that Spanish Jews, as descendants of those who brought about the death of Christ, responsible for the alleged nefarious acts of their ancestors. The end result was the same. Racial hatred and the destruction of Jewish life culminated in the expulsion of the little remnant that still clung to the religion of its forefathers in 1492. The Inquisition relentlessly persecuted the Jewish population: first the secret Jews and finally many whose only crime was to claim Jewish descent. Covetous desire for personal enrichment through pillage or *legal* expropriation of the Jews' worldly goods more ultimately governed the pogroms, the massacres, the mass baptisms, and even the Inquisition itself than did a pious desire to reap the so-called harvest of souls for the only true religion.

Fig. 3.1: Astorga. Calle de Matías Rodríguez. Formerly known as Calle del Arco and site of judería.

Fig. 3.2: Astorga. Roman wall at edge of city enclosing former Jewish cemetery, known until recently as Paseo de la Sinagoga.

3 Astorga

On entering town and searching out the main plaza, I was struck by the impression that events of modern times had bypassed Astorga. Neither factories nor well-stocked stores with goods for sale existed. Few people appeared in the streets. Along one side of the plaza, a few old men sat around a table in an outdoor cafe under the covered sidewalk. According to Cantera Burgos, Astorga once had many Jewish inhabitants. He based his judgment on the fact that two Jewish quarters, each with a synagogue of its own, had occupied the area. It is not known if both juderías existed contemporaneously, or if the first was extinguished and the second took its place. Supposedly, one judería was located in the southern part of town somewhere between the cathedral and the Church of San Bartolomé. I did not locate the other in the western part of the city.

I asked the old men to direct me to the Church of San Bartolomé, which they did; one of them actually walked me to its very door to make sure I did not get lost. The judería once had been located along the street now known as the Calle de Matías Rodríguez, formerly known as the *Calle del Arco* (Street of the Arch), a name of doubtless medieval origin. In a section of town far from the center, it was located to one side of the main body of the city, near the Church of San Bartolomé. The street turned slightly to the left, gradually widening as it ran in a southwesterly direction. It finally terminated in a small park with evenly spaced rows of trees at the very edge of town just inside a well-preserved section of the ancient Roman city wall. The little park, elevated high above the surrounding area, afforded a view over the countryside. Until the 1930s, this park was known as the *Paseo de la Sinagoga* (Synagogue Promenade); its name was changed after the Civil War.

Considering that the location of the park was on the very edge of town in an isolated and unpopulated neighborhood, I surmised that the synagogue, with the Jewish houses pressing around it, must certainly have been located in the nearby Calle del Arco. The park, outside the judería proper, possibly could have provided the burying ground for the medieval Jewish community of Astorga. I could find no trace of the synagogue; I could not look among the roots of the trees to see if Jewish bones had nurtured them.

I slowly retraced my steps back to the main plaza. After a cup of coffee, I left for Bembibre somewhat disappointed that my first exploratory venture had had such a negative result. My spirits rose when I arrived in Bembibre and found the remains of a synagogue literally blocking the road.

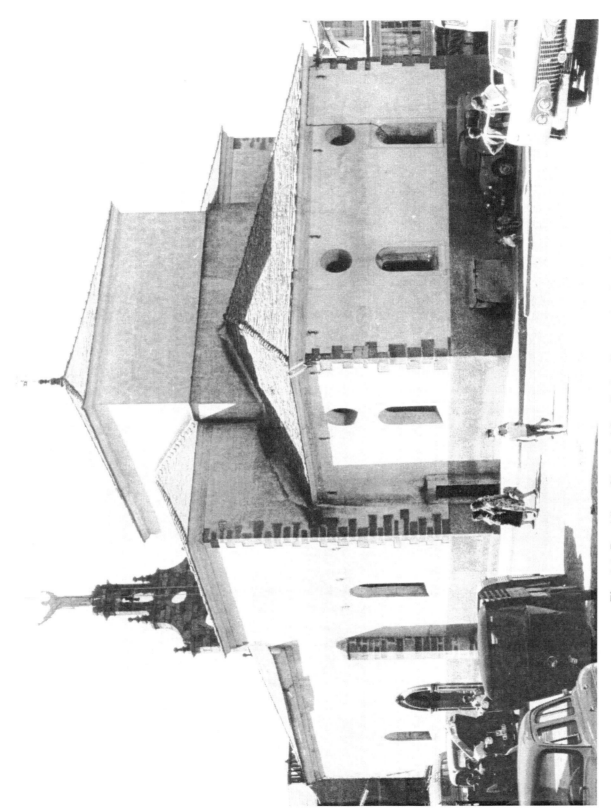

Fig. 4.1: Bembibre. Church of San Pedro. East end and south side.

4 Bembibre

From Astorga to Bembibre the road wound though mountainous and broken terrain, circling around the troughs of the slopes, ascending to the summits, and then descending into narrow valleys along river courses. Coal mining had taken over the entire region. The towns presented the dreary, sooty appearance common to coal-mining areas. Refuse piles from the diggings marred the natural beauty of the steep verdant inclines of the countryside. Cable lines carrying buckets of coal crossed and recrossed the highway at intervals, appearing and disappearing between mountain peaks. The populace, both men and women, wore black, the color of the material they extracted from the earth. Because of the dust permanently ingrained in the pores of their skin, their faces were pallid and dark. A black veil even covered the houses. Whites became grays and all the primary colors deadened, thus creating the appearance that the facades of houses and the faces of men were of one piece.

Bembibre, in the Province of León, lies on the main highway between Madrid and La Coruña. It presents such a dreary and uninviting aspect that few motorists are inclined stop there, preferring to continue on through the town. Some have thought the name, Bembibre, to be a corruption of the Hebrew *ben Ibri* (son of Hebrew). They also thought that originally only Jews had settled the town. However, this is only a romantic conjecture, not a proven philological or historical fact.

Approaching from the south, that is, from the Madrid side of the highway, I entered Bembibre over a narrow steel bridge that led directly into the main street. The highway ended abruptly at the facades of some poor timber-framed houses that conveyed a medieval air. A short turn to the right and I was directly in front of the blank west facade of the Church of San Pedro. This building projected no particular architectural distinction worth even a passing glance from the many motorists who are forced to circle it in order to pick up the main road again. This unprepossessing building had been a synagogue before it was converted to a church toward the end of the fifteenth century.

The former synagogue, that is, the Church of San Pedro, stood in the center of the main plaza of the town like an island surrounded by streets on all four sides. A puzzling feature! Usually located in an out-of-the-way corner of medieval towns, this synagogue, and consequently the judería, appeared to be in the very center of Bembibre. Why? Some investigators erroneously conclude that during most of the Middle Ages only Jews had inhabited Bembibre. These investigators submit the city's Hebrew-sounding name as support for this conclusion.

Fig. 4.2: Bembibre. Church of San Pedro, formerly a synagogue. West front.

The "synagogue plaza" actually appeared off to one side of the medieval urban complex and was originally on the outskirts of the city, just a short distance from the river. The Jewish quarter was isolated on lower ground below the main part of the medieval town, which lay higher up to the east. There the Christians lived. The streets emerging from the synagogue plaza sloped gently upward, running in an easterly direction away from the plaza. The Jewish quarter probably clustered about the synagogue, its outer limits probably extending to the river on the western side of the modern town.

The exterior of the former synagogue has been remodeled at various times during its long history. Major remodeling took place soon after it was converted to a church in the late fifteenth century, actually not very long after it had been built, and again during the twentieth century after the Civil War. The west facade is unadorned and lacks the usual main portal, which normally gives access to the nave. The statue on top of the arcaded belfry wall, *espadaña*, is of recent origin. The long north and south sides contain the main entrances to the building. No special decoration embellishes the entrances. In plan, the building is essentially a broad rectangle with a rectilinear apse projecting slightly off-center from the east end. Originally the synagogue probably did not have this apsidal feature. It must have acquired the feature upon conversion to a church about five hundred years ago.

Formerly divided into three aisles, this synagogue is similar to the interiors of the synagogues of Corpus Christi in Segovia and Santa María La Blanca in Seville. The original architectural character of the interior that survived through the centuries was finally destroyed in a fire in 1934. During the Spanish Civil War a few years later, the antireligious elements among the townspeople pillaged the building.

I wished to go inside but found both doors locked and asked the children following me how I might get the door opened. One of the children, a little boy of about nine or ten, offered to take me to the house where the sacristan lived and from whom I might get the key.

We walked uphill along a narrow street with a broken potholed cobblestone pavement, doubtlessly in a state of disrepair for decades, if not centuries. A small narrow street, a now-forgotten Jewish street, rose from the plaza. The sacristan lived in a house a few yards away. An old woman answered my knock on the door. When I said what I wanted, verbally seconded at some length by my small guide, she turned away, and in a moment the sacristan came out with an enormous iron key.

He was a tiny gray-haired little man with a child-sized, wizened, wrinkled face. After a word of greeting, he walked off at a rapid pace, inclining forward with each fast step as he unhesitatingly picked his way over the broken pavement while I kept falling behind him and the little boy as we descended to the plaza. The sacristan presented himself no different from the *shamas* (beadle), that wisp of a frail little Russian Jew who cared for the synagogue I used to go to for Hebrew lessons as a child.

Fig. 4.3: Bembibre.   Street leading away from plaza and synagogue-church of San Pedro. Probably part of judería on former outskirts near river. Main part of city lies beyond.

He was the same man and the same grandfather with his small grandson making their way hurriedly to the synagogue to open it for afternoon prayers. He put the key into the ancient lock of hand-hammered wrought-iron in the door on the south side of the building and began telling me not of the scrolls of the Torah in the sacred Ark that once occupied the east end of the hall, but of the solitary image that stood there instead, the Sacred Heart of Jesus.

I paused just inside the door and listened to his tale. The image of the Sagrado Corazón de Jesús existed as the only ancient one in the church, and the only one that the *Reds* of Bembibre did not burn when they assaulted the place in 1937 during the Civil War. They appeared in the dark of night, broke down the doors, and carried all the sacred images of the saints out into the plaza, including that of the Sacred Heart of Jesus. They burned them all in a tremendous bonfire, an *auto da fé*. They burned all except the Sacred Heart of Jesus, which they placed so He could see how all His saints were being consumed by the flames. That is why all the images in the Church of San Pedro were new—that is, except that of the Sagrado Corazón de Jesús who witnessed the sacrilege.

What a strange story to hear from a little wizened birdlike shamas! Could this great fire in the plaza have been part of a chain of events beginning in 1490 when the Torah was removed and the synagogue forcibly converted to a church? Did the twentieth-century Bembibreños revere and respect the holy image of Christ as their fifteenth-century ancestors would have the sacred scrolls of the Torah? The symbols have changed, but the faith has remained.

I left the synagogue-church, mumbled a few words of thanks as the shamas-sacristan locked the door, handed him a few pesetas, and left Bembibre. The sky had become even more sunless and overcast than when I had arrived. The green verdure of the hills had turned almost gray under the dull colorless sky.

I took the road back toward Astorga, and then went on to Zamora. A few kilometers beyond Astorga, I rushed through Benavente and after crossing the Esla River, I observed that the character of the landscape changed abruptly. The secondary road ran due south over the flat upland plains of Old Castile, a high plateau with mountains visible in the distance that reminded me of the high flat country of central Mexico. In fact, the flatness of the grasslands, parched by the sun and under a big sky, seemed so much like the plains around Guadalajara in Jalisco.

Straight ahead in the distance an eminence jutted from the gently undulating plain. Crowning it were the rooftops and church towers of Zamora, an ocher and earth-red little island rising above a sea of parched grass under a great, cloudless, ultramarine blue sky.

5 Zamora

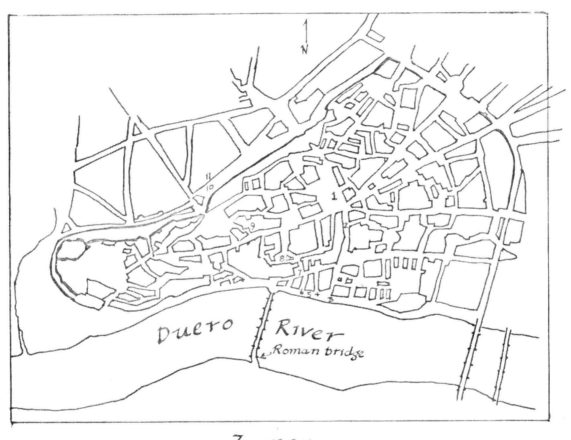

Fig. 5.1: Zamora. Map showing location of three juderías and their synagogues.

I entered Zamora from the north, into the modern part of town. The nineteenth and twentieth century and even earlier in style buildings make *modern* a relative term. The medieval section of the city lay to the south and at not too great distance. With perhaps 40,000 inhabitants more or less, Zamora is not a large city by contemporary standards. The older medieval parts of the city have remained at a

Fig. 5.2: Zamora. Calle de Ignacio Gazapo, formerly Plaza de la Judería. Full of houses, this area had been center of judería. The houses were torn down mid-twentieth century to provide access for automobile road now skirting the Duero, thereby opening up a view of medieval bridge over river.

standstill, as if frozen in time, since the fifteenth century. Many of the streets and houses are the same as they were during the period when Jews still lived in Zamora.

In plan the city looks like an outspread fan with a small handle. Situated to the north and east, the modern part of the town is encompassed within the flare of the fan. Here the streets are wide enough to accommodate automobile traffic. Confined to the narrow handle of the fan to the west and south, the medieval part restricts itself to foot traffic. Still extant in the handle of the fan are some sizeable stretches of the ancient walls of fortification. Within its perimeter, according to Cantera Burgos, three synagogues once existed. Only a large Jewish community would have constructed multiple synagogues.

Nevertheless, one cannot determine the number of Jews living in Zamora at any given time. The ratio between the number of synagogues—providing, of course, that they all existed at the same time—and the number of people using them is difficult to ascertain because of the limitations and impediments to freedom of action placed on all the Jewish communities of Spain. Jews were forbidden to build new houses of worship, both before and during the fifteenth century. Any estimate of the size of the Jewish population must of necessity be based on conjecture, es-

Fig. 5.3: Zamora. House No. 5, Calle de Ignacio Gazapo, formerly known as Plaza de la Judería. This building is on site of synagogue of local judería and is occupied by automobile repair shop.

pecially since the total population of Zamora during the late Middle Ages also is unknown. Yet some authors have said that at the time of the Expulsion in 1492, thirty thousand Jews lived in Zamora. This must be an exaggeration, for even in the 1970s and 80s the population, including the greater and modern part of town, was about forty thousand or so.

Off the main plaza a rather wide street, Calle de Balborraz, descends precipitously in a southerly direction to the river. So steep is the incline that the builders had to lay out the street in successive terraces or broad steps, making it impractical for wheeled vehicles. A thin slice of the Duero River appears in the narrow slit between the houses at the bottom of the hill. The terraces are each three to four paces wide, descending to an open area with a road running parallel to the river. According to the data assembled by Cantera Burgos, a small Jewish quarter with a synagogue had existed somewhere in the vicinity along the riverbank. Until about the middle of the twentieth century, the open space in front of the row of houses facing the river had been known as the Plaza de la Judería. The foot of the Calle de Balborraz offers an unobstructed view of the sixteen arches of the medieval stone bridge in the distance.

Fig. 5.4: Zamora. *Calle de los Baños* (Baths Street). View from Calle de Ignacio Gazapo rising to north away from riverbank and Plaza de la Judería. This street was possibly part of judería near river.

I had hardly expected to come to an open unbuilt area so unlike and out of character with the narrow streets of the medieval town through which I had just passed, crowded with houses crushed against each other. The Jews who once lived there never saw this view of the river and bridge. Accompanying the destruction of the Jewish houses to make way for it, the automobile road that skirted the river obliterated part of the medieval judería, including the street plan.

A row of houses, which once supposedly fronted on the obliterated Plaza de la Judería (now the Calle de Ignacio Gazapo), stood some distance back from the riverbank and the modern road. An automobile repair shop now occupies the area where, Cantera believes, a synagogue once stood. My findings place this in the block between *Calle de los Baños* (Baths Street) and *Calle de la Manteca* (Lard Street) on the site where house No. 5 now stands. The old building had remained intact until about 1940 when someone tore it down to make way for the coming of modern times and the automobile to Zamora.

Squeezing by the ancient automobile parked in the door, I entered the garage. There in the irreverent atmosphere of grease and oil, with the bowels of internal combustion engines and tools strewn about in anarchic Spanish disarray, a massive stone wall extended only part way, like a peninsula, across the room at the rear. The medieval synagogue retained this wall as its only remaining vestige. I edged my way through the small opening to the left into the space behind what would had been the synagogue wall. Three grease-begrimed men were peering over a recently dissected automobile engine, each one doing something to bring the work along. They were huddled about the disemboweled engine in the very spot where centuries ago men huddled around and peered into the unrolled Torah scrolls to read the weekly portion of the Law early every Sabbath morning.

I said a word of greeting. A lively conversation ensued; no Spaniard is ever speechless. I ventured the information that they were working in a former synagogue. Yes, they had heard something to that effect. I walked out of the garage into the morning sunshine turning left on the Calle de Ignacio Gazapo to the corner of the Calle de los Baños which rose gently up toward the center of town, away from the river and the Jewish quarter. The houses were of recent construction, but the street itself—that is, the lay of the land—was as it had been five hundred years before. Houses may be torn down and new ones built in their place, but property lines and building sites remain unchanged. The narrow building plots of medieval times had forced the new houses into a mold, a Jewish mold created many centuries before.

Going back downhill, turning into Calle de Ignacio Gazapo, and passing the synagogue-garage again, I continued in a westerly direction toward the bridge. The next intersection included Calle de la Manteca, which also rose uphill toward the center of town. Why Lard Street? And just a few steps from the synagogue! The Calle de la Manteca twisted up to higher ground in a manner that at the summit it obscured the Duero River below. A rough pebble roadbed lined on each side with poor houses, some with iron balconies adorned with potted plants as their only embellishment. Continuing uphill and away from the river, I entered into the Plaza de Santa Lucía. On the opposite side on higher ground, the remains of some of the old city walls still stood. Above the walls, higher still, houses made a pretty picture as they clung to the sides of the eminence upon which the city stands.

Fig. 5.5: Zamora. *Calle de la Manteca* (Lard Street). View to south from Plaza Santa Lucía toward Calle de Ignacio Gazapo and riverbank where main part of judería had once been located. This street was also within perimeter of judería.

There in the plaza a child played with a kitten. Suddenly he kicked it. I was jolted out of the past into the present and asked him with mock severity, "¿Porque pateas el gatito?"

"Para que corra," he answered laconically.

A man wearing an apron stained with and smelling of glue stood in the door of a carpenter's shop where the kitten had taken refuge. My unexpected words had taken him by surprise. I asked the little boy, hoping the man could hear, "Is that why you kick the kitten, to make it run? Do you know that this is cruelty to animals, that animals were created, just as you were by God, and that because of people like you Christ was crucified?" I said all this with a mixed expression of seriousness and levity, half grave, half jocular. For once a Spaniard was speechless. Perplexed, the child looked at me and said nothing. The carpenter shook his head pensively, but wordlessly, and agreed with me with his eyes. His expression conveyed a mixture of puzzlement and awe such as he might have feigned had a cleric uttered those overly sententious words.

I slowly crossed the Plaza de Santa Lucía and entered the Calle de Cipriano through a narrow opening in the old city wall, which followed the contour of the precipitous lower periphery of the city. This wall probably once marked the boundary between Jewish and Christian Zamora. The Jews lived below and outside the wall on the river flats and the Christians above and inside.

Fig. 5.6: Zamora. View of Calle de Cipriano, from Plaza de Santa Lucía, remains of medieval city wall to left or south. Judería located on lower ground near river, may have extended uphill as far as Plaza Santa Lucía, but not beyond or inside city wall on Calle de Cipriano, which continues uphill to city center.

Turning to the right off the Calle de Cipriano, I ascended to one of the principal streets of the town on the highest ground west of the Plaza Mayor, once known as Rua de los Francos. It is now called Calle de Ramos Carrión. Cantera Burgos believes, that the remains of yet another synagogue exists just a few steps to the north of the Calle de Ramos Carrión and the Calle de Moreno. The rear half of the house located at No. 42, Ramos Carrión did, in fact, still possess a single nondescript vestige of a Jewish synagogue, half of the door facing the Calle de Moreno.

The door was open, so I entered. Nothing remarkable struck my eye; it was just a room stacked high with rolls of newsprint and bundles of paper. This part of the building, located on the very ground where once men stood in prayer, turned out to be a warehouse where the local newspaper stores its supplies. I stood in the doorway for a while and examined it. The door arch appeared to have been mended. The half toward the north was thicker. I stepped into the street to see if it still "looked Jewish." The Calle de Moreno, where it opened at the corner of Calle de Ramos Carrión, narrowed to the point that vehicular traffic could not pass. This narrow defile originally must have been the opening in the ghetto wall because the street beyond the synagogue-warehouse widened and curved slightly to the right. The houses there were modern, but the lay of the street with its pebble and flagstone pavement had remained the same as during the Middle Ages when Jews lived on that street.

According to my guide, Cantera, the remains of a third Jewish

Fig. 5.7: Zamora. The corner intersection of Calle de Ramos Carrión and Calle de Moreno. Doorway to building where men are standing is all that remains of synagogue of second judería of Zamora. Building is now used as warehouse for newsprint and other paper products. This section of street, Calle de Moreno, extremely narrow but widens just beyond building. Narrow bottleneck of Calle de Moreno may be site of gate to judería.

quarter once had been located in the part of town known as La Vega. A neighborhood isolated from the main body of the city, La Vega lay outside that portion of the city walls originally built by the Romans. The site occurred along the north-

Fig. 5.8: Zamora. Calle de la Vega, location of third judería of Zamora on northern outskirts of city. East wall of synagogue is preserved and appears at corner of second house from right with hooded chimney on roof directly above it. Synagogue building suffered many changes and alterations when converted to church, later used as private dwelling.

western edge of the handle of the fan-shaped city. This small suburb consisted of no more than a row of houses stretching along the unpaved road, the Calle de La Vega, which circuits the northern perimeter of the town. Nearby, to the north in a neighborhood now known as the Barrio de La Luna, the Jews located their cemetery of Zamora. It has disappeared completely. Only remaining is the memory that it was contiguous to the site where the Monastery of Santo Domingo later stood.

The remnants of the former little Jewish hamlet of La Vega lay on the right, just beyond the old Roman walls. In 904, Alfonso III rebuilt and strengthened the walls. The Arabs gave up the city in 748. It changed hands several times before coming under permanent Christian rule. The medieval walls represent an accretion built on the original Roman. Yet the judería remained ever outside them. Still visible just inside the city wall high above the road of La Vega, the remains of a truly Castilian edifice, a castle, dominates the scene today. The Jewish hamlet lay well below the towering heights of the city on the very edge of the vast plain. A narrow path up the hill provides access to the city from La Vega. At the end of this path, a circular redoubt, partially in ruins, still stands as a sentinel overlooking the judería and the plain beyond.

Fig. 5.9: Zamora. Remains of Roman wall of fortification opposite former synagogue of judería La Vega.

The row of small houses lay below the present road level. All but one were of nondescript architectural character and modern. The exception was a one-story structure built of very massive stones and separated on the east from its neighbor by a narrow passageway open to the sky, in which the ancient masonry was still quite visible. According to Cantera Burgos, this building once housed the synagogue of the judería of La Vega. Later it became a small *ermita* (hermitage) dedicated to Nuestra Señora de La Vega. No longer a church, let alone a synagogue, the building then reverted to the humble home, in an isolated, poor, and undesirable neighborhood, that it had served as hundreds of years ago.

This synagogue was perhaps the last one built in Zamora on this site before the Expulsion. The judería of La Vega had been one of the first in Zamora, probably the first established in Visigothic or possibly even in Roman times. Traditionally, one synagogue or another occupied this site since time immemorial. The synagogue-church had been torn down in the eighteenth century, but the north and west walls were spared.

I walked though the narrow space between the buildings and came in to an open field behind and scrutinized the rear of the building. Only part of the west wall

emerged above the sloping roof of the contiguous buildings that obscured the major portion. Except for a small section at the corner, it displayed a character different from the long north wall. It was impossible to tell which of the walls had once been part of the synagogue and which had been added when it was converted to a church.

I returned to the dusty road and stood facing south looking for a sign of recognition. The stones remained mute and did not speak. I walked away and left the Calle de La Vega, and left Zamora.

Fig. 5.10: Zamora. Remains of Roman wall of fortification and medieval castle to south and high above Calle de La Vega and judería.

Fig. 5.11: Zamora. Narrow passageway leading from Calle de La Vega and judería to gate and redoubt in Roman walls.

Fig. 5.12: Zamora. Remains of east wall of former Synagogue of La Vega.

Fig. 5.13: Zamora. North wall of ruined Synagogue of La Vega.

Fig. 6.1: Salamanca. Map of judería.

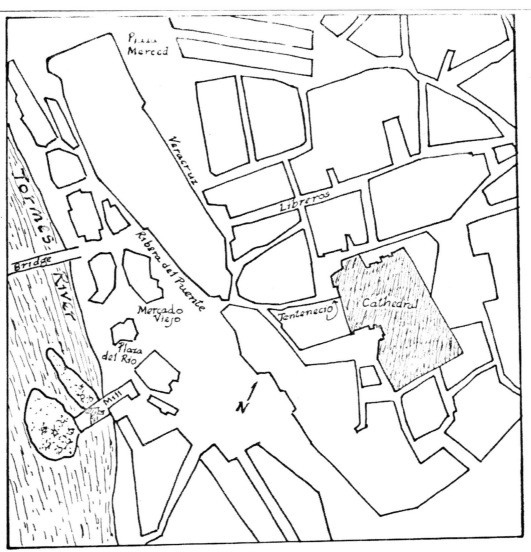

Salamanca

6 Salamanca

The countryside between Zamora and Salamanca, a little over sixty kilometers directly south, is a slightly rolling terrain cultivated mainly with wheat, yet deserted except for two or three small villages. The sky is as big here as on the high plateau of central Mexico.

The highway came to an end abruptly, and I entered Salamanca through the modern part of town. The city derives much of its fame from the older section in which sixteenth-century architecture dominates.

Salamanca is located on a gentle slope inclining in a southerly direction toward the Tormes River. A town of ancient origin, the Romans called it Salamantica. A stone bridge at the very edge of the old judería provides evidence of Roman occupation. In fact, during the Middle Ages the principal access to this bridge, which leads to the road to Avila and Madrid, cut right through the very heart

Fig. 6.2: Salamanca. Roman bridge over Tormes River. Judería located near entrance to bridge along riverbank, also extended to higher ground on bluff above.

of the judería. A gate once pierced the city wall, nonexistent now, more or less directly opposite the bridge. The judería actually extended from the very edge of the river around the accesses to the bridge up to higher ground and to the city wall. That Jews resided there is attested to by the fact that the open area slightly to the east of the bridge is still known as the Mercado Viejo. This name, in all probability, recalls the existence of a market in or adjacent to the Jewish quarter on the outskirts of town and just in front of one of its principal gates.

In the course of its long history the city passed through various hands. The Carthaginians, under Hannibal, conquered it in 217 B.C.E. Successive waves of Germanic barbarians—Vandals, Alans, Suevi, and Visigoths—occupied it as they swept across Europe following the decline of Rome. Moslems took over in the eighth century C.E., whereupon the struggle between Christian and Moslem for the city began. As late as 1085, Christians assumed permanent control.

Just when Jews first settled in Salamanca is not known. History reveals they were there as far back as Moslem or even Visigothic times. However, notices of the existence of a Jewish community in Salamanca only begin to appear in various documents from the twelfth century on. In 1178 Fernando II published his famous *Fuero de Salamanca*, which guaranteed certain legal rights to Jews on a par with Christians. This state of affairs changed radically about two hundred and thirty years later, in 1411, when according to an apocryphal story repeated as fact by the

Fig. 6.3: Salamanca. La Gota de Leche building on Plaza de La Merced on site of synagogue.

seventeenth-century historian Gil González Dávila, San Vicente Ferrer supposedly came to Salamanca and Zamora and preached to the Jews there. After a Jewish friend advised him about how he might successfully convert the Jews of Salamanca, he burst into the synagogue one Sabbath morning during prayers. A tumult arose; he quieted the assembled Jews with sweet words and expressions of love, begging them to hear him. While he was preaching, some white crosses appeared on the clothing of the Jews. (A possible explanation would be that the arrangement of their prayer shawls created the cross image.) When the congregation saw this *miracle* all as one man asked to be baptized, many taking the name Vicente in honor of the saint who had showed them the light!

The synagogue where this miracle took place has long since disappeared. During the seventeenth century the site was occupied by the *Colegio de La Vera Cruz* (School of the True Cross) of the monastic order of La Merced. The school derived its name from the miracle of the apparition of the crosses on the Jewish prayer shawls that fateful Sabbath morning more than two hundred years before. Even the name of the street, *Calle de La Vera Cruz* (Street of the True Cross), also originated in this miracle.

The monastery and school of La Merced also have disappeared. In their place, at the time Cantera was writing, a school building stood together with a charitable institution known as *La Gota de Leche* (The Drop of Milk), which distributed free milk to the poor mothers and children of this humble neighborhood.

The land pitched steeply to the south and east from the little plaza of La Merced. All had changed. Not a single vestige from the Middle Ages, except the lay of the streets remained. La Gota de Leche rose as a compassionate overbur-

Fig. 6.4: Salamanca. Tower and dome of cathedral from Plaza de La Merced in judería at intersection of Calle de Moneda on left.

Fig. 6.5: Salamanca. Calle de la Vera Cruz. Principal street of medieval judería from intersection of Calle Libreros toward east. Calle de Tentenecio in background.

Fig. 6.6: Salamanca. East of Calle Libreros from Calle de la Vera Cruz to dome of Church of La Clerecía, Jesuit seminary church, in background. Second synagogue in vicinity of intersection.

den on the site of the synagogue where the miracle of the True Cross had occurred. Diagonally across from it, the Cathedral of Salamanca rose over the rooftops of the houses. Construction of the cathedral began in 1100 and was completed a century later. At this time, the Jewish community experienced great development. This flowering of Jewish culture occurred as the result of a law mandated in 1178 that delineated the rights and privileges of the Jewish community. The modern tower presents a different appearance from that which Jews of the judería could see as they moved about their street so long ago. It was rebuilt in the seventeenth century, long after Jewish life had been extinguished in Salamanca.

The street of the True Cross was not extinguished, however, and to this very day still preserves its Jewish outlines. Somewhere along its course another and even older synagogue once had existed, perhaps near the intersection of the Calle de los Libreros. Built long after the Jews had been converted to Christianity, the dome of the Jesuit Church of La Clerecía dominated the view up the Calle de los

Fig. 6.7: Salamanca. Calle de Tentenecio at foot of principal street of medieval judería, Calle de la Vera Cruz, near cathedral tower. Street probably one of entrances to judería.

Fig. 6.8: Salamanca. View to north of Calle de Tentenecio from below near riverbank; Calle de Ribera del Puente, toward Calle de la Vera Cruz, the principal street of judería. Dome of cathedral dominates background.

Libreros from the Calle de La Vera Cruz. Except for the memory, Jewish influence completely disappeared.

The remnant of Israel that had survived in Spain after a century of dire persecution left in 1492. The Decree of Expulsion strictly prohibited the Jews from selling their communal property, such as synagogue buildings, houses of study, cemeteries, and the like. The crown claimed their property. In 1492, local church authorities took over the other synagogue, the one which had been spared the miracle and probably the one near the Calle de los Libreros. The authorities then converted it to private dwellings. They sold the property in 1507 after the building deteriorated. Not a vestige of it remains today, nor is its exact location actually known.

The cross street that once descended through the heart of the Jewish quarter down the slope to the riverbank and the Roman bridge have disappeared; new houses have been built on it. I could only approximate its location with the aid of a map as I faced the blank walls. The only access to the river now is by the circuitous way down to the lower end of the Calle de La Vera Cruz and into a narrow little alley-like street called Calle de Tentenecio. I walked the length of the Calle de La Vera Cruz to what seemed like a dead end at first. A turn to the left and then to the right brought me into what was no more than a sloping corridor between high walls open to the sky. At the bottom between the walls was the river. The Calle de Tentenecio is a steeply inclined, extremely narrow, curving street extending from the cathedral tower past the blind intersection of the Calle de La Vera Cruz down to the *Calle de Ribera del Puente* (Strand of the Bridge), a narrow strip of land at some height above the riverbank. The street was badly paved and actually inaccessible to vehicles from the the Ribera del Puente below. Steps led down to the lower ground and the site of the Mercado Viejo and the lower section of the judería near the Roman bridge.

I clambered down from the higher Ribera del Puente to the river's edge, and the urban air changed to one of pastoral calm. On my map of Salamanca I noted that the bank at this point was known as the Plaza del Río. Jewish houses must once have fronted this plaza. Groups of women from the neighborhood washed clothes, children waded in the water, and some fished. A little distance to the east, an old

Fig. 6.9: Salamanca. Ancient Roman bridge over Tormes River from Plaza del Río in medieval judería on riverbank lower down slope from Ribera del Puente.

mill framed by trees provided a backdrop to the quiet scene. The stream of water diverted under the mill gushed out like a mountain brook with a sound like the tinkling of crystal as the green ripples topped with bubbling white foam eddied by. A spot with wide-branched leafy trees grew on the very edge of the river, a spot once dominated by the strong, but no longer extant, fortification walls high up the slope where the Jewish houses once clung.

I retraced my steps up the narrow, hemmed-in Calle de Tentenecio past the blind intersection of the Calle de La Vera Cruz, the cathedral tower a guiding beacon overhead above the tops of the walls to either side. Suddenly the passage widened. It was as if I had been walking in a dense forest and had come unexpectedly to a clearing under an open sky above. I stopped and looked back down the Calle de Tentenecio once again and realized that I had passed from Jewish Salamanca to Christian Salamanca. The modern wall on the left actually rested on an ancient foundation of rough-hewn stones of great size. The street had formed a bottle-neck. The wall on the right, the one toward the Calle de La Vera Cruz, was of the same character as the remnant under the modern wall. It turned sharply to the left, almost closing the opening leading into the lower part of the Calle de Tentenecio from where I had just come. The narrow opening at this point in the clearing doubtlessly marked the gate of the judería, the gate in the wall that separated Jew from Christian in the Middle Ages.

Fig. 6.10: Salamanca. Mill just east of Plaza del Río in lower section of medieval judería.

Here, then, in the very shadow of the cathedral on the sharply pitched land tumbling down to the river, Jews once lived and had two synagogues until they witnessed the miracle of the True Cross on their prayer shawls while at Sabbath morning prayers.

Taking a circuitous route around the city, I crossed the river over a modern bridge upstream from the old Roman one adjacent to the judería. Across the broad stream Jewish houses had once clung to the steep slope from the water's edge up to the medieval city wall. The view was picturesque and appealing. The rear walls of the houses on the Jewish Street of the True Cross sat on the crest of the barren slope. The beautiful towers and domes of the churches of Salamanca rose above them in the distance. The Jews had never seen this view; these Christian edifices arose long after the Jewish community had been extinguished.

7 Avila

The road to Avila from Salamanca passed over the flat plains of Castile, but near Avila the landscape changed, becoming somewhat rolling and even broken in places with curious outcroppings of rocks and enormous weathered boulders. The whole of the scene was desolate, and were it not for some advertisements of an enterprising optician in Madrid painted on some of the more imposing rocks, I would never have known that I was not on the moon. A slight descent and a turn in the road brought the walled city of Avila into full view through the windshield. An imposing sight, the dark walls of the town blended into the stark landscape, all of a piece. The rough stone walls were so high that they hid the city within from view, except for the bell towers and domes of the many churches and religious houses barely extending above the battlements.

I crossed the dry bed of the River Adaja over a rather ugly iron bridge at the western outskirts of town and came almost immediately to one of the eight gates of the city. It was hardly wide enough to allow my American-sized automobile to enter.

Fig. 7.1: Avila. Calle de Esteban Domingo located in northeast part of town, probably street in medieval judería.

After some cautious maneuvering, I parked in an open area just inside the walls, noting before me a mass of densely packed houses as close to one another as trees in a forest. The exceedingly narrow streets rose steeply to the center of town on the summit of the hill on which the city was built. The city dominated the plain below. Inside the city was as stark as the landscape surrounding the town, high and dry and stony.

Until the Expulsion of the Jews and Moslems, the grim medieval town flourished; afterward it went into a permanent decline. In Avila, in these severe, harsh surroundings, one of the most colorful and most typical figures of Spanish history, Santa Teresa de Avila (1515-82), had been born and had lived almost all her life. Santa Teresa lived a life of piety and mysticism that is still considered exemplary. She introduced reforms which operated against any laxity in religious life and which only reinforced the existing customs of religious asceticism and mysticism in the daily life and practices of the religious orders. She reestablished a strict and rigorous observance of the rule of the Carmelite Order, which then enjoyed a great development in the Spain of her day and later. The whole of Avila is full of relics of her birth, life, and death. I was astounded when I learned from the works of Julio Caro Baroja that he had concluded, based on his extensive research, that Santa Teresa was of Jewish descent.

Teresa was born about a generation after the Jews had been expelled from Spain. If Caro Baroja is correct, it is an irony of fate that the most venerated, the most Spanish, of all Spanish saints should be of Jewish descent! Her grandfather had been a Jew who, though converted, still practiced Judaism in secret. When this was discovered by the Inquisition, he repented his "backsliding" and was condemned to wear a *sambenito*, a special garb like a smock worn by penitent convicts of the Inquisition. Teresa's brothers all left for the New World, perhaps to be out of reach of the Inquisition and the suspicion under which they had to live as grandsons of backslider. The Convent of the Incarnation, where Teresa spent twenty-nine years of her life, lies just outside the city walls to the north in the plain below.

According to Cantera Burgos, the Jewish quarter of Avila was probably located in the northeast corner of the city in the rather reduced area between the Arco del Mariscal and the Puerta de San Vicente. I searched out this part of town and came to a narrow street known as

Fig. 7.2: Avila. Calle de López Núñez, Puerta de San Vicente, medieval wall fortification, possible entrance judería.

Calle de Esteban Domingo leading off the main plaza to the judería. I followed this street for a short stretch and found it brought me into the Calle de López Núñez with the Puerta de San Vicente at the far end. The area seemed to be on the very highest point of the town. To the left was a garden, probably nonexistent in medieval times. I could find no sign or indication where the synagogue may have stood. A contemporary document records that in 1476 the synagogue had been converted to the Church of *Todos los Santos* (All Saints), thus suggesting that a synagogue had existed in Avila. Where it had stood no one knows for sure. Surely I was standing somewhere in the vicinity on that early afternoon in August about five hundred years later.

The harsh, severe, dark-red Avila, with its mighty unyielding walls that constricted and choked the physical growth of the city, provided an apt stage for the most Spanish of all Christian Spanish saints, said to be the granddaughter of a reluctantly converted Jew. At the time the rest of Europe was enjoying the fruits of the Renaissance and Spain was on the brink of entering the modern world, Spaniards turned instead to the teachings of Teresa of Avila. She had renewed, with great passion, the asceticism and mysticism of the waning Middle Ages. The ardent Christian pietism of Santa Teresa of Avila provided the natural counterpoint to the indecisive conversion of her grandfather.

Dark, foreboding Avila is still clothed in a gloom that is neither night nor day. In the half-light, no trace of the Jewish community, which gave Spain its greatest saint, appears.

Fig. 8.1: Madrid. Map showing medieval judería.

Madrid

8 Madrid

Ever since the airplane displaced the steamship, most visitors from abroad arrive first in Madrid. The first stop on most tourists' itineraries through Spain, Madrid is not, however, as important for the traveler into the Jewish past as is Toledo or Seville. Madrid came into prominence during the sixteenth century, after the Expulsion of the Jews, when Felipe II permanently established the court there. Because of its location in the very geographical center of the country, it offered good accessibility.

The earliest notices attesting to the existence of Madrid, however, reach back to the tenth century when the town was under Arab domination and known as Magrit or Magerit. Madrid passed into Christian hands in 1083 under Alfonso VI, who purified the mosque within the Arab fortress, located on the site now occupied by the National Palace. Here an image of the Virgin was found near a grain storehouse. Curiously, this Virgin bears an Arab name to this day, *La Virgen de la Almudena* (Virgin of the Granary). *Almudena* is Arabic for wheat storehouse or granary. Until 1329 when Fernando IV assembled the Cortes there, Christian Madrid was an unimportant town during most of tthe Middle Ages.

Fig. 8.2: Madrid. Calle de la Fe, formerly known as Calle de la Sinagoga, possibly main street of judería. View from higher ground in front of Church of San Lorenzo at corner of Calle de Baltasar Bachero looking down to Plaza Lavapies.

Fig. 8.3: Madrid. Calle de la Fe, formerly Calle de la Sinagoga and possibly main street of judería. View from midway down street at intersection of Calle de Zurita, looking toward Church of San Lorenzo on higher ground.

After the Reconquest of Madrid, the authorities concentrated both Jews and Moslems in separate neighborhoods. The former Moslem quarter bears the name of La Morería to this very day. By the fifteenth century the Jewish community of Madrid had become so impoverished that in 1481 it did not have the means to comply with the order to enclose the judería with a wall. The City Council of Madrid then had no other alternative but to agree to build it at its own expense.

In 1561, when Felipe II located the royal court there permanently, the town had about 25,000 inhabitants, many more than when Jews still resided there before the Expulsion in 1492. The judería lay to the south of the Plaza Mayor toward the Manzanares River, a neighborhood which preserves in vestigial form some of its medieval character, a veritable maze in contrast to the more regular sixteenth-century plan of Madrid. The difference between sixteenth-century and medieval Madrid is revealed by the regular, orthogonal grid pattern of the streets of the former and seemingly formless pattern of the latter, which developed organically without any preconceived plan over the course of time.

The Jewish quarter had been centered around the Calle de la Fe, formerly known as the Calle de la Sinagoga, or even possibly the Calle de la Judería. Standing in front of the Church of San Lorenzo on Faith Street from my position on the top of the hill and looking down toward Plaza Lavapies, I saw a most commonplace narrow city street with rather ugly tenement houses lining either side, all with uniform iron balconies and with commercial establishments, mainly grocery stores, at street level. Not a Jewish trace was in evidence. After walking down to the foot

Fig. 8.4: Madrid. The corner of Calle de Argumosa and Calle de Dr. Fourquet, former site of Jewish cemetery, located downhill in southeasterly direction from Calle de la Fe, probably outside walls of judería. Cemetery now occupied by four-story garage.

of the street and looking back up toward the Church of San Lorenzo, I witnessed again the same unprepossessing view of a typical lower-middle-class neighborhood in any one of dozens of modern European cities. Not a single Jewish spoor greeted me. The site of the present Church of San Lorenzo, with its dominatingly high position in the cityscape, could not have been the location of a synagogue during the medieval period. Hopefully, I searched for some Jewish trace up the street from where Calle de la Fe meets the intersection of Calle de Baltasar Bachero, which in turn runs uphill to the Calle de Santa Isabel. The street, as straight as the lines on the paper on which its plan was first drawn, contained no ancient traits, rather it resembled the confection of a twentieth-century real estate developer.

I walked up Faith Street again to the Church of San Lorenzo and into a narrow street, the Calle de La Travesía de San Lorenzo, on its north flank that went down the hill. I followed it along its entire length where it emptied into a wide avenue open to two-way automobile traffic, Calle de Argumosa. I had read in Cantera that at the intersection of the latter and the Calle del Dr. Fourquet skeletal remains in some quantity had been found three or four meters below the present street level. Some observers concluded this to be evidence that the medieval Jewish burying ground had been located there, truly a bitter irony. The most mundane of build-

Fig. 8.5: Madrid. Plaza Mayor. Northwest angle. Place where Inquisition executed sentences of the condemned, usually through *auto da fe*. Spectators watched from many windows in buildings surrounding plaza.

ings occupied the site. This building—a garage—exemplified the undistinguished architectural design typical of the twentieth century with its irreverence for the past.

The modern city, with its tenements, grocery stores, and garages, had eradicated the Jewish past in the old Jewish quarter of medieval Madrid. Nothing tangible remained to guide me in my search. I retraced my steps up the Travesía de San Lorenzo to the Street of the Faith with little hope of finding even a speck of Jewish dust there. Looking up at the street sign just in front of the Church of San Lorenzo, I noted in faint outline the word *Sinagoga* peering through the more freshly painted lettering of *de la fe*. The memory of the synagogue was not yet obliterated! Then I realized that all the street names in the vicinity were strange, too exhortatively Christian. The strikingly unexpected concentration of street names most strongly affirmed an adherence to Christianity. Piety demonstrated itself to an excessive extent unusual even in Spain. The Street of the Synagogue had been converted to the Street of the Faith. Faith Street emptied into the *Plaza de los Lavapies* (Washing of the Feet). Hail Mary Street and Jesus and Mary Street converged on the Plaza of the Washing of the Feet. Curiously, in the immediate vicinity of Jesus and Mary Street were many others that still had preserved their medieval secular names: Street of the Bear; Street of the Fencing Foil; Street of the Two Sisters; Street of the Three Fish; Street of Hope; Street of Spring, and others.

Traces of the ultimate Jewish tragedy in Spain exist in more material form in the Plaza Mayor where many secret Jews, and even Christians whose only crime was to have had Jewish forebears, were put to the supreme test in fire and flame. In 1959, work was in progress to restore the Plaza Mayor, which had fallen into a sad state of disrepair. The job was completed in 1961 in time to celebrate the four hundredth anniversary of the establishment of the capital of the Spanish empire in Madrid. Although begun much earlier and literally carved out of and inserted into the medieval city plan, the Plaza Mayor was originally built in 1619. It is a rectangular open space about 200 meters long by 100 meters wide (600 by 300 feet) surrounded on four sides by buildings with open arcaded corridors at street level. Casa de la Panadería, a specially designed section, sits in the center of the building on the north side. Otherwise, the four facades repeat the same elements to form a regular and severe pattern. Nine arches or gateways, which provide access to adjacent streets, pierce the buildings enclosing the plaza.

Fig. 8.6: Madrid. Plaza Mayor. North side with Casa de la Panadería. Windows in this section best for viewing spectacles of *autos da fe.*

Here during the heyday of the Spanish empire in the seventeenth century, great spectacles were enacted for the moral improvement and spiritual diversion of the populace. This plaza, with its surrounding buildings five stories high with 477 windows looking out on the great open space below, adequately provided space for assembling thousands of spectators. The Plaza Mayor witnessed fiestas, and the infamous *autos da fe* (public punishment of heretics by the tribunal of the Inquisition). After due legal process by the Holy Office of the Inquisition, *marranos* (secret Jews, or Jews who tenaciously held on to the faith of their fathers following Christian baptism) met a horrible fate. Here they were "relaxed" in person, or if no other guise was possible, then in effigy. Madrid employed its Plaza Mayor, with magnificent monumental architecture, as a setting for public executions. No other city in Spain claimed such an auspicious setting for such a purpose.

Madrid authorities built the Plaza Mayor long after they exempted the few miserable impoverished Jews from erecting the wall designed to close them off from the rest of the city, and long after they expelled the Jews. They were unable to destroy Judaism in the city, however. Fire consumed the parchment of the Torah scrolls, but not the letters.

9 Segovia

I could not imagine what the motives had been, other than geo-political, for the choice in the sixteenth century to locate the capital of Spain in the approximate physical center of the country. A reasonable answer to this question eluded me and I concluded the motives must have been more quixotic than realistic as I sped over the bare and monotonous empty plain of New Castile toward Segovia. There seemed to be no material reason, no economic or social reason, no reason of nature or of man why a metropolis should exist in the spot where Madrid now intrudes on the horizon. Madrid is where it is because of an arbitrary, autocratic, political choice. This choice is somewhat comparable to the arbitrary, though democratic, choice made in the late eighteenth century, to locate the capital of the United States of America in Washington, the then geographical center of the new republic.

Once beyond the confines of the endless streets of Madrid, with its interminable rows of red brick, high-rise apartment houses more like prison blocks than domestic dwellings and all uniformly alike in their ugliness, the twentieth century is left behind and one is speedily transported back to the New Castile of centuries past. However, the ugliness of Madrid housing structures chokes the city in ever-widening circles, encroaching more and more each year on the wild Castilian plain.

Leaving Madrid in a northwesterly direction, I traveled over a rolling plain with the mountains, Sierra de Guadarrama, as a backdrop. I turned off the main highway at the small crossroads town of Villalba on a cobblestone road. The roughness of the cobblestone surface created a whirring staccato of the automobile's turning wheels, suggesting a rapid-fire beat on a snare drum, as if the wheels had been shod with hardwood drumsticks rather than rubber tires. The sensation was that of sitting on a vibrating massage machine. The road soon began to climb higher and higher, and some of the views from the hairpin turns were breathtaking, revealing the ground just passed over as a gigantic three-dimensional relief map. The vegetation changed with the rise in elevation. The dry, barren landscape gave way to verdant hills and dark woods hemming in the road on either side. Benign rains, whose moisture does not reach the plain below, provide pine trees and clearings with a lush ground cover of grass and wild flowers. The road reached a height of 1,860 meters (6,100 feet) at Puerto de Navacerrada on the very summit of the mountains, revealing a view of the other side of the Guadarrama range and Segovia in the valley below. I had to acclimate to the thin air at this great height while enjoying the grand sight from the side of the road where I stopped for a few moments.

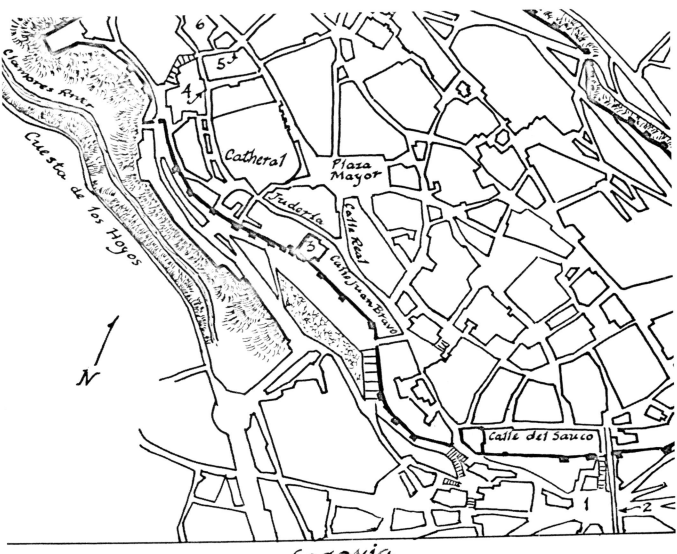

Fig. 9.1: Segovia. Map of judería.

Then occurred a hair-raising descent down the steep, tortuously winding road with many blind hairpin curves along the narrow defiles of the steep mountains. I was now breathless, not from lack of oxygen but from the tense concentration needed to avoid sailing off the road into the profound abysses that bordered the narrow pavement unprotected by guard rails. The ride seemed endless, though the distance was short; I breathed more easily when I reached level ground again on approaching La Granja. The rest of the road to Segovia was anticlimactic. The total distance traversed from Madrid was but eighty-eight kilometers or about fifty miles, but I felt I had gone five hundred.

Segovia is one of the chief tourist attractions, insistently and incessantly brought to the attention of travelers visiting Madrid. These tourists then travel there by the busload, view the principal architectural monuments, especially the Alcazar, the cathedral, and the Roman aqueduct; hear many interesting stories; eat a sumptuous lunch in a restaurant exuding "typical" Spanish atmosphere; and finally return to their hotels in Madrid with a sense of accomplishment. For me, Segovia took on a different guise. The few paltry remains of Jewish monuments in Segovia do not impress the viewer, overwhelmed as they are by the majesty of the cathedral whose spires dominate the former Jewish quarter. The narrow Jewish streets twist and wind. They are altogether most unprepossessing. The great Jewish monuments are the intangibles of the spirit, and are just as enduring as the mighty fortress, the Roman aqueduct, and the cathedral for which Segovia is famous.

The city is located on the steep slopes of an eminence in a typical Castilian landscape, all red and ocher and dry with a bright blue sky above, at the confluence of the Eresma and Clamores rivers that form its north and south natural defenses. The westerly tip of the city rises high above the fork of the two rivers. The much restored and much commercialized fortress depicted on thousands of travel posters, the Alcazar, a true "Castle in Spain," dominates the landscape. The southwesterly side of the city ends in a steep bluff. One goes from the lower part outside the ancient walls up many flights of steps to reach the higher level from the Plaza del Azoguejo, where the old Roman aqueduct, still in use, bridges the depression. The aqueduct provides an imposing stage setting before which a number of pleasant cafes on all sides of the plaza arrange themselves. Daily, these cafes receive patrons according to the position of the sun: one side in the morning, the other in the afternoon. The shade is preferred in summer, the sun in winter.

Founded by the Romans about 80 B.C.E., the city was settled previously by the native Celtiberians, who are remembered for their resistance to Roman domination. Subsequently, the Arabs conquered it and established a capital here that remained two centuries. Evidence of Jewish life in Segovia comes to light only after the Christian domination. Here in 1474, Isabel La Católica was proclaimed queen; she and her husband Ferdinand became Los Reyes Católicos. As rulers, Isabel and Ferdinand later spelled out the final doom, not only for the Jewish community of Segovia, but for all Spanish Jewry as well.

Climbing up the steps to one side of the aqueduct from the Plaza de Azoguejo, I passed inside the old walls of the city. Continuing in a westerly direction along the Calle del Sauco, I entered the Calle de Juan Bravo. Further along, the Calle de Juan Bravo emptied into the Calle Real, which terminated at the Plaza Mayor. The Calle Real is jammed with both pedestrian and automobile traffic and lined with commercial establishments. About one block before reaching the main plaza, the Calle de la Judería Vieja branches off to the left. At this junction I noted a very sim-

Fig. 9.2: Segovia. Portal to courtyard of Church of Corpus Christi, formerly synagogue. Gothic arch over entrance probably contemporary with date of synagogue, wall itself subject to alterations and repairs. Located on busy street, not far from main plaza.

Fig. 9.3: Segovia. Entrance to synagogue-church of Corpus Christi. Door located on right side of court as one enters from street, at far end of building. Nave extends to left. Horseshoe-shaped arch spans door. Above, under eaves, a two-bay window also spanned by two horseshoe-shaped arches. Wall with door and twin-arched window repaired in 1902, indicated on inscription to right at bottom of lunette just above door.

ple, narrow facade pierced by a single Gothic portal. Above the pointed arch were written the words *Corpus Christi* (the Body of Christ). The portal was the entrance to a small courtyard fronting the convent and Church of Corpus Christi. The church had formerly been a synagogue. In 1410, according to a story still current, the Jews committed a heinous sacrilege. As punishment for the alleged sacrilege, the Catholics converted this Jewish house of prayer into a Christian church.

The new Christian name given the converted synagogue was not altogether arbitrarily chosen. The extraordinary story tells how a Jew had stolen the Host, the

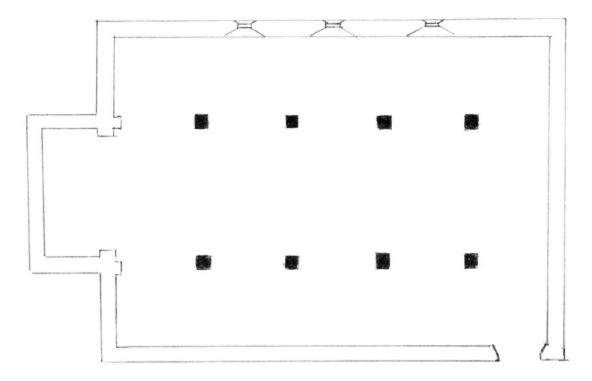

Fig. 9.4: Segovia. Plan of synagogue-church of Corpus Christi. Building suffered severe damage in fire (1899). All interior decoration in modeled plaster as well as all Hebrew inscription lost. Only its plan could be restored to original state.

symbol of the body of Christ used in celebrating Mass, from the altar of a church and had brought it to this synagogue, where the rabbis threw it into a cauldron of boiling water. The Host raised itself up in the air, and the synagogue shook as if an earthquake had rocked the place, so much so that some of the walls cracked. On seeing this portent, the rabbis were frightened and returned the Host to the prior of the monastery of Santa Cruz. The prior administered the Host to a novice by way of communion. The novice died three days later. The men who were guilty of this unpardonable sacrilege were hung from the gallows and their broken bodies later dragged though the Calle Real to the Plaza Mayor and through the streets of Segovia. Ironically, in 1459, a converted Jew, Friar Alonso de Espina, first repeated this fantastic story in print.

A religious order of nuns, whose convent is now contiguous to the former synagogue, took over the building. At the time of this writing, they still used it as a church. I walked under the pointed arch and came into a small open space surrounded by a high wall on the street side, by the convent building, and by part of the long east wall of the synagogue of the Body of Christ. I tried the door there only to find it locked. I asked a small boy playing in the courtyard how I might

Fig. 9.5: Segovia. Synagogue-church of Corpus Christi. Prayer hall toward East Wall oriented toward Jerusalem. Where Ark of Torah had been located now occupied by main altar of church. Chancel arch is horseshoe shaped as are arches of nave arcades, windows in clerestory to either side of nave, except the five windows at far end. Wall surfaces before fire decorated with designs in modeled plaster and Hebrew inscriptions comparable to those of synagogue-church of El Tránsito in Toledo.

Fig. 9.6: Segovia. Synagogue-church of Corpus Christi. Detail showing nave arcade and clerestory. Each bay spanned by horseshoe-shaped arch of mudéjar style, comparable to arches of nave arcade in synagogue-church of Santa María La Blanca in Toledo.

find someone to open the door. He led me to an entry or small vestibule with what looked like a small opening in the wall containing a cylindrical wooden revolving window or turntable. He pulled a cord hanging to one side and a muffled tinkling of bells came faintly through the heavy wooden turntable. After a few moments, I heard a high-pitched voice, a soft woman's voice from another world ask what I wanted. "To see the interior of the church," I answered. The little boy also offered the information that I had come all the way from America to see their church.

In a querulous tremolo the voice asked, "*¿Como están las cosas en América? ¿Hay paz en América?*" (How are things in America? Is there peace in America?).

I answered, not wishing to carry on a conversation with the disembodied spirit in the wall, "*Si, si, todo anda bien, y hay paz*" (Yes, yes, all goes well and there is peace). The turntable creaked as it slowly revolved a half-turn, revealing a longitudinally bisected section of the cylinder and in it a large iron key polished smooth from being handled for so many hundreds of years. I took the key, murmured, "Gracias," and as I turned to go to the synagogue door across the courtyard, I heard the turntable grating to complete the full revolution. I held the key in my hand and felt its smoothness, then inserted it into the lock, which turned effortlessly, swung the door open and entered. The interior was dark and cool, another world, a world of the past. I left behind the noisy Calle Real full of pedestrians, automobiles and motorcycles, and the hot, bright sunshine of the late afternoon in August. I journeyed back in time to afternoon prayers in August of 1410, almost six hundred years ago, just one month before the calumny and its subsequent disaster when the principals of this synagogue were hung by the neck from the gallows. Just inside the door the memory of their alleged sacrilege remained alive. In fact, a plaque, affixed to the very wall, materially preserved the event. It had cracked at the very moment when the Host rose from the boiling cauldron in 1410.

The main axis of the building stood at right angles to the door near the end of the east wall where I had entered. At the far end of the nave to the south, the main church altar had taken over the place in which the Ark of the Torah once stood. The rectangular plan was divided into three aisles, the central one the widest, by two rows of octagonal columns and horseshoe-shaped arches supporting a clerestory with an arcade of windows with the same type of arches as in the Synagogue of Santa María La Blanca in Toledo. The synagogue-church of Corpus Christi had remained more or less intact until 1899 when it was destroyed in a fire. Only the exterior walls and the two interior arcades with horseshoe-shaped arches resting on octagonal columns were left standing. The building has been restored completely. Though its plan has been preserved, nothing of the ancient wooden beamed ceiling with its decorative pattern of interlaced moldings, the *alfarfe*, nor any of the original stucco wall decoration has survived.

I returned to the little court fronting the entrance to the building proper, a quiet place between the profane world of the street and the other worldly sanctity of the house of prayer. By custom, a courtyard preceded the medieval Spanish synagogue, which did not face directly on the street. This was not unique; the synagogue court has antecedents extending back into antiquity to the first synagogues constructed in ancient Israel. The wall of the Synagogue of Corpus Christi facing the courtyard, though repaired and restored, resembled the original before the fire of 1899. The door and the arcaded window above, facing the courtyard, remained unchanged.

Fig. 9.7: Segovia. Calle de la Judería Vieja. Synagogue-church of Corpus Christi is located at place where Calle de Juan Bravo changes in name to Calle de la Judería Vieja. Street is irregular and narrow. Houses, modern now, stand on same sites as were occupied by medieval Jewish community.

Fig. 9.8: Segovia. Calle de la Judería Nueva. View from intersection of Calle de los Leones west and Calle de Almuzara. Street center of second or new Jewish quarter and center of area into which Jews were confined after 1412. It descends sharply and borders right side of Plaza de La Merced where Synagogue of Judería Nueva stood.

Leaving the courtyard I turned to the left and entered the street that still bears a name that recalls the fact that this was the Jewish quarter of the town, *Calle de la Judería Vieja* (Street of the Old Jewish Quarter). It wound in an easterly direction, widening and narrowing quite fortuitously as it skirted the lower ramparts of the city wall. Farther down, the narrow tunnel-like street widened and continued as the Calle de Almuzara. In the fourteenth and fifteenth centuries, this relatively wide section was the very center of the Jewish quarter. About midway down its length, a steeply inclined narrow street with steps intersected it. The street sign at the corner read, *Calle de la Judería Nueva* (Street of the New Jewish Quarter). Above me, on

Fig. 9.9: Segovia. Calle de Almuzara, view to northeast. This street is a continuation of Calle de la Judería Vieja. In 1412 another synagogue, located somewhere on Calle de Almuzara, turned over to monastic order of La Merced for use as hospital. High stone wall in background encloses Plaza de La Merced on higher ground where synagogue-hospital once stood.

Fig. 9.10: Segovia. Calle de Almuzara. View southeast with cathedral in background dominating Judería Nueva. Plaza de La Merced to left, behind high retaining wall. Calle de la Judería Nueva intersects at corner. High wall right encloses private houses built on highest section of precipice above Clamores River. On Opposite bank, Cuesta de los Hoyos, Jewish burial ground, location of Jewish refuge when Decree of Expulsion reached Segovia in 1492.

higher ground, I could see an open area or park, the Plaza de La Merced. I continued on the Calle de Almuzara, walking on between the retaining wall of the park and a high fence on the opposite side, behind which a garden sloped down to the city wall below. No buildings obstructed the view, and when I looked over my shoulder I saw the dome and the tower of the Cathedral of Segovia, just as the Jews of the Calle de Almuzara must have seen it before they were expelled from Segovia. Somewhere on this street, the Calle de Almuzara, according to my informant, Cantera, once was located yet another synagogue, one which was probably not as important as that converted into the Church of Corpus Christi. Try as I might, I could find no vestige of this house of prayer.

Soon after 1412, the year the edict separating the Jews and Moors from Christians was promulgated, the monks of La Merced requested that they be given the synagogue in the Calle de Almuzara by way of compensation for some land, probably on the Calle de la Judería Nueva. This street ran just behind their monastery, into which the Jews had been confined in compliance with the new law. The monks then expressed the "altruistic" desire to use the building as a hospital for the poor. They received the building as well as all the property and rents that had belonged to this synagogue.

The synagogue-hospital of the Calle de Almuzara has since disappeared, as has the monastery of La Merced. The area is now the site of the small park with a splendid view across the river gorge. At least the name of the street into which the Jews had been herded, the Calle de la Judería Nueva, the one which descends rapidly downhill crossing the Calle de Almuzara, has survived the centuries.

I looked over the top of the garden wall and gazed at the landscape beyond in a southwesterly direction from the judería. The land falls sharply there in a steep slope forming one side of the gorge carved out by the River Clamores. The equally steep opposite side bears the aptly descriptive name, *La Cuesta de los Hoyos* (Hill of the Graves). The name was an old one, but the reason for its existence had long been forgotten. As recently as the late nineteenth century, archaeologists carried out excavations on the site and finally confirmed that the graves found there were part of the ancient burying ground of the Jewish community of Segovia.

The graves were in the shape of grottoes or caves excavated from the soft limestone of the cliff, a form of Jewish burial common in the Holy Land since antiquity. The Segovia Jews used the tombs for more than one burial, separate sepulchers being dug off the central chamber exactly as had been traditional in their ancestral home in ancient Israel. It was here that the pitiful remnant of the once-flourishing Jewish community of Segovia took refuge when the edict of Expulsion of 1492 reached them. There they remained among their dead begging for more or time before departing from their native home where they had lived and died for centuries. Some of the kind-hearted people of the town, both ecclesiastics as well as ordinary citizens, moved to compassion by the suffering of the Jews living in the graves of their ancestors and wishing to take advantage of the propitious moment of their despair, clambered up the Cuesta de los Hoyos and with sweet words of love and other blandishments begged the refugees to leave the Law of Moses and see the light of the True Religion. Some of the Jews did "see the light" and were baptized, but the greater majority left the graves of their fathers and went into exile, and no Jews—neither the quick nor the dead—have resided in Segovia since.

10 Toledo

Now, at some distance in time and space from my first experience with the remains of the Jewish past in Toledo, I am able to speak somewhat dispassionately of these monuments of brick, stone, and plaster that still echo with long-stilled cries of anguish from the immolated bodies of those who died for *Kiddush ha Shem* (Sanctification of the Name of God). Synagogues of brick, stone, plaster, and wood contrived in great beauty of shape and form to survive as living memorials to the known and the unknown, the silenced of Israel. The two synagogues with such outlandish names, Santa María La Blanca and Nuestra Señora del Tránsito, are poignant, living reminders that more than synagogues were forcibly converted. Such profoundly pious Catholic Christian names with which these two synagogues were consecrated were also forced on men. Baptized Jews, converted willingly or against their will, were likewise christened with names of Catholic saints and the like to symbolize that they had traveled to the opposite pole of their faith, to prove that they had fled the greatest distance possible away from fellow Jews, from Judaism itself, and from Jewish life. The improbable name for a synagogue, Holy Mary the Virgin, summarizes the Jewish story in Toledo in the waning days of the Middle Ages in Spain.

So much then for Toledo, the Toledo that held forth as the most important city in all Spanish history, the city which Spaniards say is the most complete and characteristic ensemble of all that has been and is genuinely Spanish. The most perfect, the most brilliant, and the most suggestive resumé of the history of Spain is to be found in the streets and the architectural monuments of Toledo, a history in which the Jews played one of the principal parts.

Some, even Spaniards, would say that the Jews founded Toledo and that the Hebrew word *Toledoth*, taken from the weekly portion of that name read in the *Torah* (the Pentateuch) at Sabbath morning services, bestowed its name on the town. This is hardly a fact, rather a naive folk-story assertion concerning the remote origin of the Jewish community of Toledo. Certain evidence for the antiquity of Jewish life in Toledo points only as far back as Visigothic times. The Toledan Jewish community was one of the more important ones during the Moslem period and also the most influential during the Christian Middle Ages.

Probably the Romans founded the city, calling it Toletum. In 418 C.E., the Visigoths conquered it. During their rule, many religious councils of bishops were celebrated. These bishops were especially preoccupied with formulating laws and

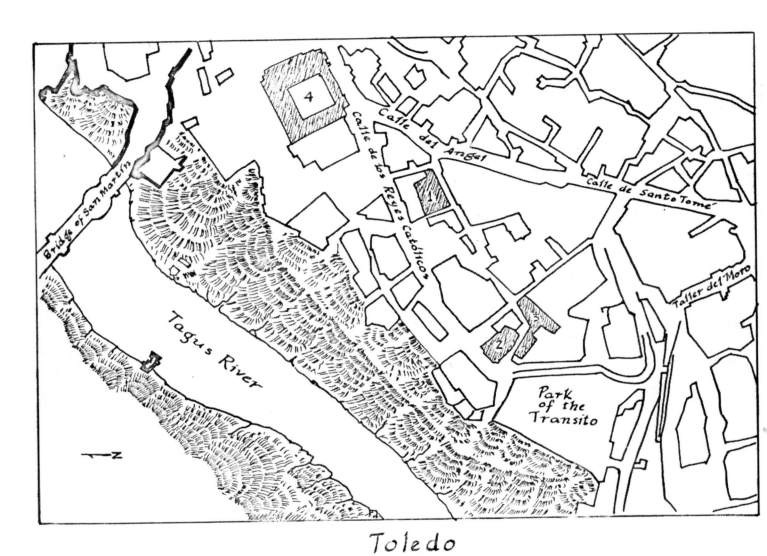

Toledo

Fig. 10.1: Toledo. Map of judería. Key: 1. Sta. María La Blanca, 2. El Tránsito, 3. Palace of Samuel ha Levi, 4. San Juan de los Reyes

regulations with regard to the Jews of Spain as a whole. The end result of their deliberations and edicts was disastrous, indeed. To these edicts may be traced the origin of the endemic antisemitism which characterized all of Spanish history until the nineteenth and twentieth centuries.

At the very beginning of the reign of the Visigothic king, Recesvinto, 653-672, the Jews of Toledo, who had been forcibly baptized by his two immediate predecessors, sent him a very touching letter that he presented to the Eighth Council of Toledo. In it they ask to be exempted from the requirement that they eat swine's flesh, declaring at the same time that they truly believe in Our Lord Jesus Christ, preserve no Jewish customs at all, do not commit incest, do not circumcise their flesh, and do not celebrate Passover. Nor do they keep the Sabbath, divide food as do Jews, keep any customs that Jews have, all believing with clean faith, agreeable will, and great devotion in Christ, the son of the living God, as ordered by the evangelists and apostles. The letter goes on to say, furthermore, that they all cling to the sacred Christian law as regards holidays, marriages, as well as other customs without deceit and with no reason against these customs, and that they do everything that they promise. However, as regards eating meat of the pig, they promise to comply eventually. If they are not able to stomach it now it is because they have not yet got used to it. Regarding other food cooked with pork, they promise to eat it without anger or disgust.

A graphic description of how forcibly converted Jews, who doubtlessly still kept the Law of Moses in secret, must have suffered. To demonstrate that he had converted body and soul to the new faith, the Jew would eat pork publicly, thus giving rise to the name *marrano* (pig). To eat pig meat was the trial, the acid proof of sincerity in the Christian faith. So great was the Jews' aversion to pork that if they ate it there could be no doubt that they had truly converted and were Christians at heart.

In the eighth century Toledo fell into Arab hands. In 1012, the local governor declared himself king and independent of the caliph of Córdoba. Nevertheless, toward the end of that same century, in 1085, Alfonso VI of Castile and León conquered Toledo, placing it once again in Christian hands. From that time until Felipe II established his court definitely in Madrid in the sixteenth century, Toledo held the position as the seat of the royal court, that is, the capital of Christian Spain, more often than any other city. During his rule, Alfonso VII established the famous school of translators (ca. 1130) in Toledo. For a short time Christian, Moslem, and Jew lived in harmony and peace in Toledo.

When the Arabs dominated Spain, the Jewish community of Toledo had been somewhat eclipsed by that of Córdoba. With the return of the Christians at the end of the eleventh century, the community of Toledo became the most flourishing in all Spain. Perhaps this expansion was due in part to the influx of Jewish refugees from Córdoba, still under Moslem rule. There Jewish life had taken a turn for the worse because of the anti-Jewish fanaticism, first of the Almoravids and later of the Almohads.

By the middle of the thirteenth century, under the rule of Alfonso X, also called Alfonso *El Sabio* (the Wise), the Jews of Toledo entered an epoch of euphoria. Alfonso X welcomed scholars from the Jewish communities of Córdoba, Seville, and Lucena, who became members of the academy he founded in Toledo. Here scientific investigations, especially in astronomy and mathematics, were carried on, not only by Jewish scholars, but also by Christian and Moslem as well. Works were translated from the Arabic into Latin and Spanish; even the Talmud and the Cabala were translated into the vulgar tongue. On the other hand, in his famous poem in praise of the Virgin, *Los Cántigos de María*, Alfonso El Sabio repeats the usual libels of the popular tradition inspired by the clergy. Yet, paradoxically enough, some of his most important and trusted officials were Toledan Jews, especially in fiscal matters.

In the fourteenth century conditions changed, not only in Toledo but in all of Christian Spain. The Jews lost their rights before the law, their prosperity, and the level of culture they had acquired. All of these attainments vanished because the endemic religious hatred, which persisted since Visigothic times, had never been dispelled. The peaceful and prosperous life of the Jews under Alfonso X had been a short respite in a long tragic history, the outcome of which was the literal destruction of Spanish Jewry in the fifteenth century. This destruction culminated in the final blow, the Expulsion in 1492.

During the fourteenth century, the rate of baptisms, both forcible and for convenience, greatly accelerated. By the end of the fifteenth century only a remnant of professing Jews remained to be expelled from Spain. Persecutions and massacres became the order of the day during the greater part of the fourteenth century, the severest taking place in 1391. Jews were thrown out of public office for good. This dismissal applied to fiscal administrators especially. Jews were prohibited from engaging in commerce, from working at a trade, and ultimately were forced to live within walled ghettos, *juderías*, where they were an easy prey for murder, pillage, and massacre. One such massacre took place on May 7, 1355, in one of the smaller sections of the judería of Toledo, the Alcana, where 1,200 men, women, and children were slaughtered. Interestingly, the soldiers of the king, Pedro el Cruel, defended the Jews, especially near the bridge of San Martín where they repelled the attackers.

Under Pedro, the Jewish community of Toledo flourished and became the most prosperous of all Spain. Some investigators believe that in 1358 there were at least 12,000 Jews residing there. During this short period of prosperity, in the mid-fourteenth century, they built the Synagogue of El Tránsito. Completed in 1360, it remains to this day one of the more splendid examples of mudéjar workmanship in all Spain. King Pedro gave special permission for its construction to his treasurer, Samuel ha Levi, despite the fact that canon law forbad building new synagogues.

The extent of the judería in the mid-fourteenth century is not exactly known. It existed near the bridge of San Martín in the southwest sector of the city high above the steep slopes rising from the gorge of the Tagus River. In this location Jews had lived even before the Christian Reconquest and had built a town, so to speak, within the city limits of Toledo. The main city wall to the north formed the boundary of this town. Within the judería, one stronghold, known as the Fortress of the Jews, served a double purpose in that it was part of the general fortifications of Toledo, protecting the city from enemies from without and the Jews themselves from enemies within.

The area occupied by the judería may possibly have comprised about one-fifth of the total extent of the city. Thus, it is quite possible the figure of 12,000 Jewish inhabitants is close to the number that actually may have lived there in the mid-fourteenth century when they constructed the Synagogue of El Tránsito. Many other synagogues of older date are known to have served the Toledan Jews. An elegy—more like a threnody—written by a Jewish author in Hebrew, one Jacob Albeneh, who lived through the massacre of June 20, 1391, enumerates the existence of eleven synagogues as well as five centers of study in Toledo, all of which were destroyed in the pogrom. The exact sites of the other synagogues are impossible to locate now. Only two have survived, the Synagogue of Santa María La Blanca and that of El Tránsito.

Santa María La Blanca

Located along the very edge of the city on the street known as Calle de los Reyes Católicos between the imposing fifteenth/sixteenth-century Church of San Juan de los Reyes to the north and the Synagogue of El Tránsito to the south, the Synagogue of Santa María La Blanca presents a most nondescript exterior. On my first visit to Toledo I almost walked right by, not suspecting that just beyond the high courtyard wall one of the few remaining Jewish houses of worship of medieval Spain stood, almost intact. Jews had used this synagogue until about 1420, at which time the Christian authorities converted it to a church. Long after I left Toledo I read the account of a sixteenth-century author who repeats the apocryphal story of almost folk folktale character concerning how the conversion to a church took place. San Vicente de Ferrer, it is said, came to the judería of Toledo during the year 1411. Accompanied by men-of-arms, he entered the synagogue, blessed the building, expelled the Jews, carried out the Torah, and celebrated Mass immedi-

Fig. 10.2: Toledo. Main door of Synagogue of Santa María La Blanca. Door has been reconstructed, not preserving original form. Originally, probably spanned with horseshoe-shaped arch similar to Synagogue of Corpus Christi in Segovia. Doorjambs finished with smoothly trowelled white plaster, which must be whitewashed from time to time to cover graffiti inscribed by Jewish visitors.

Fig. 10.3: Toledo. Synagogue of Santa María La Blanca. The central aisle looking toward door. Horseshoe-shaped arches span space between columns. Intricate designs in modeled and carved plaster decorate spandrels (space between arches) and lower section of clerestory wall. Blind arcade of clerestory above probably bricked up after synagogue converted to church. Main door transformed at some unknown date. Not original are door and square window immediately above it as well as pair of windows higher up and the circular window in gable.

ately. The story is not corroborated by any historical evidence, nor is it certain that Ferrer, in fact, had anything to do with the conversion of this particular synagogue. The process, as described however, is well known from other instances of the conversion of synagogues to churches: expelling the Jewish worshipers; removing the Torah scrolls from the Ark; and, in its place, setting up an altar for the immediate celebration of the Mass. After its conversion to a church about 1420,

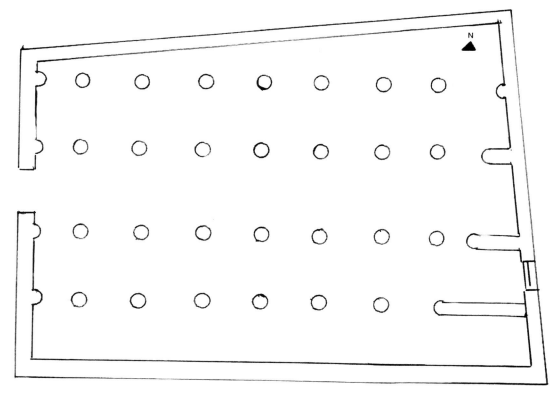

Fig. 10.4: Toledo. Plan of synagogue of Santa María La Blanca. This building subjected to radical alterations when converted to church. Neither two short walls nor two long walls parallel to each other. Except for southwest corner where facade and south long wall meet, walls do not meet at right angles. Building divided into five aisles by four rows of seven octagonal columns, except for extreme right-hand row of only six. Seventh column replaced by spur wall that projects from rear cross wall.

some changes were made to accommodate the needs of the Christian ritual. Santa María La Blanca was restored some time in the eighteenth century, and again in the mid-nineteenth, at which time the building was declared a national monument.

As is typical of other medieval Spanish synagogues, and even of the earliest ones in ancient Israel itself, the building is not located directly on the street but is set back in a forecourt surrounded by a high wall on three sides shielding the main facade from view. Though a traditional Jewish feature, the forecourt was also a necessary element in synagogue plans since, according to canon law, it was forbidden for synagogues to be so situated that they might be seen from the street. The medieval Spanish synagogue forecourt, however, actually served a triple purpose: that of complying with the requirements of ensuring that the synagogue proper should be unobtrusive; as an extra measure of protection against mob violence; and finally, the traditional one, as a place to congregate before and after prayers, that is at midpoint between the profane of the street and the sanctity of the prayer hall.

Fig. 10.5: Toledo. Synagogue of Santa María La Blanca. Column capital. This capital in mudéjar style of Islamic inspiration and derived from much older Byzantine prototypes. Note profusion of scrolls and interlace of delicately carved bands or ribbons defining space occupied by each scroll.

Entering from the street through the gate in the high stone wall, I stood in the forecourt. A small garden altered it; a few trees obstructed the most unprepossessing facade whose only adornment was a nondescript wooden door. Unpainted white plaster covered the brick doorjambs, which required repeated white-washing to obscure graffiti scribbled there by Jewish visitors. The inscriptions ranged in tenor from the banal to excerpts from the Psalms written in Hebrew characters.

The ground plan of the building is most curious indeed. It is not a regular rectangle, but skewed. The four walls are not set at right angles to each other. Neither the east and west walls nor the north and south walls are parallel to each other. The interior is divided into five aisles by four rows of octagonal columns supporting horseshoe-shaped arches. The surfaces of the shafts are plastered and left spotlessly white, providing a most dramatic contrast to the rather intricate capitals surmounting them. These are typically mudéjar in style and are remotely derived from the classical Corinthian capital. Like the column shafts below, the arcade is also finished in a hard smooth, trowelled coat of plaster.

The present roof, according to Czekelius, is not original, for the clerestory windows above the central aisle or nave display evidence of having been bricked up at some date later than that of the original construction of the building. More likely, the roof of the central aisle once soared above the roofs of the two side aisles immediately adjacent to it so that the windows of the clerestory illuminated the interior. Originally the roofs of the aisles adjacent to the side walls were lower still.

Departing from the norm, this synagogue does not have a womens' gallery. It probably disappeared during conversion to a church. In medieval Spanish synagogues, a stairway, usually on the exterior of the building, provided access to the women's gallery. Quite possibly, the women's gallery of the Synagogue of Santa María La Blanca once projected on the main facade above the main door.

A strange disparity in style exists between the windows of the clerestory above the nave arcade and the windows on the west end. There is a circular window in the gable, immediately below which are a pair of large rectangular window openings. Lower still, a smaller almost square window is most unlike the lobulated-arched windows of the clerestory. Also, the plaster decoration of the arcades of the central aisle ends abruptly at the west wall. This is a strange feature and out of concert with the overall style of the building. The implication is that the wall of the west front and the main door are not original, but rather represent alterations carried out after the building was converted to a church.

The exact date when this synagogue was built is debatable, with a number of investigators each offering a different solution to the problem. Some place it about 1180. Others place its construction during the reign of Alfonso X, somewhere between 1250 and 1300. This implies that the synagogue functioned for about one hundred and fifty years at most before being converted to a church.

Synagogue of Nuestra Señora del Tránsito

The second extant synagogue of Toledo stands a few blocks from the Synagogue of Santa María La Blanca, at the end of the

Fig. 10.6: Toledo. Synagogue of El Tránsito. Main door, located at end of one of long side walls, does not preserve original form and seems out of place when compared to double window opening of mudéjar style above. Two pointed horseshoe-shaped arches share short column in center. Arches enclosed within frame called *alfíz*, mudéjar in style. Main door probably spanned by similar arch. Note masonry, also typical mudéjar. Wall laid up with courses of rough undressed stones of varying sizes separated at intervals by leveling courses of brick. Brickwork of door opening recent construction, different in character from adjoining section of original wall.

Calle de los Reyes Católicos and to one side of a little park. The steep ravine carved out by the Tagus River forms the southern boundary of the park, which was probably part of the Jewish quarter in the fourteenth and fifteenth centuries. The rather plain exterior of the synagogue provides no hint why this building is considered one of the most excellent examples of mudéjar architecture in all Spain.

Fig. 10.7: Toledo. Synagogue of El Tránsito. Exterior view of clerestory that lights prayer hall inside. Clerestory is above roof of women's gallery that projects along this side of prayer hall. Note mudéjar type of masonry walling of women's gallery and also cornice, a brick corbel table with closely set brackets, under eaves of roof above clerestory.

Samuel ha Levi Abulafia, the treasurer of Pedro el Cruel, constructed this second synagogue in mid-fourteenth century, perhaps as early as 1357 or by 1366. After the tragic occurrences of 1391, the pogroms that decimated the Jewish population of Christian Spain, this synagogue remained as the most important, if not the only one in Toledo. Soon after the Expulsion, about 1494, it was converted to a church and turned over to the military order of Calatrava. In the eighteenth century, by which time the religious military orders declined in influence, the building became a hermitage under the advocation of *Nuestra Señora del Tránsito* (Our Lady of the Transit). In 1877 the building was declared a national monument.

The exterior is hardly impressive. Although the door is not, the twin horseshoe-shaped windows above it probably are original. When first built, the synagogue did not stand directly on the street as it is today, but rather inside a walled courtyard as in the case of Santa María La Blanca. Also, the separate entrance and the stairway leading to the women' gallery have disappeared. The clerestory rising above the shed roof of the women' gallery is divided into ten panels alternately pierced by five windows with pointed horseshoe-shaped arches. The cornice of the clerestory wall has a course of dentils or a corbel table to mark the transition to the roof.

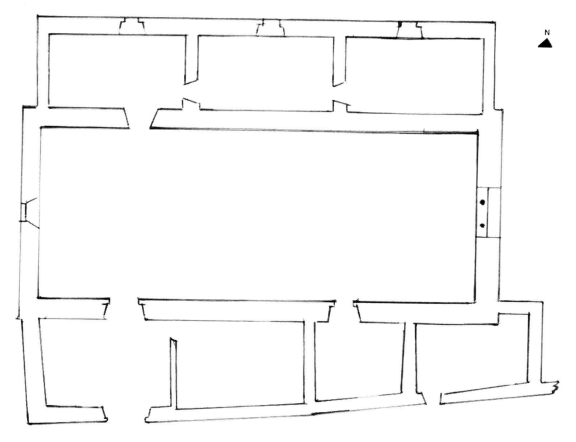

Fig. 10.8: Toledo. Plan of the Synagogue of El Tránsito. Main prayer hall flanked by section with entrance vestibule and other rooms above which is women's gallery. Rooms on other side, now housing gift shop and museum, probably not part of original construction but added when synagogue converted to church.

I was unprepared for the sight I beheld on entering the high-ceilinged prayer hall. The rectangular room, devoid of any special architectural features that might obscure the simple spatial volumes, was nevertheless most splendid and variegated in details. This was particularly true of the complex painted stucco decoration running along the tops of the walls and also covering the entire surface of the east wall where the Ark of the Torah once stood. The impression was that of intricately patterned Oriental rugs hung on the walls. Reminiscent of Moslem usage, Hebrew inscriptions are woven into the decorative scheme. As a fitting climax to the wall treatment, the room is spanned by a splendid beamed and coffered wooden ceiling decorated with an overall geometrical, angular interlace of entwined moldings, probably original and dating to the fourteenth-century. Typical of all such ceilings, *artesonados*, the rafters and purloins of the roof framing form the structural skeleton or framework on which the decorative elements composed of moldings assembled in variegated geometric designs are affixed. The overall shape of the ceil-

Fig. 10.9: Toledo. Synagogue of El Tránsito. Interior, East Wall. Space divided into three panels decorated with intricate overall patterns or arabesques. Effect like that of oriental rugs or tapestries hung on walls. At bottom and center of each of side panels is a tablet with inscription in Hebrew six lines long, forming a single text of twelve lines between two tablets. Inscriptions give details of synagogue furnishings and mention that Samuel ha Levi built it.

ing is like that of the overturned hull of a wooden ship with its keel up and viewed from inside and below.

The east wall is divided into three vertical panels. The middle one is a triple-arched opening forming the front of the niche where the Ark of the Torah was placed. The three lobulated, slightly pointed arches rest on two slender columns. A complex double molding, decorated with an inscription consisting of excerpts from various Psalms, frames the panel. The surface of the panel is overlaid with a continuous pattern of lozenges, within each of which other motives are worked, the whole looking like a finely woven tapestry.

The two panels to either side are quite symmetrical and are framed with moldings ornamented with leaves and acorn-like fruit intertwined in a lacework. The panel proper is covered with a vine that undulates up into two rows, leaving eight more or less reserved spaces where a motif somewhat like a lily is placed against a field of an intricate, fine lace-like pattern. At the bottom of each side panel, a square tablet with an inscription in Hebrew is surmounted with an oval-shaped element decorated with the coat-of-arms of León and Castile. A blazon or coat-of-arms, depicting what appears to be the facade of a castle with three towers, appears in the bottom corner of each border of the panel.

This is probably the escutcheon of Samuel ha Levi, the chief benefactor and builder of the synagogue. The main area of each tablet is filled with an inscription in Hebrew six lines long, forming a single text of twelve lines between the two, giving details of the construction of the synagogue. The quotation that follows is the result of what I was able to make out in the inscription with the help of Cantera's epigraphical reconstruction:

"Look upon the sanctuary which has been consecrated in Israel, the house built by Samuel, and the pulpit of wood in the center thereof for the reading of the Torah, and the scrolls and the crowns, and the *pateras* and lamps, and the windows, like those of Ariel, and the courts for those devoted to the perfect law, and the house of study for those who sit in the shadow of God, being such that those who see this synagogue may say that it is like that built by Bezalel. Come, all ye people, enter the doors and seek God, for this is the House of God, Beth El."

Immediately below each side panel more inscriptions of twelve lines appear, each written in much larger characters than those of the tablets within the panel proper. Unfortunately, these are in a very poor state of preservation, and I had difficulty in making out words, let alone what they said. Efforts by various epigraphers, including Cantera, have made the meaning clear though the exact wording remains problematical. The two inscriptions form part of a single text and are interspersed throughout with biblical quotations in which Samuel ha Levi and King Pedro el Cruel are praised as protectors of Israel. However, my interest was aroused more by the figured decoration rather than the calligraphy. The topmost section of all four walls of the prayer hall is treated as a clerestory with an arcade of lobulated, pointed arches resting on paired columns. Some of the bays of the arcade are blind, that is, filled with masonry. Others are perforated by windows with grilles of varying geometric patterns. A broad band running beneath the arcade is covered with delicate painted stucco decoration of intricate design. Immediately below and above the clerestory arcade are moldings decorated with Hebrew inscriptions executed in bold square letters, the texts of which are from the Book of Psalms.

According to most architectural historians, the plan of the synagogue is fraught with problems because of the changes carried out during its use as a Christian church for about four hundred years. The prayer hall proper is a rectangular space, a large room approximately 23 meters long by 9 meters wide, or about 70 by 28 feet. The women's gallery is located above the rooms on the south side of the building. The present anterooms on the ground floor are entered directly from the street and may not be contemporary with the prayer hall. The rooms along the south side of the prayer hall under the women's gallery have been modified considerably in the course of the centuries. Another projecting section abuts on the north side of the prayer hall. Though connected with the sanctuary today, it may in fact date from post-Jewish times, for here the archives of the Order of Calatrava were housed. Yet, it is also possible that this part of the plan once served as a house of study or school.

The women's gallery is located in the second story over the rooms on the south side of the prayer hall. Though now reached by a set of stairs in one of the rooms

Fig. 10.10: Toledo. Synagogue of El Tránsito. East Wall, left-hand panel. Inscription below panel proper also has one in
Hebrew, from Book of Psalms. In worse
repair than that in right-hand panel.

Fig. 10.11: Toledo. Synagogue of El Tránsito. East wall, right-hand panel. Moldings around panel decorated with Hebrew inscriptions. In bad state of repair,
some of text obliterated, large inscription
below panel taken from Book of Psalms.

Fig. 10.12: Toledo. Synagogue of El Tránsito. East wall, right-hand panel. Detail of Hebrew
inscription below panel containing texts from Book of Psalms interspersed with references
praising Samuel ha Levi and King Pedro el Cruel as protectors of Israel.

Fig. 10.13: Toledo. Synagogue of El Tránsito. Clerestory windows north side of prayer hall. Arcade has lobulated pointed arches. Alternate bays of arcade blind. Each open window has delicate lace-like grill, no two alike. Intricate vine with leaves and interspersed blazons entwined on broad continuous band below clerestory. Horizontal moldings above/ below clerestory arcade decorated with Hebrew inscriptions taken from the Psalms.

Fig. 10.14: Toledo. Synagogue of El Tránsito. Interior, West Wall. Three windows lower part of wall. Middle largest with lobulated pointed arch. Other two have simple semicircular arches. All three arches framed by panel, each filled with delicate lace-like grill. Four windows in clerestory above, spanned by lobulated, pointed, horseshoe-shaped arches filled with grills.

Fig. 10.15: Toledo. Synagogue of El Tránsito. Capital from supporting pier in women's gallery. Design worked in carved plaster. Horizontal band above capital has moldings above and below, decorated with Hebrew inscriptions. Medallion immediately above capital has Arabic inscription.

below, originally it was probably entered by means of an exterior stairway in the former synagogue courtyard. Only scant vestiges remain of the stucco decorations that once graced the wall and the piers on the open side of the gallery facing the prayer hall. The decorative motives on each of the pier capitals remain intact and appear similar to those on the side panels of the east wall of the prayer hall. A continuous decorative band bounded by Hebrew inscriptions above and below is still visible in part, where it once ran around the gallery just under the ceiling. Various Psalms provide the text.

In recent years some wealthy and well-intentioned members of the Jewish community of Madrid covered the bare white-plastered side and rear walls of the prayer hall with silk cloth. This detracts somewhat from the beauty of the carved plaster decoration and the magnificent ceiling. A museum shop where tourists may buy mementos now occupies the rooms on the north side. And it has been reported that the Jewish community of Madrid, in recent years, has celebrated services for *Rosh ha Shonah* and *Yom Kippur* (New Year and the Day of Atonement)!

The Palace of Samuel ha Levi

The house of Samuel ha Levi still stands within sight of the synagogue he built. Today it is known as the House of El Greco; the famous seventeenth-century painter lived there for some years before his death. Over the years, the house has suffered many changes including those effected recently, which were necessary in order to turn the building into a museum. It is difficult to tell which parts date from the fourteenth century as distinct from those of later date.

The tragic fate of Samuel ha Levi, whose synagogue became a church and his house a museum, is the story not only of Spanish Jewry, but also a fable of how the mighty are often humbled. Samuel ha Levi was appointed royal treasurer of Pedro

Fig. 10.16: Toledo. The street between Synagogue of El Tránsito on left and palace of Samuel ha Levi on right. In seventeenth century, palace home of renowned Spanish painter of Greek origin, El Greco.

Fig. 10.17: Toledo. Palace of Samuel ha Levi, House of El Greco. Door leading to patio has carved plastic decoration around top in style of carving inside synagogue.

el Cruel (1350-69), who also entrusted him with important missions of political character. Samuel reorganized the tax-collecting system. Two castles were placed in his charge, Hita and Trujillo. This possibly clarifies the meaning of the two three-towered castles depicted in the lower corners of the panels of the side bays on the east wall of his synagogue. In carrying out his duties, he often employed Jews, mainly relatives, as well as Christians. For some reason, he and all his kinsmen fell out of favor with the king and were arrested. Samuel was confined to prison in the Torre del Oro in Seville, where, after enduring excruciating tortures, he died. Many legends still persist as to his wealth. Guides continue to show visitors subterranean chambers in the garden of his house, once supposedly connected by tunnels with the synagogue, and describe these chambers as the place where Samuel stored all his gold and other valuables for safekeeping.

So powerful had Samuel become that Pedro allowed him to construct the Synagogue of El Tránsito, though it was strictly forbidden by cannon law to build any new synagogues at that time. Just why Pedro turned on his most faithful servitor is not clear; perhaps the reason was to assuage the antagonism of his Christian subjects, especially that of the nobility, who traditionally resisted the royal authority and who resented that so many Jews were directly connected with the gathering of taxes. Or did the king turn on him for the money Samuel ha Levi had accumulated? Popular legend has it that in the secret subterranean chambers of his house, the newly appointed Christian treasurer of the king, who replaced Samuel, found three mounds of bars of gold and silver so high that a man of ordinary stature could hide behind them. According to the legend, the king had demanded money of Samuel, money which he accused Samuel of pilfering from the royal treasury, but which Samuel refused to give him. On seeing all that gold and silver, Pedro exclaimed that had Samuel given him but one-third of even the smallest pile of gold and silver he would not have ordered him tortured. Instead, Samuel allowed himself to be racked to death without revealing its hiding place. Today, in the museum of El Greco, once the palace of Samuel ha Levi Abulafia, nothing tangible remains of the Jewish past—not a vestige of Samuel's life there, not even a single gold coin from his earthly treasure.

11 Córdoba

The word *Córdoba* (Cordova) had been stored in my memory as some fantasy ever since the days of my childhood when my schoolteacher, a dour New England spinster, obliged the class to memorize sizable portions of Henry Wadsworth Longfellow's poem, *The Courtship of Miles Standish*. I still remember the opening lines describing Miles Standish, especially about his boots:

> Clad in doublet and hose and boots of Cordovan leather,
> Strode, with martial air, Miles Standish the Puritan Captain.

Cordovan leather. Leather from Córdoba! Only years and years later did I associate the cordovan leather of Miles Standish's boots with Córdoba, or the deep russet brown color of cordovan leather with Córdoba. What had Córdoba been to me all those years of my childhood? It was a never-never world, a world that was a word, a word that sounded beautiful in a poem, a word to use in a figure of speech. I never knew that there was really a Córdoba under the Andalusian sun, a Córdoba rooted in the ocher and brown earth harmonizing with the color of cordovan leather and surrounded by olive groves, a Córdoba of the broad, silent, mighty Guadalquivir River. Nor had I known of a Córdoba possessing the most beautiful mosque in all Islam, a Córdoba of the indescribably beautiful ensemble of streets and houses of men in the old Jewish quarter. This was a Córdoba of which I never had dreamed.

Yet this was the Córdoba I came to for the first time one hot summer day some forty years ago. This was not only the Córdoba of the leather of Miles Standish's boots, but also the Córdoba of one of the greatest Jewish minds of all time, in fact one of the greatest minds of all Western civilization—Maimonides.

Only after I had wandered through the streets of the judería did I realize that this Córdoban Maimonides was the same Maimonides whose *Guide for the Perplexed* (*Dux Dubitans* in Latin and *Moreh Nebukhim* in Hebrew) I had read as an undergraduate in Friedlander's English translation. He was the very same Maimonides of whom my father's father had told me so many stories as a child. These stories were folktales of a great folk hero, not a warrior, God forbid, but a thinker who carried out many outstanding feats of the mind, whose intellect towered above all men, the great *Rambam* (Rav Moshe ben Maimon). I had visualized the Rambam as an East European Jew, a Russian Jew who spoke Yiddish like my grandfather with a Podolian accent. Only as a grown man did I finally associate the Rambam

Fig. 11.1: Córdoba. Map of judería.

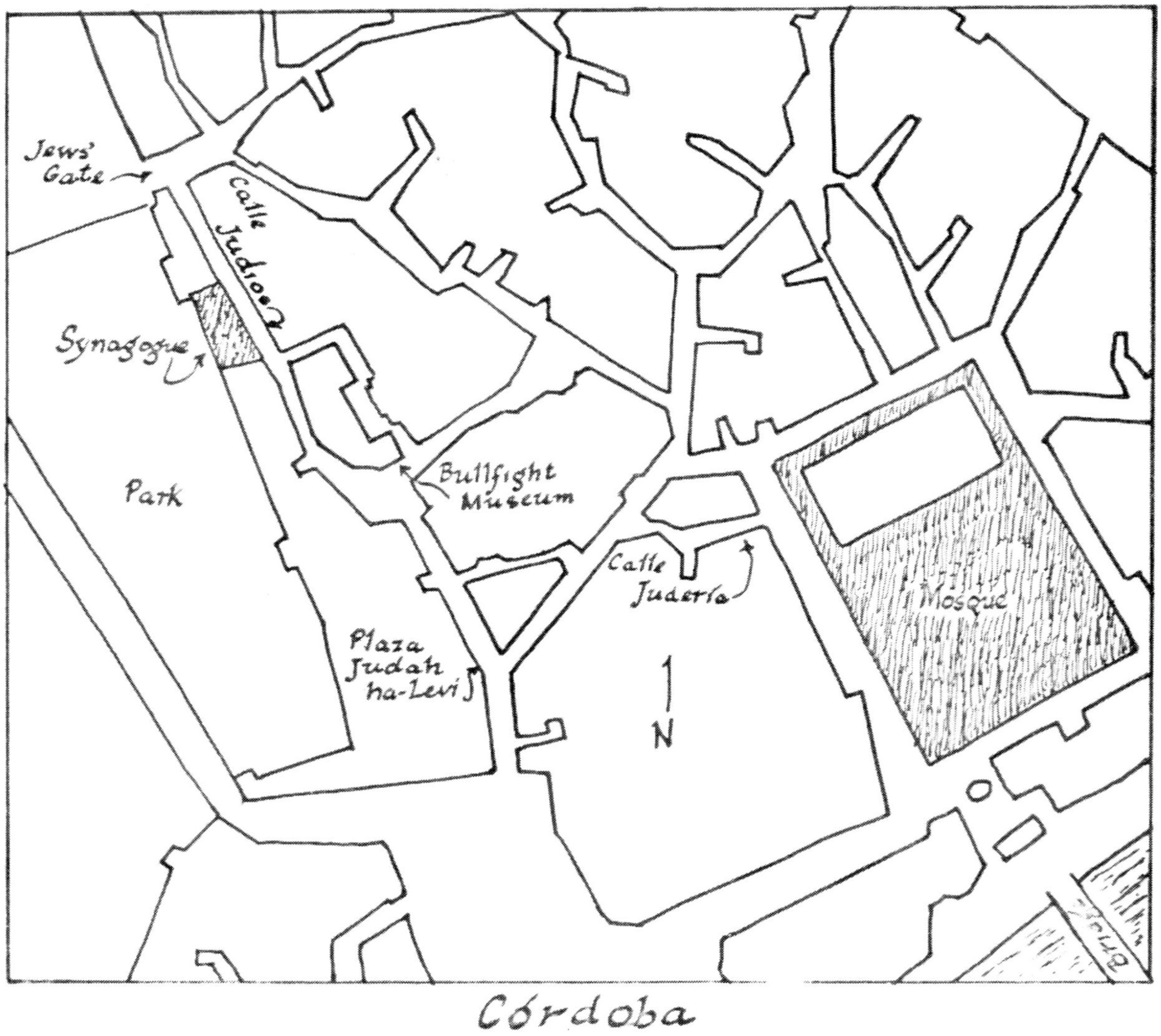

Córdoba

of my childhood with the medieval philosopher Maimonides, the man who sought to rationalize reason and faith long before Thomas Aquinas was to do the same for Christians. It was here in Córdoba, in the narrow twisting streets of the judería that it dawned on me that I was in Maimonides' native home. I suddenly realized that the Rambam had spoken Arabic and Hebrew, not Yiddish. It was here that the Rambam and Maimonides fused into the one man he had always been.

Córdoba is another Spain: the south, Andalucía. This was the Spain that was carried to the New World, the Spain of bright sunlight, ultramarine blue skies, white houses with red-tiled roofs, orange trees, and olive groves. It was the Spain with a flavor of the cantillation of the cantor in the synagogue and the ululating call to prayer of the muezzin from the minaret of the mosque. In its time, Córdoba was the most important city in the Western world and the setting of a glorious epoch in Jewish history. The Arab role in Spain is well known. As intermediaries, Arabs brought Greek philosophy and science to the medieval Christian world of Europe. That Córdoba was the actual locus, the very spot from which this civilizing influence emanated is not so well known. The judería itself—the narrow streets, no more than narrow slits between high, whitewashed blank walls except for a door or a window grille here and there—comprises the tangible, the concrete form, the material reflection, the physical counterpart of this abstract historical concept that was Oriental Córdoba. This Córdoba of Moslem and Jew provided the bridge between the ancient civilizations of Greece and Rome and the emerging Christian West during the early Middle Ages.

Except for the great mosque, still standing remarkably well preserved and serving as a Christian cathedral, and the jumbled ruins of the Alcazar, the Arab fortress and palace, few physical vestiges of the Moslem past exist in Córdoba. Not even one identifiable ruin or any physical remnant can be found that might reveal Averroes the Moslem (1126-1198) and Maimonides (1135-1204) as contemporaries. These men might have had direct personal contact with each other, even walking the same streets. Córdoba thus was the principal theater where for centuries the prologue of the great drama of the rebirth of classical learning in Europe was enacted. Córdoba also provided the principal stage for the enactment of the struggle between the Crescent and the Cross. In this contest, Jews were sometimes important actors, but never the leading protagonists; yet they were always victims caught in the crossfire between the contestants, Islam and Christendom.

The city is located on the Guadalquivir River (*Wadi al Quibir* in Arabic, the Great River) on a plain near the Sierra Morena. Phoenicians first settled the region at some undetermined date, perhaps in the eighth century B.C.E. In order to dominate the western Mediterranean, they later allied themselves with Carthage during the wars with Rome. The name Córdoba is said to derive from the Phoenician word *corteb* (olive-oil press). An appropriate moniker this since the surrounding countryside remains one of the chief olive-growing regions of Spain. The Romans, who colonized the town near the end of the third century B.C.E., followed the Phoenicians. In 151 B.C.E., Córdoba became an administrative center of the Roman province. It is not known if Jews had resided there during the Phoenician period. That they had exerted considerable influence in the population, during the time of the Romans before the arrival of the Visigoths in the fifth century C.E., may be inferred from the malevolent treatment the newcomers accorded Jews.

As elsewhere, the Visigoth Germanic barbarian conquerors displayed hostility toward the Jews, especially after the latter renounced the Arian form of Christianity in favor of Roman Catholicism. When the Arabs initiated their conquests of Spain in 711, the Jewish population of Córdoba sided with the invaders against the Visigoths and helped take the city. The Jews looked upon the Moslems as their deliverers. As the object of special discriminatory legislation that had imposed many economic, social, and religious liabilities on them, the Jews welcomed relief. They had suffered merciless persecutions and forced conversions at the hands of the Visigoths for almost three centuries.

In 711 there began an epoch of greatness for Córdoba—Oriental Córdoba, Córdoba of the Crescent—to which the light of the Menorah added its own particular brilliance. Manolo Machado, the Andalusian poet, characterized the cities of Andalucía in pithy verse. Of Córdoba he wrote: *"Roman y mora, Córdoba callada"* (Roman and Moorish, Córdoba the taciturn). In truth, Córdoba, both Roman and Moorish, is quiet, restful, peaceful, thoughtful, pensive, and lost in evanescent vagaries of thought often expressed not only with words, but also with feelings. It is "Córdoba the taciturn," Córdoba of the philosophers and thinkers from the Roman Seneca to the Moslem Averroes to the Jewish Maimonides. All share a common character, though they were pagan, Moslem, and Jew. All were thinkers who left their mark on the city to this very day.

Fernando III, known as the Saint, took the city in 1236. In favor of the Cross, he essentially extinguished the feats of mind that were the glory of Moslem Córdoba. Actually Jewish life had ceased to flourish in Córdoba about a century before the Christian Conquest. Maimonides himself, along with the entire Jewish community, had fled the city when the fanatical Moslem Almohads, Berbers from North Africa, invaded Spain in 1146. Allowing death as the only alternate choice, they began a campaign to convert not only the Jews, but Christians as well, to Islam.

The actual battle for the city, led by Fernando III, utterly destroyed not only the Moslem monuments, but also what remained of the Jewish, abandoned about a century before (soon after 1146). The city was depopulated for a while. Settling them in the former judería, Fernando brought in Jews from Christian Spain in the north. The street plan of the judería as it exists today is perhaps the only part of Córdoba still retaining something of its former Moslem and Jewish flavor.

The great mosque, now a cathedral, and the twisting winding streets of the Jewish quarter represent silent witnesses to a city that existed during the centuries when classical learning was spread to the barbaric west. The mosque-cathedral, still one of the outstanding artistic and architectural monuments in all Islam, reflects the glory of the Arab past in Córdoba. What of the Jewish past? What remains of Jewish architectural monuments or religious buildings? A synagogue of lilliputian dimensions dating from after the Reconquest still stands today as a reminder of the Jewish role in the history of Christian Córdoba.

Those Moslems who come as tourists to Spain today, almost as pilgrims, go mainly to the Alhambra in Granada and the mosque in Córdoba. The mosque serves as a cathedral where Catholic rites are performed daily to the understandable disquiet of the Moslems, many of whom weep unrestrainedly when beholding the former greatness of their people and their faith reflected in the vast and beautiful building.

Fig. 11.2: Córdoba. Puerta del Almodóvar. Gate in ancient city wall giving direct access to judería had been known in Arabic as *Bab al Yahud*, in Spanish as *Puerta de los Judíos*.

And the Jewish visitors, hardly pilgrims, yet conscious of the Jewish past, what can they do when they enter the tiny little synagogue less than twenty feet square and see excerpts from the Psalms worked in stucco relief on the walls? They say Kaddish, the memorial prayer for the dead praising the Name of God, and weep, recalling not the former glory of the Córdoban Jews, but rather the martyrdom of the little remnant of Israel who came there to say the daily prayers some six hundred years ago.

The judería is largely of Christian origin, having been rebuilt in the thirteenth century on the ruins of the Moslem city. The rebuilding includes the Jewish quarter, which was destroyed during the conquest. The Barrio de la Judería, as it is called today, comprises the area of the southwest corner of the city extending from just south of the Church of San Nicolás, where the Avenida del Gran Capitán ends, to as far south as the mosque and the western city wall along the Avenida de General Primo de Rivera. The exact eastern limits are not well known. The area of the city known now as the judería is far more extensive than that of Christian times when the Jewish community of Córdoba was of rather slight importance and considerably smaller than those of Seville or Toledo.

After settling in the very same hotel on the Avenida del Gran Capitán where I had stayed during my first visit to Córdoba two years before, just a few steps from the beautiful octagonal Tower of San Nicolás so reminiscent of a minaret though a Christian monument from the first, I walked down the wide and expansive Paseo

Fig. 11.3: Córdoba. Calle de Maimonides, formerly called Calle de Judíos. View to south from intersection of Calle de Fernández Ruano.

Fig. 11.4: Córdoba. Calle de Maimonides. East Wall of synagogue on right. Too narrow for automobiles, street displays channels gouged out of house walls to accommodate hubs of wheels of horse-drawn carriages.

de Primo de Rivera. I came once again to the monumental gate opening into the old Jewish quarter, now known as the Puerta del Almodóvar. The Almodóvar gate during Moslem times was known as *Bab al Yahud*, in Arabic. It is popularly known today by the same name, but in Spanish, *Puerta de los Judíos*, which is a translation of its pristine Arabic name, Gate of the Jews.

The gate itself is probably of Arab construction, but was altered when the city walls were strengthened some time after the Christian Conquest in 1236. The slightly pointed arch frames the view into the Calle de Fernández Ruano and marks the border between modern Córdoba and the Córdoba of times long past. Just a few paces from the gate, a narrow corridor-like street opens to the right and twists in a southeasterly direction. Inscribed high up on the whitewashed wall of the house at the very corner is the word, *Judíos*. Some of the recent city maps refer to this street as Calle de Maimonides, having been so renamed in the 1930s by the republican government of Spain. The name still marked on the corner is the traditional one and goes back to the mid-thirteenth century when Fernando III resettled Jews on this same street and in the very same neighborhood, which they most probably had occupied during the Moslem domination of the city and before their flight from the Almohads in the twelfth century.

Fig. 11.5: Córdoba. Plazuela de Maimonides. Prior to commemoration of eight-hundredth anniversary of death of Maimonides, plaza called Plazas de las Bulas. Site of building of large synagogue in thirteenth century. A Papal Bull issued in 1250 halted construction, thus providing original name, Plaza of the Papal Bulls.

A few hundred feet beyond the corner, the street swerves slightly to the right and narrows even more. In fact, the street becomes so narrow that a deep concave channel has been gouged out in the walls to either side, about three feet above the pavement, to allow the projecting hubs of the wheels of the horse-drawn carriages to pass through. The wall to the right is unlike the others on the street; it has been neither whitewashed entirely nor re-plastered in places where the stucco coating has fallen off, revealing the brick masonry. A door in the bare brick wall, the jambs of which also have been hollowed out to accommodate the hubs of the carriages, is the only opening in the otherwise high blank wall. On the lintel are painted two words in bold capital letters, *LA SINAGOGA*.

I went through the door and into a tiny patio. To the left was a private dwelling from which came the sounds of women and children talking, singing, and even squabbling. Immediately in front of the door, affixed on the high wall opposite, was a marble plaque. It was partially covered with foliage that clung to the wall growing from a tiny garden plot below. Not deeply incised, the letters read:

VIII CENTENARIO DE MAIMONIDES
1135 – MARZO – 1935
———

ESPAÑA. POR EL GOBIERNO DE LA
NACION EXPRESA SU HOMENAJE AL
INMORTAL GENIO DEL JUDAISMO
———

CÓRDOBA, SU PATRIA LE OFRENDA
LA VENERACION DE SU RECUERDO

VIIIth centenary of Maimonides
1135 – March – 1935
———

Spain, through the government of the
nation, expresses its homage to
the immortal genius of Judaism.
———

Córdoba, his native home, offers him
the veneration of his memory.

The Spain of the Inquisition had come a long way. Spain and his native city claim Maimonides as their own! This is the same Rambam revered in the Yiddish tales of my grandfather. A memorial plaque honoring him exists in the courtyard of a synagogue and in Córdoba where he was born.

Fig. 11.6: Córdoba. Synagogue patio. Memorial plaque to Maimonides, native son of Córdoba, commemorates eight-hundredth anniversary his death.

As I stood there reading and rereading the inscription, a wizened little old man appeared in the door of the synagogue, standing there exactly as he had when I saw him for the first time about two years before. He lived in the house on the other side of the patio and seemed to be of the same material and the same age as the ancient walls of the house of prayer.

I entered the synagogue and he followed me with a slow halting pace, his evenly measured and clearly defined footsteps brushing the pavement softly like rustling silk as his cane beat a counterpoint between swishes. There he stood on the same spot I had first seem him two years before, in the middle of the room, the place of prayer, and resting a brief moment to catch his breath after the exertion of taking the few steps. With a settled look on his face, he began his discourse in a thin voice, a high-pitched, monotonous voice lacking the timbre or the tonal range of youth.

His words sounded as if they were coming from a small jar. He had memorized his oration, and intoned each word for me once again as if repeating the piece from a music score. His oration was about the long dead; he presented it as one who was more spirit than flesh. Speaking without stopping, like a soothsayer in a trance, he used his cane as a pointer. His feet spread far apart for better balance, he recited the words as if repeating the cadences of the Kaddish prayer,

Fig. 11.7: Córdoba. Synagogue. Old man in synagogue door with cane in hand awaits visitors to relate history of synagogue.

Fig. 11.8: Córdoba. Synagogue. "This is the Synagogue of Córdoba, the church of the Jews...."

"This is the Synagogue of Córdoba, the church of the Jews, built by Isaac Makheb in 1315. Here sat the rabbis—rabbis are the priests of the Jews—and there stood the Torah—the Torah is the Bible of the Jews. Above in the balcony there sat the Jewish women."

After taking a breath and pausing as if waiting for the "Amen" from the congregation, in a rising voice he continued,

"Nowadays many Jews come here, from Israel, from Jerusalem, from France, from America, but *solo de paso, no viven aquí* (they only pass through to visit. Jews do not live here)."

His chant ended; silence once again took its place.

The existence of this synagogue was discovered in the late nineteenth century. Declared a national monument in 1884, it was subsequently restored to the fullest extent possible. The actual structure of the synagogue is nondescript and hardly worthy of note, nor can it be compared with major works of architecture. It is a tiny little building with no exterior sign or embellishment that might serve as a prelude to the surprises of great beauty within, a beauty reflective of the riches of the spirit more than that of earthly possessions. The little patio measures about fourteen by twenty feet. Just beyond the door, a small anteroom with a modern stair rises to the women's balcony above. The main room, the prayer hall for men, is diminutive in scale to an unexpected degree, measuring approximately twenty-two by twenty-one feet. The pyramidal-shaped, wood-beamed ceiling is modern. The upper portions of the walls still preserve much of their original character and are covered with intricate designs in carved stucco in a manner similar to those of the Synagogue of El Tránsito in Toledo. Excerpts from the Psalms written in bold, square Hebrew letters, as in Toledo, form part of the decorative scheme.

The most interesting feature of the room is on the east wall, where a deep niche or alcove projects almost like an apse from the building proper. The Ark and the scrolls of the Torah most likely were kept there. To the right and left of the niche

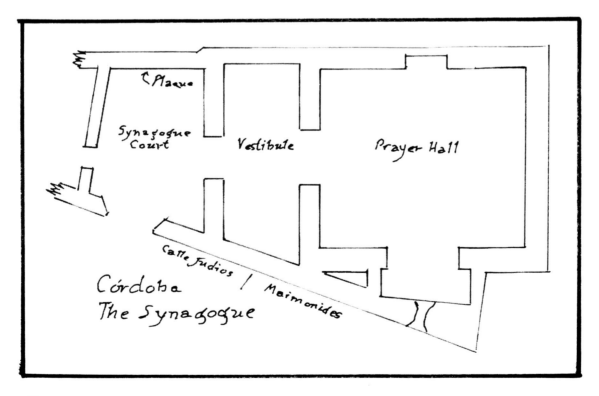

Fig. 11.9: Córdoba. Plan of synagogue. An extremely small building, the prayer hall measures approximately twenty-two by twenty-one feet. Women's gallery directly above vestibule.

Fig. 11.10: Córdoba. Synagogue. Interior, NE corner. Decoration in carved plates executed with arabesques/repeated geometric designs on individual panels. Similar to textile wall hangings.

Fig. 11.11: Córdoba. Synagogue. Niche for Ark of Torah on East Wall. Upper portion over niche extant. Mudéjar style, framed within alfíz covered with carved plaster decoration. Hebrew inscriptions almost obliterated.

Fig. 11.12: Córdoba. Synagogue. Women's gallery. Wall once covered with carved plaster.

Fig. 11.13: Córdoba. Synagogue. East Wall, right-hand panel with Hebrew inscription below, stating that synagogue was built by Isaac Makeb in 1314/1315. "Arise, O Lord, hasten to rebuild Jerusalem."

are decorated panels. On the one to the right, or south, an inscription is preserved in the lower part which says, in part, that the synagogue had been built by Isaac Makheb in the year 5075 (1314–15 C.E.) and ended with the words, "Arise, O Lord, hasten to rebuild Jerusalem."

The west wall opposite is unusual. It has a small niche spanned by an elaborate lobulated arch set in a beautifully decorated panel in the center of the wall. There have been various discussions as to what purpose the niche served, some insisting that here the rabbi sat. In fact, the old man had intoned thus. As I was standing in the tiny room another explanation occurred to me. Here in Córdoba, because of the limitations of the restricted floor space, the reader's desk, where the Torah scrolls are traditionally brought to be read during services and which is usually located on a raised platform in the center of the prayer hall, had to be placed in front of the niche in the west wall and opposite from the Ark on the east wall. In such a small room a centrally placed reading desk would have been most impractical.

This, then, is the Synagogue of Córdoba, where Jews from all over—from America, from France, from Jerusalem—come to visit, but not to stay. Jews live here no longer. I gave the old man a few *pesetas*, which he accepted without a word of thanks. In truth, they were his in the first place for daily calling to life once again the long extinct congregation.

Fig. 11.14: Córdoba. Synagogue. East Wall, right-hand panel. Overall geometric pattern carved plaster. Pattern simulates that of mudéjar carpentry *alfarje* (wood-paneled ceiling) with carefully joined moldings creating overall geometric pattern. Dedicatory inscription below panel.

Fig. 11.15: Córdoba. Synagogue. Niche center panel of west wall opposite niche for Ark of Torah. Niche spanned by lobulated, pointed arch inset in elongated alfíz, surface covered with interlace of repeated pointed arches containing interior designs. Moldings once decorated with Hebrew inscriptions.

Two little girls burst into the prayer hall arguing and squabbling as they both held on to a large cat. Each wanted the cat for herself. The black-haired, beautiful, and smiling one let go, and the smaller, blond, more aggressive child, with a triumphant and satisfied look on her face, pressed the cat to her. I went into the synagogue court and looked at the memorial plaque to Maimonides once again. I turned for a moment and saw all three of them, the old man and the two little girls with the cat, in the doorway. "Do they look Jewish?" I asked myself. "Could the old man and the two children be descendants of the Jews who had lived on this street so many centuries ago?" They stood still while I took a photograph.

I left and walked further down Maimonides Street, or Jews' Street, and entered the Plazuela de Maimonides, which until the 1930s or so was known the *Plaza de las Bulas* (Plaza of the Papal Bulls). There on the north side of the little square, a large house of ancient fabric, much restored, contains a museum dedicated to bull fighting, of all things. Some of the more imaginative guides tell Jewish tourists that Maimonides himself lived in that very same house, which is of course impossible since it probably dates from the sixteenth century. However, the site does have a Jewish past and has been identified as the one where in 1250, about fourteen years after Fernando III wrested the city for the Moors, a large synagogue had been under construction. The local bishop had become outraged and appealed to Pope Innocent IV to stop the building; the Jewish house of worship was destined to be too large, too tall, and exceedingly sumptuous. Thereupon, the pope issued a bull in Lyon, France, on the 13th of April 1250, authorizing the bishop to put a halt to the illegal construction. The Papal Bull still exists and probably accounts for the name of the plaza, Plaza of the Papal Bulls. Not a single trace remains of the stillborn synagogue. Ironically, the bullfight museum is housed in a beautiful building. Even if Maimonides did not live there and no synagogue was ever under construction there, the site is ideal for a synagogue, facing, as it does, a quiet plaza in the heart of the judería.

Another anachronistic street name is that of a small open area further along where the configuration of the streets form the letter *Y*. The open space where the two branches of the fork join the vertical stem has been named for another great Jew, the poet Judah ha Levi (1085-1140). Judah ha Levi was a native of Toledo, who, in mid-twentieth century, apparently was awarded honorary citizenship in Córdoba and a place of honor not far from the synagogue on Maimonides Street.

12 Ecija

I left Córdoba and, after crossing the Guadalquivir River, drove in a southwesterly direction toward Seville. The distance to Seville over the heavily traveled potholed road, the principal highway, is one hundred and thirty-eight kilometers, or about eighty-five miles. The road sweeps in a wide arc away from the Guadalquivir, first southwest and then west beyond Ecija, passing through rolling terrain with countless olive groves and fields of wheat. Since it was late in August, the wheat was tall and golden-colored, responding in undulating billows to the early morning wind.

Another road, older and slower, hugs the north bank of the Guadalquivir and passes through many small and picturesque villages, each with its own particular flavor and manner of speech. These villages have such mellifluous-sounding names as Almodóvar del Río, Posadas, Palma del Río, Peñaflor, Lora del Río, Cantillana del Río, Alcalá del Río, and finally La Algaba just on the outskirts of Seville. Most of the names of these towns are rooted in the Moslem past, as are their very inhabitants. Some once had Jewish communities, of which no single trace remains today. The main and better highway, the one that swings away to the south from the Guadalquivir passes through two towns, Ecija and Carmona, both with a Jewish past.

Ecija is located on the left bank of the Genil River, a tributary of the Guadalquivir, about halfway between Córdoba and Seville. Approaching from the higher ground, I viewed a thread of towns with many beautiful tall, elegant, and graceful towers in the distance. These towers, inspired by the Giralda of Seville, pierced the clear blue, cloud-

Fig. 12.1: Ecija. Tower, Church of San Juan. Medieval judería possibly located in vicinity. Destroyed during race riots (1391), four hundred years before Church of San Juan with tower was built in eighteenth century.

less, hot summer sky. As the terrain dipped down to the river, I entered a pocket of intensely heated dry air. For good reasons, indeed, Ecija is known as *la sartén de Andalucía* (the frying pan of Andalucía). In all of southern Spain, the heat of summer is oppressive; in Ecija it is especially so. To me, the fiery climate of Ecija seemed to be a poignant and living remembrance of the flames that raged in this beautiful town during the latter part of the fourteenth century when fires consumed its Jewish community.

The spark that first ignited and set aflame all the Jewish communities of Andalucía, the source of the conflagration that spread to the rest of the Iberian Peninsula in the ominously fateful year of 1391, was generated by a native of Ecija, Ferrand Martínez, the archdeacon of the Cathedral of Seville. Here he was born and here he had his first fateful contacts with Jews, undoubtedly while still a child. In his heart a bitter religious hatred must have been kindled early, a hatred that smoldered for years and burst into a raging passion when he was a grown man and a cleric. Supposedly speaking for the church, sometimes even defying his ecclesiastical superiors, he went up and down the countryside preaching against the perfidious Jews, the Christ-killers, who stubbornly persisted in their refusal to accept the true faith and who must be wiped off the face of the earth. When he temporarily occupied the archiepiscopal throne of the archbishopric of Seville in 1390, he found himself in a position of even greater authority and influence. Then did his preachments reach a culminating fury to the extent that he ignored the express orders of the king, who took more than a dim view of the inevitable results. These results amounted to the destruction of the Jewish communities and, consequently, the loss of an important source of royal revenue. In 1390, Ferrand Martínez ordered the destruction of the synagogue of his hometown, Ecija, as well as those in Alcalá de Guadaira, Coria del Río, and Cantillana del Río, all in the vicinity of Seville.

The history of the founding of Ecija places it in remote antiquity, probably by Greeks. Its history continued on through the Roman, Visigothic, and Moslem periods. Very few remains of these cultures are in evidence today, due largely to the earthquake that destroyed the city as well as much of Andalucía and Portugal in 1755. Fernando III reconquered the city from the Moors in 1240, four years after taking Córdoba and eight years before he vanquished Seville. The few vestiges of Ecija's walls of fortification, the walls Fernando stormed and broke through, still standing are of Arab date. Very little else of the medieval Christian period remains. If anything of the synagogue was left standing after its destruction at the hands of the inflamed rioting mob in 1390, it was surely reduced further to rubble in the earthquake of 1755. The town today is quite eighteenth-century baroque in architectural character. The great number of beautiful church towers, all dating from the second half of the eighteenth century, adds to the picturesque charm of its tortured, twisting streets.

The earliest documentary reference to the existence of a Jewish community in Ecija dates from 1332, in which, among other matters, the Synagogue of Rab Yocef or Yucaf el Levi Aben Shabad is mentioned. Its location cannot be ascertained. The Jewish community probably had been founded there earlier than the date of the document mentioning the synagogue. The timing would place it either at the same time as, or soon after, the establishment of the Jewish community in Seville after its conquest by Fernando III in 1248. The Jewish community of Ecija was probably not very large; one synagogue apparently was sufficient for its needs.

I walked and re-walked the streets of Ecija, the part where the medieval street plan is still preserved, looking for a trace, for some sign that might indicate where the Jewish community possibly could have lived before it was extinguished in 1390. Judging by the nature of the street plan, the judería might have been located on the

Fig. 12.2: Ecija. Calle de Garcilópez, probable location of obliterated judería.

Fig. 12.3: Ecija. Calle de Garcilópez and intersection of Calle de Estudio, probable part of judería before destruction of 1391.

Calle de Garcilópez. This narrow little street, which bends away a short distance to the north of the main plaza toward the Genil River, has the same look as so many other identifiable juderías. Ecija—medieval Ecija—has disappeared just as its Jews, their houses, and their synagogue have disappeared.

The synagogue that had been dismantled in 1390 was never rebuilt. The following year, in 1391 during the hot summer month of June, the massacre of the Jews, which had started in Seville and spread to the rest of Christian Spain, also brought with it the final destruction of the Jewish quarter of Ecija. Most of the Jews of Ecija were forcibly baptized, so that to all intents and purposes the Jewish story in Ecija ends in that evil-omened year. Almost a century later, in 1473, one hears of another riot when the *marranos* (secret Jews), the New Christians of Ecija, suffered a pogrom. Finally, the last dying ember of Judaism in Ecija was put out forever.

13 Carmona

Carmona is but forty-three kilometers (about twenty-five miles) from Ecija, over a broad plain and through seemingly endless fields of wheat. The road is level and straight most of the way. After a sharp turn to the left or south, the road climbs gently. There in the distance, high above the undulating billows of the wheat fields on an eminence above the plain encircled by its ancient walls, stands the town of Carmona. The walls are of ancient lineage and are still preserved to some extent. With its towers and battlements signaling the visitor from a distance, the old *alcázar* (Arab fortress), now in ruins, dominates the landscape from afar.

Fig. 13.1: Carmona. View to plain, to east from Alcazar, the ruined Arab fortress.

The view from the alcázar is breathtaking, the limitless expanse of the vega stretches to either side. To the east toward Ecija and Córdoba a sea of wheat waves; to the west toward Seville a sea of olive groves cover the hillsides. Somewhere in this beautiful setting, in the western part of town on the very fringe and abutting on the city wall itself, a Jewish community existed—its synagogue, according to

Fig. 13.2: Carmona. Puerta de Sevilla, main gate in wall of fortification. Romans built first city wall, later Arabs strengthened it. Semicircular horseshoe-shaped arch spans opening. Ancient judería located inside wall at short distance to left of gate.

Cantera Burgos, embedded in the Church of San Blas. A broken remnant, a paltry token of Jewish life was destroyed by a bolt of lightning one fateful and ominous day, June 6, 1391. This Jewish community became the victim of a conflagration that had been ignited in Seville, a scant thirty-three kilometers away. This conflagration spread here, to Ecija, and eventually to all the Jewish communities of Christian Spain.

Carmona is a little known treasure house of Iberian history, art, and architecture. On the western outskirts of the town and to one side of the Seville road are the remains of a Roman necropolis with well over one thousand tombs, some of which are of monumental proportions and range in date from about the second century B.C.E. to the fourth century C.E. The Romans first built walls that gird the city. Later, the Arabs strengthened and rebuilt the walls. The *Puerta de Sevilla* (Seville Gate), with its horseshoe-arch spanning the door remodeled by the Arabs, still functions. The interior portion of the gate has remained intact since Roman times. Whether a Jewish community had existed in the Roman "Carmo" or the Arab "Karmuna" is not known. Certain it is that Jews settled the place, in part, soon after the Reconquest of the city in 1247, a year before Seville fell to the victorious Christian armies under Ferdinand III.

With a small boy to show me the way, I set out from the Puerta de Sevilla following the city wall in a westerly direction and came to the Church of San Blas, once a synagogue. The long south side of the church, with the main door, faces a small open area or plaza. The west side, the shorter side, fronts on a long narrow street. This narrow street descends sharply in a northerly direction so that the lower part of this wall is considerably below the level of the side facing the little plaza. Standing there and viewing the two sides of the building at once, I observed not a single vestige of medieval construction, let alone anything even remotely Jewish. The church building, according to Cantera, had been rebuilt completely in the eighteenth century, leaving precious few vestiges of its former existence as a synagogue. Where were these precious few vestiges?

Suddenly I found a clue! I noted that though the church is oriented east-west, as is to be expected in a church, the main entrance is on one of the long sides, the south facing the plaza on the higher ground where I stood. Normally, the entrance to a church is on the west front, but here the west side is a blank wall abutting on the very right-of-way of the steeply descending street. I looked up and saw another curious and most unusual feature. The single bell tower, reduced to a belfry, rises from the very ridge of the roof over the gable on the west end. Bell towers are normally placed to one side of the main or west facade of churches, especially in eighteenth-century churches. I reasoned that the unusual location of the bell tower, just as that of the main door, was predicated by the existence of an older structure, the medieval synagogue, which had been utilized in the eighteenth-century reconstruction. Judging by the nature of the exterior of the building, the synagogue had been totally obliterated.

Fig. 13.3: Carmona. The west end of Church of San Blas, formerly Synagogue of Carmona. Belfry rising from ridge of roof is from eighteenth century.

Some small boys played "bullfight" in the plaza. One put his hands to his head, extending his forefingers to simulate the horns of the bull. Another stood off with an old torn shirt in his hands that he fluttered shouting, "*Olé, toro, toro,*" while the other, head down, charged at him. The toreador kept his ground, stood erect, chest out, and executed a fancy twirl, an incipient *verónica*, as the bull charged by, brushing the torn shirt from his hands. "*¡Olé, olé!*" These boys were playing at bullfight on the very ground where Jewish boys and girls once assembled in the synagogue court while their elders remained at prayers inside.

I walked down the narrow street running past the west end of the church and, at the bottom of the incline, turned right into an extremely narrow alley-like street, the Calle de San Blas. Because the street lies at a considerably lower level than the

Fig. 13.4: Carmona. Synagogue-church of San Blas. Main door, eighteenth-century date, located on south side of building near western end.

Fig. 13.5: Carmona. Synagogue-church of San Blas. Main door, north side of building, only remnant of synagogue. Located above Calle de San Blas, accessible through second story of house in street below abutting foundation of church above. Door original construction of synagogue 13th/14th centuries.

plaza on the other side, the long north side of the church building towered above me. Small river-borne boulders and pebbles pave the narrow, little street. The street, where the Jews of Carmona once had lived, rises in an easterly direction. Some poor little houses, really no more than one-roomed hovels, huddle below the foundation level of the church.

I noted one house built right against the north wall of the synagogue-church of San Blas. A triangular pediment spanned its plain door; the decorative feature seemed out of concert with the humble building it graced. I hesitated about knocking to ask permission to enter. I wanted to see exactly how the rear wall of the house was joined to the north wall of the church. Instead, I advanced a few yards up and looked back in a westerly direction down the street. The houses on the cross street leading down from the plaza along the west wall of the church, the one from which I had turned into the Calle de San Blas, nestled against the partially ruined city wall rising high above them. These were also Jewish houses.

Fig. 13.6: Carmona. Calle de San Blas, principal street of judería. View to west, section of ancient city wall of fortification with houses abutting. Former synagogue, now Church of San Blas, towers above street to left out of picture.

A little girl with her water pitcher stood opposite me in the doorway. Her smile encouraged me, so I turned and knocked on the door where I had hesitated a moment before. It opened. A man in faded and patched blue-denim pants and shirt invited me in after I told him I wanted to see the north door of the church hidden from view by his house. I came into a tiny room with an extremely low ceiling. To the right, an opening in the wall permitted access to a narrow and steep ladder-like flight of stairs. When I hesitated, he bade me go up. The stairwell was so low that I had to clamber up on all fours to reach the top, to my astonishment, I found myself not in a room, but in a tiny garden open to the sky on the second floor of the house! Directly in front of the north door of the church, the garden was the counterpart of the one on the long south side facing the plaza. The north door is one of the few original and unbaptized parts of the building still extant. It had escaped the eighteenth-century reconstruction its south counterpart had suffered. In style it is truly mudéjar, probably dating from the thirteenth or fourteenth centuries. This one door, then, is the only remnant left of the synagogue so willfully destroyed by the mob of pogromists in 1391.

The arch and the jambs of the door are of hard-baked brick laid with extremely thin mortar joints. Even the decorative architectural moldings are also executed in brick. The arch itself is slightly pointed and set within an *alfiz,* namely, the arch is bounded by moldings so that it appears to be within a rectangular frame. Above the door arch with its alfiz, a corbel table or a cornice molding supported on brackets, also a decorative mudéjar device, completes the scheme.

According to contemporary accounts, the synagogue building was set afire in 1391, causing the whole of the roof and parts of the walls to fall. The north door escaped destruction and could therefore be utilized later when the building was re-constructed and converted to a church. The curious orientation with the doors on the long sides, unusual for a church, is best explained if one compares this building with the synagogues of Córdoba, of Bembibre, of El Tránsito in Toledo, and of Corpus Christi in Segovia. In these four synagogues the main entrance is on one of the long sides. It would seem, therefore, that in rebuilding the burned-out syna-gogue for the Church of San Blas, the location of the doors of the original Jewish house of prayer were preserved. The slope and the lower lay of the land on the west side as well as the extremely narrow width of the street made it impractical to place the main door of the church elsewhere. To have done so, the builder would have had to construct a flight of steps inside the door to reach the nave higher up at plaza level. The orientation of the entrance scheme of the Jewish synagogue thus survives in the Christian church.

The Jewish community of Carmona was completely destroyed in 1391, its mem-bers extinguished as Jews. Those whom the sword did not slaughter, the holy water of baptism sprinkled. However, the water apparently washed off, leaving the Jews as stiff-necked as before, for another massacre occurred almost a century later, in 1474. The *conversos* (Jews recently converted to Christianity) were actually *mar-ranos* (secret Jews) and so were completely extinguished in a final pogrom as the clandestine Jewish community of Ecija had been the previous year. But what of the children playing at "bullfight" in front of the synagogue-church? And what of the little girl with the water pitcher, and the man in the patched, faded blue-denim pants and shirt? Who are they: Celtiberians, Romans, Moslems, Jews, or Christians? They are Andalusian Spaniards!

14 Alcalá de Guadaira

Leaving Carmona at the western edge of town near the Roman necropolis, I took the left fork where the main road branched off to a secondary road, a round-about way to Seville. The bumpy road passed through a benign wheat-and-olive- growing countryside. The little villages of this countryside peeked above the crests of the low hills, looking more like man-made mounds than natural formations. They were scattered here and there over the otherwise flat terrain, a peculiar characteristic of this particular landscape. These small eminences breaking above the horizon are still known by their Arabic name *alcor*. Therefore, the names of these towns have the word *alcor* as a descriptive appendage, El Viso del Alcor and Mairena del Alcor, each with its own particular savor, manner of speech, and picturesque streets lined with whitewashed houses with red, barrel-tile roofs. The "big-city" people of Seville, with a patronizing smile of self-evident superiority, dub the natives of the alcor villages as *catetos* (country bumpkins), especially because of their peculiar speech—really not too different from that of the "sophisticated" Sevillanos—that I came to understand only after weeks of conscious effort.

In general, the people of the region around Seville, and the less-urbane Sevillanos too, in their speech convert the *l* to an *r*, so that words such as *balcón* (balcony), *soldado* (soldier), and *alcalde* (mayor) come out sounding as *baRcón*, *soRdado*, and *aRcaRde*. This I did not know when I first came to Alcalá de Guadaira and Carmona by bus from Seville some forty years ago. A young woman sitting next to me, a native of Alcalá de Guadaira on a visit back home from Barcelona where she was working as a housemaid, explained why all the towns of the region had the appendage *alcor*. The word *alcor*, she quietly confided to me so that the other passengers would not hear and so not be offended, was a *cateta* mispronunciation of the word, *alcol* [sic] *alcohol*, spelled the same in English as in Spanish and similarly pronounced. According to my authoritative informant, a resident of the great city of Barcelona, much *alcol* is manufactured in these towns; that is the reason they are called "Mairena of Alcohol," and so forth. It was a long time later, after I had heard *l* becomes *r*, that I learned the moral of the story of the enchanting "alcohol towns." The young woman wished to impress me that she was no longer a *cateta* though born and raised in Alcalá de Guadaira, which she nevertheless still pronounced *Arcará* de Guadaira.

During the year I spent in Seville, I went to Alcalá de Guadaira quite often, just for an outing or to wander about the streets or, best of all, to buy freshly baked

Fig. 14.1: Alcalá de Guadaira. View to south of Barrio de San Miguel, former judería, from plaza before main entrance to Alcazar. Synagogue, converted to Church of San Miguel, top left of photograph. Olive grove just beyond judería, wheat fields in distance.

Fig. 14.2: Alcalá de Guadaira. View of northern side of *Alcazar* (Arab fortress) on western edge of site as seen from Seville road. Ancient judería lies on sloping ground outside fortress on other side.

bread. The bread of Alcalá de Guadaira is excellent and much sought after in the city of Seville. The skilled bakers use superior flour, from grain grown locally, for baking bread. For centuries, Alcalá de Guadaira has been the hub of an important wheat-growing and milling region. Because it is a pleasant town to visit, many Sevillanos also go to Alcalá de Guadaira to spend a pleasant Sunday afternoon. The town is only some fifteen kilometers distant from Seville over the direct road. In fact, the bullfight season, right after *Semana Santa* (Holy Week), traditionally begins there a little earlier than in Seville. During its famous annual April fair, the *aficionados* (fans), eager for a foretaste of the taurine spectacle after the long winter interim, go to the *corridas* (bullfights) there before the opening of the season in Seville. The bakers still carry their bread daily to Seville, where it finds an eager and hungry market the entire year round (not that the bread of Seville is bad, but that of Alcalá is better). Even more than bread, what attracted me to make repeated visits to Alcalá de Guaidara was the old judería, hidden from view from the rest of the town and inhabited by the poorest people in town.

To go to the judería of Alcalá was to go back to the fourteenth and fifteenth centuries, or even earlier, to the times before the Reconquest. Alcalá still preserves its Oriental (that is, North African Moslem) air, though most of its churches underwent much restoration and change in the eighteenth century. High up on an eminence overlooking the Guadaira River on the western edge of town there still exists the imposing fortress originally constructed by the Romans, but completely rebuilt and strengthened by the Almohads in the twelfth century. Its most imposing aspect would come into view across the wide valley, with the river below, on my approach from Seville. The road makes a wide arc, hugging the side of the steep hill. Hidden from view on the other side, the south, of this ancient mole and huddled under its shadow, remnants still exist of the judería and the Synagogue of Alcalá de Guadaira. The synagogue, now the Church of San Miguel, had been largely rebuilt about mid-twentieth century, its original style having been preserved more or less.

The natural defensive position of Alcalá was first recognized by the Romans and later by the Arabs. The Alcázar of Alcalá served as a military outpost within the system of fortified towns guarding the approaches to Seville. In fact, before Fernando III could conquer Seville, he had first to eliminate this very fortress, which he took in 1246, just two years before his conquest of Seville.

The entrance to Alcalá from the Carmona road is not dramatic; it is nothing like the approach from Seville on the opposite side of town. On my first visit, I parked my automobile in the main plaza, an open space bordered by buildings of no particular architectural merit, and walked to the outskirts of town, the Guadaira River on my left. Then I climbed up the road leading to the Alcázar through an ancient gate of Almohad construction, a vestige of the outer perimeter of defensive walls that once encircled the lower reaches of the entire citadel itself. At the summit there is a splendid view of the town with its eighteenth-century church towers and the limitless plain beyond. Just over the edge of the terrace wall of the *Plaza del Aguila* (Eagle's Plaza), on the summit and in the shadow of the Arab fortress, lies the judería, now known as the Barrio de San Miguel.

A simple box-like church dominates the few houses arranged in picturesque disarray. I walked to the edge of the terrace and

Fig. 14.3: Alcalá de Guadaira. Alcazar from south. Barrio de San Miguel, former pre-1392 judería, nestles up against wall between two enormous redoubts.

Fig. 14.4: Alcalá de Guadaira. West front of synagogue-church of San Miguel, principal street in barrio of same name.

Fig. 14.5: Alcalá de Guadaira. Main door of synagogue-church of San Miguel, converted to church after 1391, ceased to function as church at later date. Building restored and converted (ca. 1957) to elementary school for children in neighborhood.

sat on the wall, enjoying the view of the poor houses in the crooked unpaved streets conforming to the accidented, uneven lay of the land that rose to the very walls and battlements of the old Arab fortress. The judería was and is located in the most isolated part of town, on a steep slope outside the city walls. Yet it enjoys one of the most splendid views: the Alcázar on the right; the Guadaira River below; and the flat landscape with wheat fields and orange and olive groves in the distance under an immense sky.

The fate of the Jewish community of Alcalá during the troubles of 1391 was even more horrible than that of Seville. In 1390 Ferrand Martínez, in defiance

Fig. 14.6: Alcalá de Guadaira. Puerta Almohade in outer ring of walls of Alcazar, one of entrances from city to judería, which lay west.

Fig. 14.7: Alcalá de Guadaira. View to east from inside Puerta Almohade. Ancient Roman bridge spanning Guadaira River to right in distance.

of the royal will, had ordered that the synagogue be dismantled and its site serve as a church under the advocation of San Miguel. He also ordered that the Jewish communal property be confiscated. If the synagogue was actually torn down is not known. That the Church of San Miguel, still in evidence today, took its place there is no doubt. The synagogue-church was restored in 1957, adhering to some extent to the mudéjar style in which it was originally built some time in the fourteenth century.

By the middle of the fateful year of 1391, on June 6 to be precise, those Jews of Alcalá, who were not massacred by the mob, were baptized wholesale against their will. Just how many died for *Kiddush ha Shem* (the Sanctification of the Name) or survived for the Sanctification of the Cross is not known. The Jewish community of Alcalá is heard of no longer. However, if the history of the Jews of Alcalá is like that of so many other *juderías*, those who had been baptized in 1391 continued to live in their old neighborhood as Christians and attended divine services in the same building that had been their synagogue. There, instead of an Ark for the Torah, an altar with a crucifix doubtlessly was installed.

Fig. 14.8: Alcalá de Guadaira. Father and son, residents of Barrio of San Miguel. *"¡Ríete, Currito!"* (Smile, little Curro!)

A crucifix still stands to this very day on the east wall, although the Church of San Miguel is no longer a house of prayer, neither Jewish nor Christian. Instead, the building serves as a school for the poor children of the neighborhood. In this large one-room school, bare except for some wooden benches, a young woman teacher stands before garrulous, squirming children facing the cross on the east wall. In a loud voice rising above the high-pitched resonant children's babble and hubbub, she recites maxims, which the children repeat in full-choired soprano unison. The traditional synagogue since time immemorial has many functions: *beth ha knesseth* (house of assembly); *beth ha tefillah* (house of prayer); and *beth ha midrash* (house of study). The Church of San Miguel still survives as a *beth ha midrash*.

Fig. 14.9: Alcalá de Guadaira. View to east of city from Plaza del Aguila on summit of hill where Alcazar located. Ancient judería, present Barrio de San Miguel, on slope to west.

Fig. 14.10: Alcalá de Guadaira. View from Plaza del Aguila to west of Barrio of San Miguel, built up against walls of Alcazar. Olive groves and wheat fields in distance.

15 Seville

The first time, so many years ago, I came to Seville was by the train from Córdoba and Ecija, arriving late one hot August afternoon at the neo-Moorish brick depot near the Guadalquivir River just opposite Triana on the other bank. The neighborhood of Triana is famous for its pottery and tile factories, but even better known for its gypsy flamenco music, and possibly the hometown of the converted Jew, Diego de Triana. Legend has it, because he knew both Hebrew and Arabic, Diego de Triana sailed on Columbus' first voyage as an interpreter. Destiny chose him to be the first member of the crew to espy land, the land of the New World on October 12, 1492.

My first impressions on the day of my arrival are somewhat blurred now. All I remember is that I found the place neither as distinctive nor as remarkable as Toledo and Córdoba. I had no notion then of what lay in store for me in the remembrance of Jewish things past in Seville; I was still agitated by the experiences I had had so recently in Toledo and Córdoba. Not until I had walked the streets of Seville during that first visit, the purpose of which was to study the baroque architecture of the churches with which Seville abounds, did I inadvertently come into physical contact with the Jewish past as well.

Thus, some years later I already knew what awaited me inside the city. I now approached it as a motorist at the wheel of an automobile from Alcalá de Guadaira, some fifteen kilometers (about ten miles) distant over the flat plain roofed with a vast vaulted azure sky. The skyline of Seville with its famous tower of the cathedral, the Giralda, came into view almost at once after leaving Alcalá. In its very shadow lies the ancient Jewish quarter of Seville, the *Barrio de Santa Cruz* (Ward of the Holy Cross)—one of the chief tourist attractions served up to foreign visitors.

The Romans established the city. It is not known if there were Jews in Seville during the Roman domination, but legend has it that its Jewish community was one of the oldest in Spain, having been established soon after the destruction of the Second Temple in Jerusalem in 70 C.E. Judging by the repressive laws enacted against them, Jews must have been living there before the Germanic barbarians, first the Vandals in 411 and later the Visigoths in 441, conquered the place. It is said that when the Arab warrior Musa took Seville in 712, he placed the city in charge of its numerous Jewish inhabitants, who had welcomed him as a deliverer.

The Jews of Seville lived in peace under Arab domination until the time that Spain fell into the hands of the invading Berbers, also Moslems, from North Africa.

Jewish Remnants

Fig. 15.1: Seville. Map of Barrio de Santa Cruz, location of judería.

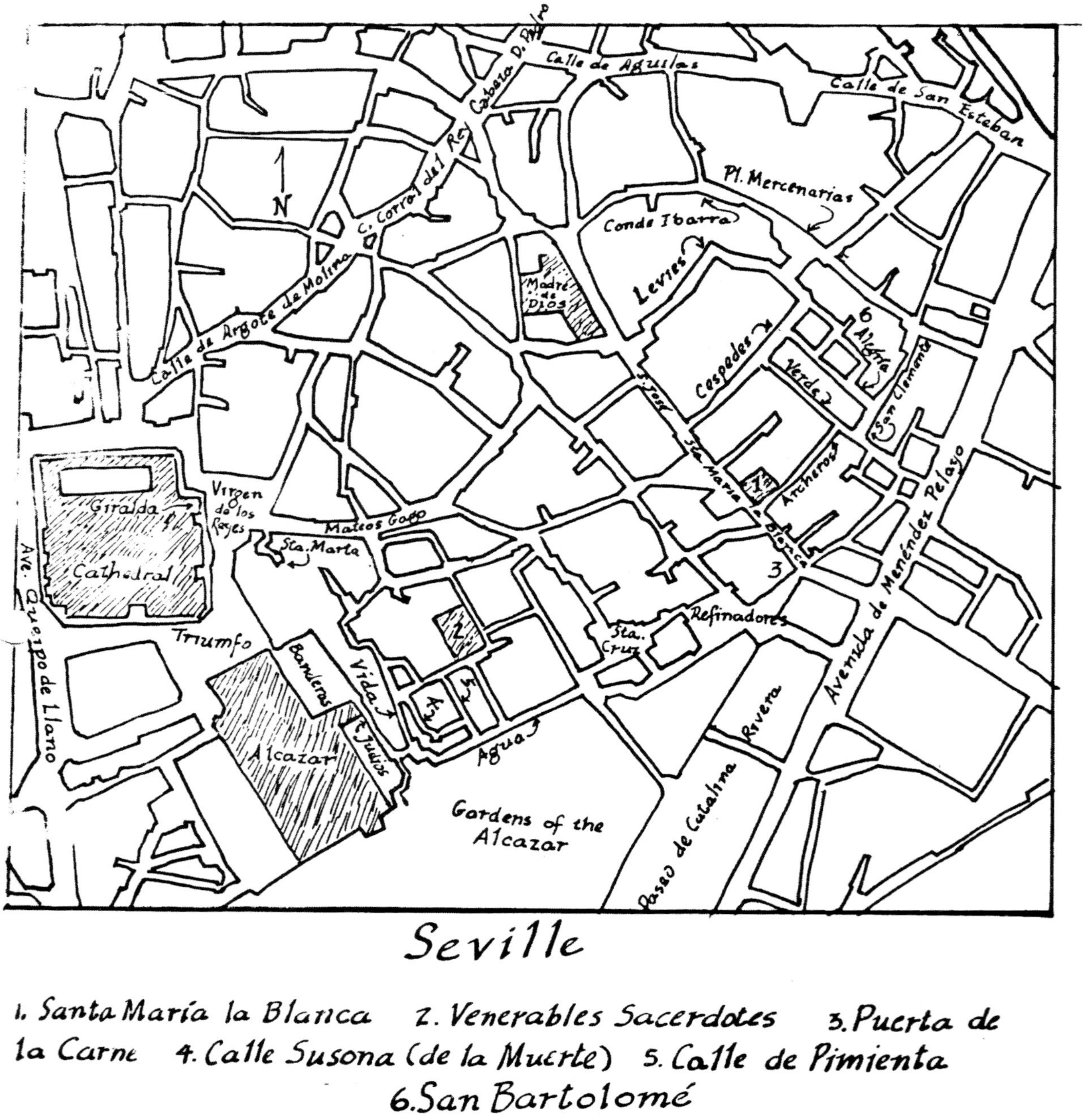

Seville

1. *Santa María la Blanca*   2. *Venerables Sacerdotes*   3. *Puerta de la Carne*   4. *Calle Susona (de la Muerte)*   5. *Calle de Pimienta*   6. *San Bartolomé*

The Almoravids (1091) invaded first and the Almohads (1148) later. The latter instituted an inhumane policy of repression against Jews, who had been tolerated as "people of the Book" since the first Arab conquest some four hundred years previously. The Almohads ordered the Jews of Seville and of all Moslem Spain to accept Islam. Many refused and became slaves. Because the period of Almohad rule in Seville was extremely trying for the Jews, the Jewish community probably did not exist very long after 1148.

Apparently some individual Jews did continue to live there during the twelfth and thirteenth centuries. When after a siege of six months, the Castilian conqueror, Fernando III, took Seville (1248), records state that the Jews of the city came to meet him carrying Torah scrolls. They presented him with a key to the judería that bears an inscription in Hebrew saying, "The King of Kings will open, the King of the earth will enter." This gilt key supposedly is still to be seen in the treasure room of the cathedral. The Jews were not alone in welcoming Fernando; the Moslem population also gave him a key to the city, a silver one. It would seem, then, that there was a Jewish community. It had probably lived in straitened circumstances for about a century until Seville once again fell under Christian rule in the middle of the thirteenth century.

A friend of Israel, Fernando III favored Jews in many ways. He assigned three, or possibly four, mosques to the newly revived Jewish community. He also invited Jews from Christian Spain to settle in the town and the surrounding countryside, allotting them olive groves and fields for cultivation. His son, Alfonso X, *El Sabio* (the Wise), while still crown prince and doubtlessly with his father's approval, also assigned certain villages in the region to Jews. Known as *aldeas de los judíos* (villages of the Jews) were the following: San Juan de Aznalfarache, now a suburb of Seville on the other side of the Guadalquivir River; Paterna, in the region known as El Aljarafe toward Huelva and to the west about thirty kilometers from Seville; and a third town, Aznalcazar, about thirty kilometers in a southwesterly direction from Seville.

I visited these towns many times during the year that I spent in Seville, always looking for some signs, some spoors, some traces, no matter how faint, of the former Jewish presence. I found nothing, absolutely nothing, no physical remains at all, except perhaps the inhabitants themselves, charming and earthy Andalusians in mien and in speech. The demeanor of the people seemed to indicate that these villages were once exclusively inhabited by Jews. Such an assumption, though possible, is not very probable. It is romantic, quixotic, and unrealistic to conclude that the modern inhabitants of San Juan de Aznalfarache, Paterna, and Aznalcazar are lineal descendants of the original Jewish settlers placed there by Alfonso El Sabio and therefore constitute evidence, albeit biological, of the Jewish past in these Andalusian towns.

Fig. 15.2: Seville. View to southeast of Barrio de Santa Cruz, former judería, from campanile of Giralda. Modern, long after Jews no longer resident, aesthetic ensemble of whitewashed walls, red-tiled roofs, and greenery of patios. Ancient layout of streets, dating from Moslem (Arab) period of Spanish history.

After the devastations caused by the war in the latter part of the thirteenth century, the new Jewish settlers played a part in the revival of agricultural production. A fossilized name, indicating that Jewish landowners once lived around Seville, came to my attention one day as I studied the Firestone Road Map No. 9, which covered the southern part of Spain. There, in tiny letters, I found a locality that turned out to be a resort hotel to the northeast of Seville still called *Cortijo del Judío* (Jew's Ranch or Farm). Hence, Jews remain in the toponymy, at least in the Sevillano countryside where Fernando III had granted some of them agricultural lands.

Jews, Moslems, and Christians lived side by side in a tolerant symbiosis in the thirteenth century. That Fernando III was considered a protector of the Jews is further attested to by the fact his sarcophagus, located in the *Capilla Real* (Royal Chapel) in the Cathedral of Seville, bears an epitaph written in four languages: one is Hebrew; the others are Arabic, Latin, and Castilian. His death is recorded according to the Hebrew calendar as the 22nd of Sivan 5012 (1252 C.E.)

Fig. 15.3: Seville. Plaza del Triunfo at rear of cathedral. Entrance gate in Alcazar wall to left opens on large rectangular courtyard, Patio de las Banderas. At opposite end, covered passageway leads to Calle de la Judería.

Physical vestiges that recall the Jewish presence in Seville all date from after 1248. Little or nothing at all remains from the Roman, Visigoth, and Arab or Moorish periods. The Jewish community that existed in the century and a half or so between 1248 and 1391 has left a permanent stamp on the city of Seville. This stamp is deeply impressed in the picturesque, narrow, winding streets of the former Jewish quarter, the *Barrio de Santa Cruz* (Ward of the Holy Cross).

By the fourteenth century, after that of Toledo, the Jewish community of Seville was probably the most prosperous and most populous in all Spain. Ferrand Martínez first kindled the spark that set off the wholesale massacres and mass forced conversions precisely here in Seville. The archdeacon from Ecija had been carrying out his anti-Jewish campaigns since mid-century. When the archbishop of Seville died in 1390, Martínez took over the administration of the archbishopric and preached his inflammatory sermons in the very cathedral, his frenzied shouting almost within earshot of the judería. The Crown did not like this anti-Jewish movement. The royal chamber considered the Jews in Seville, and of all Spain as well, as serfs and, in a sense, property of the king, to whom they directly paid taxes.

King Juan of Castile died (1390) while the crown prince was still a child. The regency in control while the new king was still a minor, having more important prob-

Fig. 15.4: Seville. View of Patio de las Banderas from Calle de la Judería looking back to Alcazar walls, Plaza del Triunfo, and Giralda of cathedral. Giralda, cathedral tower, looms above Alcazar walls. Topmost stories above main shaft of Giralda added in seventeenth century long after Jewish community of Seville extinguished, true, also, of present Gothic cathedral, largely of fifteenth and sixteenth century date. Original cathedral dating from Moorish times, replaced mosque that had been converted to Christian use after Reconquest in 1253.

lems to cope with than the crazed archdeacon, did little to curb Ferrand Martínez. His inflammatory preaching had its due effect. On June 1, 1391, disorders ending in pillage, murder, baptisms at the point of the sword, and the burning of synagogues broke out in the judería of Seville, spreading from there to the rest of Andalucía, to New Castile, Old Castilla, and even to Catalonia and the Levante. Ultimately the disorders extended throughout the Iberian Peninsula during the rest of that summer and fall. A new *Tish b'Ab* (the ninth day of the Hebrew month of Ab, when the Romans destroyed the Temple of Jerusalem) was repeated in every city, village, and hamlet where Jewish communities had existed for centuries. For Iberian Jewry, the immediate effects were dire indeed, leading to mass conversions of those who had escaped the fury of the mob and were not slaughtered. To all intents and purposes, the community of Seville ceased to exist in 1391; no remnant of outwardly professing Jews remained by the time of the Expulsion a century later in 1492.

A perusal of the archives of the Inquisition attest, though Jewish communal life had ceased, that there is no doubt Jews still lived in Seville as *marranos* (secret Jews). Hundreds of baptized Jews who were found guilty of holding on to their ancestral faith in secret were burned at the stake in *autos da fe*.

The construction of the many apartment houses mid-twentieth century on the southern outskirts of the medieval town, in the neighborhood known as La Tablada, provided physical testimony of the holocaust. Jews' broken bodies were uncovered during the building excavation. Here *autos da fe* had taken place. Time and time

Fig. 15.5: Seville. Entrance passageway of Calle de la Judería from Patio de las Banderas. Entrance street cuts through walls of Alcazar.

Fig. 15.6: Seville. Calle de la Judería. View to arched entrance passageway leading back to Patio de las Banderas. Alcazar walls of fortification and redoubt rise high above street. Calle de la Judería runs under private residence abutting against wall, continues through redoubt.

again, as foundations for buildings were dug, skeletal remains of *relaxed* heretics were uncovered. One of the most prominent *heretics*, Luis de Santangel, a supporter of Columbus and an official at the court who lent money to Ferdinand and Isabella, marched to La Tablada in 1491 and there was consumed alive by fire as a *relapsed* Jew.

In vain I tried to form some idea concerning the number of Jews that had lived in Seville during the period from the Reconquest in the mid-thirteenth century to the extinction of Jewish life in 1391. I traversed the streets of the judería over and over again to gain some notion of its possible physical size in relation to the city as

Fig. 15.7: Seville. Calle de la Vida in judería. View from Plazuela de la Vida toward Plaza de la Doña Elvira. Old man and his cat walk slowly up street.

a whole within the perimeter of the medieval walls. I even tried counting houses, allowing five persons per house. Too many unknown factors and inconsistencies in my count, as well as no way to count or even approximate how many houses possibly could have existed on each street more than five hundred years earlier, precluded accuracy. I gave up, despairing of ever reaching any reliable conclusions by this cumbersome and inconsistent method.

From literary sources I had learned the boundaries and something of the street plan of the old Jewish quarter. Taking a map in hand and walking around the now almost obliterated medieval perimeter of the city and then circling the supposed former boundaries of the judería within that city plan, I realized that the Jewish part of the city might possibly have constituted one-twelfth of the area as a whole. However, even this method of determining the size of the Jewish population of Seville is fraught with many problems and can only provide impressionistic results. In all likelihood, these results are far from reality because the physical size of the judería varied from time to time.

Countless times I walked the boundaries of the greatest extension of the judería of Seville at the time the community was destroyed in 1391. My route follows: I began at the Alcazar not far from the rear of the cathedral in the Plaza del Triunfo; went through the Patio de las Banderas to the Callejón de la Judería; passed the Calle and Plazuela de la Vida; turned left into the Callejón del Agua; proceeded up to the Plaza Alfaro; skirted the Murillo Gardens on the right and on past the Plaza de los Refinadores; and then continued up to the Calle de Santa María La Blanca. At that point, I arrived at the location of the principal entrance to the judería, the Puerta de la Judería, now known as the Puerta de la Carne. From there I continued in a northeasterly direction up the Calle de Cano y Cueto to the Plaza de los Curtidores. There I followed the line of the ancient city wall and went out

Fig. 15.8: Seville. Plazuela de la Vida from intersection of Callejón del Agua. Redoubt in Alcazar wall through which Calle de la Judería cuts in background. Wall with arched opening on opposite side of street leads back to Calle de la Judería.

Fig. 15.9: Seville. Callejón del Agua from corner of Calle de la Pimienta. Street marks southern boundary of medieval judería. City wall to right.

to the wide street full of traffic, the Avenida de Menéndez Pelayo. Following that street to the Calle de San Esteban, I arrived at the former location of the Puerta de Carmona, another city gate, and the northern extent of the judería. Thus, I physically traced with my footsteps the limits of the judería along the southeastern city wall. From the Puerta de Carmona I followed the northerly limits, turned left into the Calle de San Esteban and continued in a westerly direction to the Calle de Aguilas. Turning left here, in a southwesterly direction, I looked forward to going down the beautiful and picturesque *Calle de la Cabeza del Rey Don Pedro* (Street of the Head of King Don Pedro), which led me on to the Calle del Corral del Rey. I then turned slightly left, or south, into the Calle de los Abades. Here, I continued

Fig. 15.10: Seville. Calle de Santa María La Blanca, formerly principal street in medieval judería. It continues to city gate now known as Puerta de la Carne, formerly Puerta de la Judería. Main facade of Church of Santa María la Blanca with pointed arch on left. Church converted from synagogue after 1391. Jewish cemetery lay outside Puerta de la Judería, no trace visible, area has been developed.

Fig. 15.11: Seville. The Giralda from Calle de Mateos Gago one of boundaries of judería, reduced in size after 1391. Giralda continued to dominate reduced judería although not as tall as now. Arcaded section on top crowned with weather vane, *giralda*, added in seventeenth century.

on to the Calle de Mateos Gago, made a right turn, again in a westerly direction, and came out from the narrow hemmed-in streets into a view of the Giralda. I walked down the broad Calle de Mateos Gago past a little hidden street, no wider than a corridor in a house, leading to the delightful and beautiful Plaza de Santa Marta to the south or left, and on to the Plaza de la Virgen de los Reyes just in back of the cathedral. There, I went around the cathedral apse and returned to the Plaza del Triunfo and the entrance to the Patio de las Banderas where I had begun the circuit. The walk, which took less than an hour, included many pauses to enjoy the beauty of the scene.

Fig. 15.12: Seville. Plaza de los Curtidores (Plaza of the Tanners) in former judería. Tower of Church of San Bartolomé in background occupies site of one of three synagogues left standing after riots of 1391.

How many Jews lived in this section of the city at the end of the fourteenth century? Perhaps a count based on the number of synagogues might provide a securer basis for making such a calculation. In 1248, or soon thereafter, Fernando III assigned the Jews the three or four mosques, alluded to earlier, to be used as synagogues. These buildings were located in the areas that later, after the pogroms of 1391 during which the Jewish community was obliterated, became the parishes of Santa Cruz, Santa María La Blanca, and San Bartolomé.

In his firebrand sermons, Ferrand Martínez enumerated twenty-three synagogues as existing in Seville. This may have been an exaggeration; from the records twenty are known to have existed. Except for the three main synagogues—that is, Santa Cruz, Santa María La Blanca, and San Bartolomé—all were probably small. Allowing a conservative number of twenty to twenty-five families of five persons each for each synagogue would result in a Jewish population in Seville at the end of the fourteenth century of from between 2,000 and 2,500 individuals, occupying about one-twelfth of the total area of the city.

Just what the overall population of Seville was in the late fourteenth century is not known, but if the above calculations have any figment of fact in them, the

Fig. 15.13: Seville. Calle de Santa Marta opening from foot of Calle de Mateos Gago near Plaza de la Virgen de los Reyes at apsidal end of cathedral. Tiny passageway leads to Plazuela de Santa Marta.

whole of Seville might have included twelve times the number of Jews, or about 24,000 to 30,000 inhabitants in all in 1391. That this seems a reasonable figure, is concluded on the basis of some estimates deduced for the population of Seville in later centuries. For example, during the sixteenth century after the discovery and conquest of the New World, the total population of Seville is estimated to have been about 70,000. This may be considered to represent an acceptable increase over the 24,000 to 30,000 I ventured to estimate for the late fourteenth century. This time period existed long before the prosperous era that ensued in Seville following the discovery of America when many people were drawn there from other parts of Spain.

The Jews, as I have ventured to conclude, probably represented no more than one-twelfth of the total population of Seville in 1391. Yet, some authors have calculated the Jewish inhabitants to have numbered about 30,000 in the fourteenth century, that is, between 6,000 and 7,000 families. If this was the case, it would follow that the city, on the basis of its physical size at the time, was inhabited almost entirely by Jews. This is, of course, impossible. Even accepting the exaggerations of Ferrand Martínez as fact that there were twenty-three synagogues in Seville in 1390, these would have not have been sufficient to fill the needs of so large a Jewish population. This assumption implies that there was a ratio of about 1,300 to 1,500 people per synagogue, or about five or six times the number that could fit in the reputed largest one, Santa María La Blanca, still standing today. I estimate it possibly might have room for about three or four hundred congregants at most.

By the sixteenth and seventeenth centuries, the city of Seville had lost its medieval and Jewish character. Yet the Barrio de Santa Cruz, except for its buildings, has remained very much as the Jews left it after the massacres and mass conver-

Fig. 15.14: Seville. Calle de los Levies. View at intersection of Calle de San José, continuation in northerly direction of Calle de Santa María La Blanca. Street bears name of prominent Jewish family who lived there before destruction of judería.

sions of 1391. The streets remain intact. The Jewish cemetery, however, located in the vicinity of the Puerta de la Carne, the former Puerta de la Judería, has disappeared. This cemetery, though abandoned, existed to the end of the fifteenth century, when, soon after the Expulsion, it was converted to a public garden. Finally, it was obliterated in 1580 when the area was built up. The exact location of the graves and their moldering cargoes of Jewish bones may never be discovered, for they were probably unwittingly destroyed and disinterred when foundation trenches for the houses of the living were dug almost two hundred years later.

After 1391 and the subsequent loss in population, the few professing Jews that had survived were compressed into a judería of considerably diminished size, but which still huddled against the southeastern city wall. Its new northern and western limits were bounded by a wall that followed the curved contour of the present Calle del Conde de Ibarra, which begins just beyond the Calle de los Levies. This is located on the extreme end of the Calle de Santa María La Blanca, where, near the present Church of Madre de Dios, it becomes Calle de San José. The Church of San Nicolás, at the dead end of this street, was originally just outside the western limit of the judería and directly opposite one of its gates. Of the twenty-three synagogues reputed to have existed in the fourteenth century, possibly only four remained

Fig. 15.15: Seville. Calle de San José. View from intersection with Calle del Conde de Ibarra. Convent of Las Dominicans across street probably site of synagogue.

standing after the holocaust. These were converted to churches. Only one of the four known synagogues, Santa María La Blanca, contains physical vestiges.

Many times during the year I lived in Seville, I climbed up to the belfry of the tower of the Giralda to enjoy the general panorama of the whole city. From the great height, at my very feet, I had a close bird's-eye view of the judería below teeming with white houses roofed with red terra cotta barrel tile. The greenery of a little park, the Plaza de la Santa Cruz to the south, the occasional palm in many patios, and flowerpots hung from the windows and balconies that added harmonious accents of color to the stark white walls all worked together to provide an aesthetic ensemble impossible for any one individual to preconceive, to plan, or to carry out. The centuries created the judería. The centuries provided an aesthetic ensemble as the end result of a continuing tradition in which Celtiberian, Roman, Visigoth, Jew, Moslem, and Christian all played a part during more than 2,000 years. Although the Jews did not create the aesthetic tradition, they were an integral part of it.

The entrance to the judería, the one most frequently used today, opens from the Plaza del Triunfo through a gate in the enormous crenellated wall of the Alcazar, which was built by Pedro el Cruel in the fourteenth century. It is a Christian version of an Islamic royal palace. Passing through the arched gateway, I would enter the Patio de las Banderas and turn my back momentarily to get my fill of the view of the Giralda, the most beautiful of all towers in all Islam and all Christendom.

The Giralda represents the whole history of Seville. Its foundation stones were taken from some Visigoth buildings, which in turn had been cannibalized from even older Roman buildings. The main shaft was built between 1184 and 1196. Because of the Almohad persecutions, it is unlikely that many Jews ever beheld it before the Reconquest of Seville in 1248. It served—it still serves—the Christians as a bell tower just as it had served the Moslems as a minaret for the adjacent mosque, subsequently converted to the Cathedral of Seville. The topmost part of the Giralda, four stories high, dates from 1568. The Jewish community of Seville had been extinguished long before that date. Construction of the present cathedral itself actually was begun in 1402. It replaced the former mosque building that had fallen into ruin by that time. The few Jews of fifteenth-century Seville, confined to the nearby judería, viewed this building of enormous proportions rising within sight of their dwellings.

The contrast between the cathedral and its magnificent bell tower and the humble, diminutive, but man-sized streets of the judería impressed itself on my very being each time I turned away from the grandeur and beauty of the Giralda and entered the Jewish quarter, the Barrio de Santa Cruz. I entered through a street, really a roofed corridor cut through the Alcazar walls, but still a city street bearing the name Calle de la Judería. As I would come out from the tunnel-like street and turn around again to look, an ensemble of great beauty, a beauty created by time and by generations, would fill my eyes. To the left was the massive high wall of the Alcazar, to the right, one of the high walls of the judería, and at the far end closing the narrow slit of space, one of the fortified redoubts, a crenellated tower piercing the clear blue Andalusian sky.

Reluctantly giving up the pleasure of the sight, I would turn and continue my walk back into the Jewish past through an arched opening in the wall and enter the little *Plazuela de la Vida* (Life Plaza), dominated by the tower, through which the Calle de la Judería passes underneath. The Calle de la Vida, on the other side of the wall of the Calle de la Judería, is almost lifeless now; rarely does anybody appear in the street. I once saw an old man with a cane in hand there. He stopped and looked back to see if his cat was still behind him as he proceeded on to the little Plaza de Doña Elvira at the far end. I watched him until he was out of sight and then I entered the *Callejón del Agua* (Water Alley) from the Plaza de la Vida. The street is actually bounded on the right by the southeastern city wall and always teems with pedestrians. A number of streets that figure in the popular folklore of Seville to this very day open to the left of it. The *Calle de la Pimienta* (Pepper Street) is where the Jewish spice merchants lived and carried on their trade. A folktale still current

Fig. 15.16: Seville. Calle de la Pimienta from Callejón del Agua. Street in heart of judería where Jewish spice merchants lived.

Fig. 15.17: Seville. Calle de Susona, known popularly as Calle de la Muerte, runs parallel to Calle de la Pimienta. Susona family lived here as marranos. Daughter unwittingly revealed secret to Christian lover; as consequence, father burned at stake. Daughter converted to Christianity, entered nunnery. Years later, she repented betrayal, requested that after death her corpse be hung in front of house where she and family once lived.

in Seville tells how a pepper tree had sprung up full grown overnight in front of a Jewish merchant's house who had appealed to the Virgin for help in business matters. When he saw this miraculous portent, he converted to the *true* religion.

Another street in the immediate vicinity, Calle de Susona, which does not cut through to the Callejón de Agua, is the scene of another story—probably true. The best way to find the Calle de Susona is to walk a short way down Pimienta where it parallels Agua before making a right angle turn leading to the Plaza de Doña Elvira. Calle de Susona runs parallel to Pimienta and Vida, that is, it lies between

Pepper and Life Streets. The Calle de Susona is also popularly known as *Calle de la Muerte* (Street of Death) because of the tragic end that came to a daughter of the Susona family in 1481. The Susonas had been baptized almost a century earlier during that terrible summer of 1391 but had secretly clung to the Law of Moses, their ancestral faith. The foolish girl had a Christian lover to whom she revealed a supposed family plot against the Holy Office of the Inquisition. He betrayed her secret and her father was burned at the stake, most likely in La Tablada, a Jewish martyr for *Kiddush ha Shem* (the Sanctification of the Name of God). She went into a nunnery, a true and pious Christian. Remorseful and repentant, as her dying wish years later, she ordered that after her death her corpse be hung from in front of her house in the street which still bears the family name. For the people of Seville, the name of this street has always been Calle de la Muerte just a few steps away from the Street of Life.

In the nearby vicinity of Life and Death Streets there is a home and church for *venerable sacerdotes* (superannuated priests). The church building is an important milestone in the development of the local baroque architectural style, the interior of which is decorated with some interesting, if not outstanding, mural paintings. I had been there many times, not only to study the architecture, but also to enjoy the

Fig. 15.18: Seville. Church of Los Venerables Sacerdotes. Painting with Hebrew inscription over door leads from patio into church. Painting by baroque Spanish painter, Valdés Leal, from early eighteenth century. Letters of ineffable name of *Yaveh* (God) incorrectly written.

beautiful, verdant, typically Sevillian patio on one of the long sides of the church. It was ever a delight of sight and sound, with gently splashing water in the fountain and the chirping of birds in cages hung from the arcaded corridors enclosing the patio. One day I paused in the side door of the church leading out to the patio and looked up. There on the soffit, the underside, of the lintel right over my head within an oval-shaped blazon with an ornate floral frame supported by two winged *putti* (infant angels). Painted in bold, square Hebrew letters was the word *Yahveh*, the Tetragrammaton, the ineffable name of God! Why! How could this be? The church building dates from the latter part of the fourteenth century, but the murals on the interior were painted almost four centuries later by Valdés Leal. Early in the eighteenth century, this was a time when Hebrew was indeed a dead language in Seville, not even read let alone sounded in prayer. Valdés did not quite know the exact shape of the Hebrew letters and must have been working from a copy of a copy for the letters he drew are deformed as if awakened from the long oblivion of centuries of time. He elongated the first letter, *yad*, the smallest letter in the Hebrew alphabet to look like a *vav*, but included the diacritical mark below, two dots, one above the other. The letter, *hey*, the second and fourth letters of the Tetragrammaton, have both vertical strokes attached to the upper horizontal bar

Fig. 15.19: Seville. Plaza de la Santa Cruz, site of one important synagogue of pre-1391 judería, originally a mosque assigned by Fernando III to Jewish community (ca. 1248).

whereas only the right one should be so. The third letter, the *vav*, looks more like a *daled*, but Valdés was careful to include the proper diacritical mark below, the *kametz*. That the artist meant to inscribe the ineffable and never pronounced, never sounded, never voiced Name of God there can be no doubt. The word itself is placed within a circular field enclosed by a triangle, probably representing the Trinity, with rays emanating from it, a halo representing the *Shekhina* (the Gracious Presence of God)—a symbolic syncretism of the Law of Moses and the Law of Christ!

I frequently visited the Plaza de la Santa Cruz, the site of one of the mosques that Fernando III had allotted the new Jewish settlers (about 1248) to be used as a synagogue, and one of the three or four left standing after the pogroms and conflagrations of 1391. The center of the plaza is now a verdant park, a note of green in the geometric pattern of red roofs when espied from high up in the belfry of the Giralda. The synagogue probably was located on the west side of the plaza, though no physical trace remains of it today. In 1391, its was converted to a church under the advocation of the Holy Cross. Some two centuries later, the great painter

Fig. 15.20: Seville. Plaza de la Santa Cruz, site of synagogue-church of Santa Cruz after anti-Jewish riots (1391). Spanish painter, Murillo, a native of Seville, buried in church as noted on commemorative plaque affixed (1858) to building fronting plaza. Synagogue-church with remains of Murillo destroyed during Napoleonic invasion of Spain, early nineteenth century.

Murillo was buried in this church, a fact now commemorated on a memorial tablet, affixed in 1858, on a wall in front of the site where the mosque- synagogue-church once stood.

According to contemporary descriptions, the building must have been a rather simple one, its plan divided into three aisles by two rows of granite columns supporting a wood ceiling of typical mudéjar joinery. The mosque-synagogue-church remained intact until the early nineteenth century, when during the French invasion of the Iberian Peninsula in 1810, it was burned to the ground. A few steps from the Plaza de la Santa Cruz to the west on the Calle de la Santa Teresa a Carmelite convent stands. Here some personal objects were kept that once belonged to the Christian Spanish Saint of Jewish extraction from Avila, Santa Teresa herself. How Spanish indeed! A mosque, a synagogue, a church, all in the same building, and sacred relics of a Jewish-Christian saint just a few steps away.

Taking a sharp turn to the right and proceeding in a northerly direction up the extremely narrow Calle Ximénez, a short cut to the one synagogue still standing in Seville, I would come into an open area, the Calle and the Plaza de la Santa María La Blanca leading in turn to the site of the ancient Jews' Gate, now called the Puerta de la Carne. This area, the plaza and the street, was the very hub of the ancient Jewish quarter and the location of the principal synagogue. Embedded in the Church of Santa María La Blanca and still standing today, though remodeled in the late seventeenth and early eighteenth centuries, is what were originally a mosque and later a synagogue. Some of the original architectural elements are still discernible.

The entrance with its pointed arch was probably constructed in the fourteenth century and is not the original one that existed when Fernando III gave the building to the Jewish community soon after 1248. The style of the portal is commonly known as *mudéjar*, that is, a Gothic form with a Moorish overlay reflecting not only the blending of architectural styles, but also of the melding of Christian and Moslem elements in the population of Seville. The upper part of the facade was completely changed when the building was rebuilt in the late seventeenth and early eighteenth centuries and is entirely out of keeping in style with the simple portal with its pointed arch, the archivolt of which is carried out as a saw-toothed molding, a device common to the fourteenth-century mudéjar building style.

Partially bricked up and probably dating from Moslem or even Visigoth times, the side door is around the corner on Calle de Archeros. Two short, slender columns with Corinthian capitals of early medieval style flank a niche in which the door is inset. These columns survive from the original mosque and may have been removed and reused from an even older Visigoth building in mosque construction.

Now, the interior is entirely Christian. Overlaid with grossly exaggerated and ponderous baroque ornament, it dates from late-seventeenth-century reconstruc-

Fig. 15.21: Seville. Church of Santa María La Blanca, former synagogue. Church extensively remodeled in seventeenth and eighteenth centuries; original main portal with pointed arch remains.

Fig. 15.22: Seville. Santa María La Blanca. West facade with main portal and southwest corner on Calle de Archeros. Low pointed arch with saw tooth molding typically mudéjar style, probably constructed after building, former mosque, given to Jewish community by Fernando III (1248). Upper parts of facade rebuilt during seventeenth and eighteenth centuries.

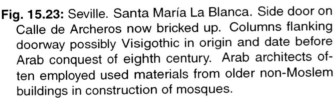

Fig. 15.23: Seville. Santa María La Blanca. Side door on Calle de Archeros now bricked up. Columns flanking doorway possibly Visigothic in origin and date before Arab conquest of eighth century. Arab architects often employed used materials from older non-Moslem buildings in construction of mosques.

Fig. 15.24: Seville. Santa María La Blanca. View toward main altar. Interior completely altered in seventeenth and eighteenth centuries, baroque in style. Nothing of medieval Jewish or earlier Moslem origin remains.

tion. All that remains of the mosque and the synagogue is the general layout of the plan, which outlines a rectangular hall divided by two rows of columns into three longitudinal aisles. Essentially, this is a wide central nave with two narrower side aisles. A mudéjar exterior, an Oriental robe clothes a baroque Christian body.

At the far end of the nave an ornate baroque retable or altarpiece with spiraling salomonic columns occupies the same spot where the Mihrab of the mosque once stood, and later the Ark of the Torah. Mihrab or Ark seemed impossible, even inconceivable and certainly out of place within the ensemble of the gilded, florid, overblown, and exuberant decoration that covers all surfaces veiling the tectonic or structural architectural forms to which this decoration is appended. However, the sanctity of the spot has been preserved. A large life-sized, draped statue of the Virgin stands at the far end of the nave, the last in a series of sanctified objects in that spot and still the focus of pious devotion.

Embedded in the wall of the main facade outside between the portal and the corner, a ceramic painting of the Virgin faces a beautiful hanging wrought-iron lamp. I observed that the lamp was never extinguished whenever I wandered by either at night or during the day. It is as if a *Ner Tamid* (Eternal Light), such as once burned in front of the Ark of the Law at the far end of the nave, had been moved outside. Or, is this light also a Memorial Light for the Jews of Seville interred in

Fig. 15.25: Seville. Calle de Verde from corner of Calle de Archeros up the street from Santa María La Blanca. Once a typical Jewish street near principal synagogue. Because of narrowness, sun rarely reaches down to street level except in midsummer.

Fig. 15.26: Seville. Calle de la Virgen de la Alegría from Calle de San Clemente. Once in heart of judería, end of street one side of the Church of San Bartolomé, site of another important pre-1391 synagogue.

the now lost and forgotten burying ground outside the Puerta de la Judería (now Puerta de la Carne) just a few yards down the street? Or could this be a light, a flame of remembrance, for souls of the Jews of Seville slaughtered for *Kiddush ha Shem* in June of 1391?

The immediate vicinity near the mosque-synagogue-church is rife with Jewish memories. The Calle de Archeros bounds on the south side of Santa María La Blanca and comes to a dead end at the Calle de Verde. The street names have survived from the time when Jews lived in this neighborhood. Calle de Verde is no more than a narrow passageway in which the hot sun rarely enters even in summer. Up Archeros, a right turn into Verde, then left at the first corner, and into the Calle de San Clemente, then another turn to then left into the *Calle de la Virgen de la Alegría* (Virgin of Joy Street), and there one corner of the Church of San Bartolomé would come into view. San Bartolomé was the third of the three synagogues left standing after the destruction of 1391 and was one of the former mosques Fernando III granted the Jews in 1248.

The little narrow street of the Virgin of Joy must have been teeming with life before 1391, the life of the observant Jews who lived literally in the shadow of the synagogue. The street skirts the synagogue-church on the left, opening up on the

Fig. 15.27: Seville. Main facade of Church of San Bartolomé, which is on site of synagogue dating before widespread attacks on Jewish communities in 1391.

Calle de San Bartolomé where the main front of the synagogue, of which not an original vestige remains, was once situated. The present building was remodeled completely in the eighteenth century; not a single remnant of the Hebrew inscriptions that once adorned the door and the interior are in evidence today.

Continuing on to the Plaza de Mercenarias, I took a left turn that brought me into the Calle de Levies. Levy Street describes a number of twists and right-angle turns so that on the printed plan of the city a dogleg outline is formed before terminating in front of the Convento de Santo Angel on the Calle de San José. Levy street is named for a family of that name who lived there during the heyday of Jewish life in Seville.

Down the Street of San José at the intersection of the Calle del Conde de Ibarra, one of the boundaries of the judería after 1391, stands the Church of San Nicolás. A gate to the constricted judería once pierced the wall here. The Convent of Madre de Dios and possibly the site of a synagogue, the fourth mosque that Fernando allegedly gave to the Jewish community at the time of his conquest of Seville, are located on the Calle de San José. It is interesting that some of the windows in the modern building that exists today on the site are in the shape of a *Magen David* (Star of David). This resemblance is only co-incidental and does not represent an example of the afterlife of Jewish influence.

Fig. 15.28: Seville. Calle de los Levies, small section of street up from Calle de San José. Street named for prominent Jewish family that lived there before 1391. Street twists and turns, forming a dogleg shape.

This motif was very popular with the Moorish and later mudéjar workmen and did not have a religious or nationalistic connotation at all. In fact, the Star of David became a Jewish symbol only in modern times. Little remains of the original structure of the convent that had been founded in 1472 and rebuilt in 1572. Little is known of the history of the building from the time of the pogroms of 1391 to the time it was taken over by the Christian religious order. The synagogue is said to have been comparable in plan and decoration to that of El Tránsito in Toledo.

Fig. 15.29: Seville. Plaza de Santa Marta on a Sunday morning with stamp market in operation. A little plaza, part of post-1391 judería, entered from near the foot of Calle de Mateos Gago.

Leaving the front of the Church of San Nicolás, I frequently continued along the boundary of the post-1391 judería, winding my way through the maze of streets and finally coming out into Calle de Mateos Gago, with the Giralda in full view down the street. It was always a delightful and new experience each time the exquisite grace and beauty of the Giralda filled my eyes as I turned the bend into the street. Calle de Mateos Gago is wider than normal, and probably follows the line of the ancient judería wall.

Proceeding down the street and just before arriving at the Plaza de la Virgen de los Reyes, behind the cathedral and the point of departure of the walk through time and Jewish history, I often entered a little passageway that opened to the left. The remains of a Moorish building, now a church, stood on the right. Taking a sharp turn to the right and another to the left in a little alley, which embraces the church so to speak, I entered a tiny plaza no bigger that a house courtyard. This was a public street, nevertheless, with the name Plaza de Santa Marta. It provided a hidden corner of tranquility in the maze of streets of the judería, and still preserved its ancient character as when Jews lived there.

Sunday mornings, the weekly philatelic market of Seville meets here. Groups of men come to sell and exchange postage stamps. Boys arrive with meager collections looking for an advantageous swap with their elders. A low hum of conversation echoes from the pebble pavement, a type of pavement known to Moorish craftsmen a thousand years before. As buyers, sellers, and enthusiasts mingle, creating ever-changing groups, harmonious pictures form and re-form to delight the eye.

Leaving the judería meant moving from the Middle Ages to a different world, to the Seville of the days of discovery and conquest of America, the opulent Seville of the days when the gold from the New World was unloaded on the wharves on the banks of the Guadalquivir River. On the left bank, downstream, stands an edifice that once served as one of the fortified towers in the Moslem defensive walls, the *Torre del Oro* (Golden Tower) built in 1120. Its name derives from its original sheathing with gold-colored tiles. Used as a temporary warehouse for the treasure of the Indies in the sixteenth century and later, the Torre del Oro had figured poignantly in the Jewish threnody long before the discovery of the New World. Duodecagonal in plan (twelve-sided), it is crowned by a dome of much later construction. The interior has vaulted chambers; a spiral staircase winds to the top.

Just a short distance downstream on the opposite bank of the river is the quay,

Fig. 15.30: Seville. Torre del Oro on left bank of Guadalquivir River with cathedral and Giralda in distance. Torre del Oro one of redoubts in walls of fortification of city of Seville during Middle Ages, built by Moslems (1120). Here King Pedro el Cruel had his once trusted official, Samuel ha Levi of Toledo, tortured and put to death.

Puerto de Mulas, from which Magellan set sail to circumnavigate the globe. Columbus assembled men, materials, and ships for one of his later voyages to America a few kilometers upstream at the Carthusian monastery.

Unfortunately, the Golden Tower was the setting for a Jewish tragedy that occurred long before the days of Columbus and Magellan. It was within its massive walls that Pedro el Cruel imprisoned his royal treasurer, Samuel ha Levi of Toledo, the Jewish magnate who built the Synagogue of El Tránsito. Here in the Torre del Oro, Pedro had Samuel tortured and put to death despite the fact he had been

Fig. 15.31: Seville. Callejón de la Inquisición, right bank, Guadalquivir River in Barrio de Triana. Modern door with iron gate approached by short flight of steps. Inquisition inaugurated in Seville (1480). Place of judgment/execution probably located here, name *Inquisición* preserved in local toponymy.

one of his most trusted and loyal officials. Pedro's true motives are shrouded in mystery, for his treatment of Samuel was paradoxical to an extreme. In the beginning he had raised Samuel to the greatest heights in social rank, prestige, and trust. Though the construction of new synagogues was forbidden by canonical law, he still gave Samuel permission to build one, a synagogue of great beauty still admired by thousands of visitors until today. In the end, Pedro brought him down to the lowest level of degradation and to a dishonorable death such as meted out to the meanest criminal.

Across the river a short distance upstream in Triana there remain some sad and pitiful mementos of the last moribund stages of Jewish life in Seville. Judaism was not altogether extinguished with the massacres and forced conversions of 1391. Agonizingly, it lingered on. A certain death awaited the marranos when one by one they were found out by the Inquisition.

Those Jews who did not die in the riots of 1391 were forced to convert to Christianity. It is unbelievable that the majority of these conversions were more than for convenience to save a life—one's own. And it is most unlikely that the majority of these conversions were based on religious conviction and a change of heart. They sought to save their lives and thereby save their world and preserve the faith of their fathers, reciting the *Kol Nidre* prayer each Day of Atonement, begging God's forgiveness for vows falsely taken.

To judge by the activities of the Inquisition, particularly after 1483 when it was headed by the Haman of Hamans, Torquemada, it appears that a great many of the baptisms had only been superficial. The Inquisition was inaugurated in Seville in 1480, and with it began the merciless persecution of Christians who practiced

Judaism in secret. Between 1481 and 1488 seven hundred and fifty men and women were *relaxed* (burned at the stake) and another five thousand who had been Jews in secret were *rehabilitated* and taken back into the true faith. There is no way of knowing how many secret Jews escaped discovery. Even the figures, taken from the records of the Inquisition, reveal that a sizable proportion of the population of Seville still must have been practicing the Jewish religion a century after the wholesale forced baptisms. Counted among the forced baptisms were many notables and people of high station. As mentioned above, even Luis de Santangel, treasurer of Queen Isabella, supporter of Columbus' enterprise before the court, was consumed alive by the flames in an *auto da fe* in 1491.

The tribunal, where those accused of crimes against the True Faith were tried, and the prison of the Inquisition, where they were incarcerated, was not located within Seville proper, but on the other side of the Guadalquivir, opposite and upstream from the Torre del Oro in Triana. The area is now famous for its ceramic tile factories, gypsies, and flamenco music. During the fifteenth and sixteenth centuries, this was a remote suburb removed from the hustle and bustle of the city streets. Here prisoners could be brought

Fig. 15.32: Seville. Callejón de la Inquisición. Iron gate in door looks down Callejón de la Inquisición. Office of Inquisición probably stood on site of private buildings that flank narrow alley, ending on bank of river. Dam upstream from Seville cut off Guadalquivir; no water fills this narrow alley except when sluice gates open.

in the dead of night without danger of revealing the methods employed by the Inquisition. The actual Inquisition building no longer exists, but its memory is still alive in the local toponymy.

I walked across the Triana bridge one day; a few steps away, I came to an alley bearing the name *Callejón de la Inquisición* (Inquisition Alley). The alley opens from a street of utterly innocuous character in the midst of a commercial area with stores selling all sorts of merchandise and food. I stood there and read the posters and signs affixed to a lamppost just in front of a short flight of steps. These steps led up to a doorway, the entrance to Inquisition Alley. An iron gate, with an ancient lock and slide bolt, blocked passage into the alley.

The narrow alley was hemmed in by buildings to either side. A blank wall closed the view to the river except for an arched opening at its very bottom through which the waters of the Guadalquivir sometimes overflow, coming up to the very door itself. The stains of high water were visible on the walls. From this narrow passageway prisoners were disposed of, or surreptitiously transported in boats to other places in the dead of night while the city slept.

The waters of the Guadalquivir that wash its banks at Seville and Triana are tranquil now. A dam, constructed a short distance upstream, diverts the course of the main channel of the river away from the city. Thus the city is no longer subject to the raging floods that frequently inundated it after the spring rains. The river is tamed, undisturbed, quiet, tranquil, and at peace. The Jews of Seville, also, are tranquil and at peace.

16 Jewish Vestiges in Andalucía

During the course of the year I spent in Seville, I traveled constantly throughout the surrounding countryside, and even further a field in Andalucía, to the many picturesque villages and towns to study the local architectural monuments. These villages and towns, especially those near Seville, were always a delight to the eye, and the inhabitants, with their unique speech full of colorful metaphors and aphorisms and their proud bearing yet courteous manner, made conversation a joy. The architectural and urban complex of each village is different from the others, representing an accretion of centuries of development. A mélange of part added to part, each blending into an integral whole so that Islamic, Renaissance, baroque, and even later stylistic elements are frequently seen side by side. All, nevertheless, meld into an harmonious and seemingly unitary composition as naturally as nature itself. The history of these towns and the lineage of its inhabitants are traceable in the lay of their very streets and in the repertoire of architectural styles of the edifices lining them. Two and even three different styles often are represented on a single building.

Only in a few instances, and only in those towns located on main traffic arteries, have the tasteless devastations of the nineteenth and twentieth centuries scarred the organic beauty of the whole. The blight is largely due to the automobile, with its need for gasoline stations and garages. Of course, the billboards, which call the traveler's attention to the local hostelry or restaurant, contribute to the ugliness of the surroundings. In general, however, the plastic, material ugliness of the twentieth century is absent from most of these towns. When it is there, it is confined to the sides of the highway, which frequently runs right down the main street.

The aesthetic blight of the twentieth century has, for the most part, affected only the centers of the towns; the peripheries remain the same as in years past. Fortunately, the former Jewish quarters invariably are located in some inaccessible corner of town, somewhere on the outskirts far from the highway and the automobile traffic in the center. The result is that if any vestiges of the Jewish presence remain, they are not overwhelmed by the ugliness of twentieth-century progress. Unfortunately, Jewish life and Jewish streets and synagogues were extinguished in these villages in the late Middle Ages. The sticks and stones of the Jewish past are often hidden in the least desirable and poorest neighborhoods by the aesthetic accretions of the succeeding centuries. The few remnants of the Jewish presence have at least been spared conversion to garages, newspaper storehouses, or sites for

Fig. 16.1: Cazalla de la Sierra. Calle de la Virgen del Monte. According to informant, until first part of twentieth century this narrow street known as Calle de la Judería. Jewish community of Cazalla de la Sierra destroyed (1391); its existence lives on in folk memory of inhabitants.

apartment houses as happened in Zamora, Madrid, and Seville.

The general attack on the Jewish population in 1391 so devastated most of the Jewish communities of the smaller towns of Andalucía that they never recouped their former size. They failed to recover not only because of the first wave of destruction and slaughter, but also because of the continued persecutions during the fifteenth century. The devastation finally culminated in the Expulsion in 1492 of the miserable but steadfast remnant of Israel that had escaped death or baptism.

This devastation prevailed in all of Spain, but in Andalucía it was even more tragic, since the Jews had been brought in from the north as colonists in the thirteenth century to settle the newly reconquered lands. Nearly every village or hamlet in the region around Seville had, at one time or another, a Jewish community; in some places Jews were the majority of the actual population. For example, as already mentioned before, in Paterna, San Juan de Aznalfarache, and Aznalcollar were Jewish towns. Street names that have persisted to this very day attested to the presence of Jews in most of the towns in the countryside around Seville. Sometimes the local inhabitants still know the limits of the judería or its principal street. In some instances, the exact location of the Jewish quarter can easily be found, in others no spoors are left at all.

In 1264, Alfonso X conquered Jerez de la Frontera, about one hundred kilometers south of Seville. There he established a Jewish community, which flourished in the town. He gave houses and land to the Jewish settlers. Many of the Jews were engaged in viticulture, for which the region is still famous today. The word *sherry* is an English corruption of the Spanish name *Jerez*, the famous wine from Jerez de la Frontera. Among the eighty to ninety householders of the judería, which flour-ished till the end of the fourteenth century, tailors, shoemakers, and rope makers plied their trade. The community had one or possibly two synagogues. Even as late as the nineteenth century, the street on which the synagogue once stood was known as the Calle de la Sinagoga.

I must have gone to Jerez on twenty different occasions and each time, following the lead of Cantera Burgos, tried to find the Jewish streets, but could not. It seems the city plan must have been altered since the late fourteenth century, obliterating the Jewish streets.

Other towns in the same region where the memory of the Jewish presence still persists are Lebrija, Sanlúcar la Mayor, Cazalla de la Sierra, and Santa Olalla; not a visible, physical Jewish trace remains. Frequently a very archly religious name, usually associated with the Virgin, offers the only suspicion or clue that a street might once have been inhabited by Jews. I could find no Jewish trace in any, except Cazalla de la Sierra.

Cazalla de la Sierra is famous for its *aguardiente* (distilled spirits). It is in a remote area in the mountainous part of Andalucía. While having lunch in the local social club, I asked, on the spur of the moment, an old man where the judería was located. I acted on a hunch; I actually did not expect him to know. After silent thought he awakened as from a dream and in a pensive voice slowly said he remembered that the street now known as the *Calle de la Virgen del Monte* (Street of the Virgin of the Mount) was once called Calle de la Judería.

I hurriedly left the dining room and found the street. Strange that the name, Jews' Street, should still exist in living memory after almost six hundred years, for the Jewish community of Cazalla de la Sierra was completely destroyed in June 1391, never to be established again. Nevertheless, there it was, a long, narrow cobblestone street flanked with whitewashed houses, a steeply inclined street, up the hill of the Virgin, but not a single trace of Jews, not a single stone or brick with a Jewish physiognomy.

Fig. 17.1: Granada. Winter's day in Granada with a view of Acera del Darro. Darro River, once running through this part of town open to sky, now channeled underground. Although no certain evidence exists, the judería possibly located in vicinity of river on medieval outskirts of city. Sierra Nevada hidden behind clouds in distance.

17 Granada

Granada, just the word *Granada*, I sit here at my table and write G-R-A-N-A-D-A. The act of writing evokes memories in my eyes and my whole being. Pictures and feelings of great and unparalleled beauty appear that transcend the moment and leave me pensive and joyously sad like the baleful sweet, heart piercing litany of a transfixed cantor chanting the *Kol Nidre* on the eve of Yom Kippur. Not only the modern city lying in a cup of a valley surrounded by the ochre-brown hills and the majestic Sierra Nevada in the distance, clothed with snow most of the year, but also the visual music of the Alhambra, seen from a thousand viewpoints as I wandered about the city below looking for spoors of the city's long disappeared Jewish community. To behold the Alhambra, not just to see it, but to behold the Alhambra and feel its grip and embrace in my eyes, no matter how often, always caused emotions so strong that my breathing was interrupted; indeed, breathtaking was the beauty that filled my eyes so that I was always transfixed, hypnotized, transported beyond the physical senses of the moment. The Alhambra of legend; the Alhambra of Washington Irving; the Alhambra of Boabdil el Chico, the last Moslem king in Spain; and the Alhambra where the Catholic Kings, Ferdinand and Isabella, issued the decree expelling the pitiful remnant of the Jews from their native home in 1492. The Alhambra!

The Alhambra impresses the viewer with its orange-ocher walls and the red-tile roofs of the vast web of buildings adorned with the dark green of elongated, tall, candle-like cypress trees in the gardens within its compass. Its open courts with pools of water reflect the sky above; fountains, with but a single spout, trickle thin streams of water that bubbles with a sweet guitar-like tremolo. The high-ceilinged rooms stand regally with walls and vaults covered by intricate carving in plaster and stone. The silence is audible, the silence that is not an absence of sound, but rather a silence filled with a music that is heard by the inner ear close to the heart. All combine to create the beauty of the Alhambra. I remember well the spot where I would stand each time. I would place myself in an arched window in the Hall of the Ambassadors. There I would listen to the silence around me, and hear from afar the sounds welling up from the city below. These sounds did not penetrate the silence. Their blended voices mingled into a harmony that cannot be set down with notes on paper and played on a violin or flute. The song rose gently up to my ears like a distant surf far from sight, an undertone from the voice of the sea that is not seen.

The sight that filled my eyes, the indescribable beauty of the geometric pattern of streets and rooftops of the city below with the greenery of gardens and the snowy mountains embracing the city, is best expressed in a few words, words that gave voice to the beauty I beheld, inscribed on the *Torre de la Vela*:

> Dále limosna mujer
> Que no hay nada en la vida
> Como la pena de ser
> Ciego en Granada

> *Give him alms, o woman,*
> *for there is nothing in life*
> *equal to the anguish*
> *of being blind in Granada*

This beauty is that of the Moslem past of Granada, a past that is also Jewish. However, the tangible, touchable, seeable Jewish remnants are all gone; not even a faint spoor can be detected. All that remains is the memory of the Jews of Granada who, on one evil-omened day in 1492, were wrenched away, cut off, blinded so they could no longer look upon the face of Granada. They were sent into exile by a harsh and iniquitous evil decree, signed and sealed in the room where I was standing transfigured by the current sights and sounds and a remembrance of that woe-filled event.

The history of the Jews of Granada is unique, representing the longest symbiosis with Moslems in the whole Iberian Peninsula. Granada was the last Moorish kingdom taken in the long drawn-out Reconquest, falling irretrievably to the Catholic monarchs, Ferdinand and Isabella, in January of 1492. Jews and Moslems had lived side by side in Granada for more than seven hundred years.

An important Christian city during late Roman times, Granada was the center from which missionaries went out to evangelize the Province of Betis, which contained most of the southern part of the Iberian Peninsula. Jews probably already were living there while it was still under Roman rule, for the first Christian religious council ever held in Spain was celebrated in Granada about 300 c.e. This Council of Illiberis, or Elvira, enacted the first anti-Jewish legislation in Spain. Later, under the Visigoths, Granada became an important military center. No material evidence has come to light associated specifically with the Jewish presence in Granada during the Roman and Visigoth periods.

When the Arabs invaded Spain in 711, they found a Jewish neighborhood located on a hillside in Granada. They called it *Gharnata al Yahud*, that is, *Gharnata* or *Granata* of the Jews. In fact, according to the folk legends during the Moslem period, Granada was originally founded by Jews. The word *granata*, or *gharnatha*, in

Arabic means pomegranate. It is interesting that in Jewish writings and literature, the city of Granada is called *Rimon*, Hebrew for pomegranate. Also, the Spanish word for pomegranate is *granada*. The Arabs, however, called the city *Medina Elvira* (Elvira City). Its present name, Granada, was adopted after the Christian conquests, but without the descriptive epithet "of the Jews."

While under Arab domination, the Jews of Granada lived in freedom and achieved some of the highest positions at court, in commerce, and in the social life of the kingdom, producing a number of men of genius in philosophy and poetry. The Jewish community of Granada had been equal in intellectual splendor to that of Córdoba until one fateful day, December 20, 1066, when a general riot and mutiny broke out among the Moslem populace, resulting in a wholesale massacre of Jews. It is said that some fifteen hundred families fell in one day. Upon their arrival in mid-twelfth century, the Almohads forced Jews to convert to Islam. They subjected the rest of the territories to this same mandate. The persecutions continued until 1232 when the Almohad rulers were driven out of Granada, with the assistance of the Jewish and Christian communities. A new Moslem dynasty was founded, the Nazarí, which remained in power until 1492.

During the fifteenth century, Jews in Christian Spain lived on an erupting volcano. The many tumultuous riots and massacres led to the practice of baptism as the only alternative to slaughter. Those who escaped conversion or death, a stiff-necked remnant, were herded into walled ghettos. Some of the Jews escaped, taking refuge in the Moslem kingdom of Granada. According to the German traveler Jerome Münzer, who visited Spain in 1494, there were some twenty thousand Jews then living in the kingdom of Granada. This must be an exaggeration, for by this time Granada already had been conquered by Christians and there were probably no openly professing Jews left anywhere in Spain at all when he was there two years after the Expulsion. The edict expelling the Jews from Spain actually had been signed in Hall of the Ambassadors in the Alhambra by Ferdinand and Isabella in 1492.

A great number of Jews resided in the city of Granada and the former Moslem kingdom as a whole during the period of its reconquest beginning in 1484. I searched the older parts of the city, traversing each street and alley day after day on at least six occasions when I was in Granada to study its architectural monuments. I found no certain leads as to where the Jewish community had been centered before the fateful year of 1492. I could only speculate in which part of the city the Jewish quarter might have been located. The area I selected—not on the basis of any fact, however, but rather by intuition—was on the south slope of the hill where the Alhambra stands extending down to the bend of the Darro River, now running underground in the street known as the Acera del Darro. This part of town is entirely modern, and it is impossible to find any tangible trace or vestige of Jews ever having lived in this location, or any other for that matter, though Jews had been in Granada for well over a thousand years. The Jewish presence in Granada, though not visible to the eye in the form of brick and mortar, nevertheless lives on in the immortal poetry of Solomon Ibn Gabirol and Moses Ibn Ezra. The streets they walked, the synagogues they frequented, the houses they lived in—all are clothed in oblivion now, but not their words.

18 Málaga

I frequently went to Málaga, sometimes for the day, sometimes for longer. Málaga offered an escape from the rainy, damp, bitter-cold winter months when the large unheated stone house made the process of getting into bed at night pure torture. The sheets were always damp and the cold in the room so penetrating that I could see my breath.

That Málaga lies on the Mediterranean is a geographical fact only recently discovered by Europeans and Americans. Now, Málaga has become the new Miami Beach, not so much the city itself as the nearby coastal towns both to east and west. Aptly, this coast is dubbed *La Costa del Sol* (Sun Coast) by promoters of tourism and entrepreneurs whose merchandise is that which they do not produce themselves, the climate. Tourists, seeking refuge from the cold winters of northern Europe, come by the thousands to the Costa del Sol, arriving by air, train, bus, and automobile. They rush off to the once-beautiful towns along the coast whose beaches are now preempted for the most part by skyscraper hotels with balconies facing ancient Homer's "wine-dark sea." These towns are now occupied by swimming pools, marinas for small pleasure craft, nightclubs, and restaurants—all the modern, garish appurtenances of a raucous commerce dealing in sun, sand, and sea.

Modern "swinging" Málaga once had a flourishing Jewish community during the Middle Ages, that is, during the Moslem domination of the city until the end of the fifteenth century. Málaga was a name known to me since my childhood by association with the Passover holiday and the *Seder* in my grandmother's house at which four cups of wine were quaffed, usually sweet Málaga wine, which caused me to fall asleep even before I drank the second.

It was a familiar Málaga, the Málaga of the Passover wine, that I journeyed to from Seville over a road I took so often that I got to know every turn, every village, every sight during the four hours or so to drive the two hundred and twenty kilometers. Alcalá de Guadaira, with the Arab fortress on my right, greeted me as first town I would pass through. This fortress had a special meaning for me; I knew that the old judería lay snuggled against the brown-ocher mole on the other side. Then I traversed the flat plain with wheat fields around El Arahal and Puebla de Cazalla. Not far beyond, I would stop by the road for a view of white-walled, red-roofed Estepa on a green eminence in the distance and the broad endless expanse of the Guadalquivir River plain to my left and beyond the horizon. Off to the north and out of sight, but fixed in my mind, lay the tragic, hot, fiery city of Ecija.

Once beyond Estepa, the scenery changed; mountains rose majestically on the right, and the terrain remained hilly as the road turned south to Antequera. From Antequera to Málaga is but sixty-two kilometers. The road skirts the *Sierra de las Cabras* (Mountains of the Goats) through the rolling countryside before entering Colmenar, a poor mountain town with ramshackle houses lining the potholed cobblestone main street overlaid in places with asphalt. This town appeared to be in need of a new coat of whitewash. From Colmenar the road climbed abruptly; within a few moments it reached a height of about 1,000 meters above sea level at a mountain pass, grandiloquently and aptly named *Puerto del León* (Lion Pass). From this point, the road descended rapidly in ever tighter and tighter zigzags. It proceeded ever downward, at first permitting fleeting glimpses of the sea around the hairpin turns and finally a bird's-eye view of the broad Mediterranean. In the distance, covered by a soft mantle of haze that melted into the sea, emerged the continent of Africa. Another turn, another drop, and Málaga appeared below. The road became a spiraling staircase that dipped behind the hills embracing Málaga; then it turned sharply to the left leading to the entrance to the city down a wide modern street past the Plaza de la Victoria and into the broad avenue with its park

Fig. 18.1: Málaga. Paseo de Reding with Alcazaba in distance. Judería located to right of low stone wall. Area, occupied by Paseo de Reding, nonexistent in medieval times. Part of ancient harbor filled in, creating a new shoreline in twentieth century. Medieval judería possibly located near shore of Mediterranean before configuration of harbor of Málaga altered.

skirting the waterfront. The park was thick with frondose, broad-leafed trees that were never sere even in winter, and flowering shrubs, a subtropical garden with the smell and the sound of the sea, and the dim voices of the city in the early morning hardly heard over the shrieking shrill cries and whirring wings of the birds, unseen flying to and from their nests overhead.

The history of Málaga, like that of Granada, is more Semitic and Oriental than Christian and European. The Phoenicians founded the city, perhaps in the eighth century B.C.E. Later, Roman hands held it until the Visigoth intrusion. In 711, the Arabs and Semites reconquered the city and it remained Moslem until the Catholic monarchs, Ferdinand and Isabella, took it 1487. Thus Málaga has been uninterruptedly Christian only for the last five hundred years or so after having been Moslem for about seven hundred. Its roots, its people, and its way of life, except for the tourist invasion from the north in the twentieth century, remain closer to North Africa and Islam than to Europe and Christendom. The adage I had heard repeated so often, "Europe ends at the Pyrenees," or put the other way around, "Africa begins at the Pyrenees," certainly applies to Málaga. This city is the last outpost of Spain, which is as much a part of North Africa as it is of Europe. Spain ever has been marginal in culture, in people, in religion, and in politics, standing between the Cross and the Crescent, the no-man's land where North Africa and Europe blend. Geographically, that is, in space, Málaga is nearer to Fez in Morocco than to Rome or Paris; and curiously it is also slightly nearer to Fez than to Madrid, the capital of Spain.

The history of the Jewish community of Málaga, like that of Granada, is one of Jewish-Moslem symbiosis rather than Jewish-Christian. The Jews of Málaga, like those of Granada, still spoke Arabic in the fifteenth century. At the time Málaga fell to the Christian conquerors in 1487, there were some four hundred Jews living in the city. The triumphant host of Christian warriors treated the Jews as prisoners of war. As was customary in the Middle Ages in Spain, the victors threatened to sell them into slavery, holding them for ransom, raised and paid by the majority of the surviving Jewish communities in Christian Spain, whose own death knell was soon to be tolled.

Among the four hundred or so people in the Jewish community of Málaga in 1487 were many who had fled there as refugees after having been involuntarily baptized in Seville and Córdoba. After being ransomed, those who had escaped baptism went to North Africa; the *new* Christians had to remain. At the time of the Expulsion in 1492, five years later, there were no openly professing Jews left in Málaga at all. However, the Jewish memory was not completely obliterated. Some marranos continued their precarious existence for almost three hundred years; in the eighteenth century, they were found out. Jewish communal life, with its synagogues, schools, and even its burying ground, was totally extinguished in 1487.

Fig. 18.2: Málaga. Plaza at foot of Subida de la Coracha. Synagogue possibly located on this little plaza, center shaded by wide-branching tree. Paseo de Reding and Plaza de Toros in distance to right. Narrow and steep little street, Callejón de Aragoncillo opens just to left of parked motorbike behind tree. Possibly one entrance to medieval judería.

Málaga is quite a modern city today, making it almost impossible to ferret out vestiges of its medieval past. Except for the *Alcazaba* (Arab citadel) and the fortress of the *Gibralfaro* (Arab fortress), little of its Moorish past is visible. The judería, it is believed, was located in the eastern part of town somewhere near where a broad boulevard, the Paseo de Reding, begins and not far from the bullring. Hugging the lowest point of the slope between the Alcazaba and the Gibralfaro and separated from the Paseo de Reding by a low stone wall of indeterminate date, there is a tiny little plaza surrounded by some poor houses. In the center of the little plaza is a large tree whose spreading branches almost shade the entire area.

When I first visited the place some forty years ago, the poor people, who lived in the houses clinging to the nearly vertical inclines of the slope, used to come to this plaza to draw water from a tap fixed to the wall. The open space with its tree possibly could have served as a synagogue courtyard. It is located in the center of a maze of streets so narrow that they can be entered only on foot. For example, the Callejón de Aragoncillo rises up the hill in steps and opens on a somewhat wider dead-end alley surrounded by hovels. The area has been transformed significantly. As recently as the end of the nineteenth century, the land on which the bullring

Fig. 18.3: Málaga. Callejón de Aragoncillo. Narrow bottleneck entrance to street from little plaza behind low stone wall on Paseo de Reding. Narrow sloping passageway laid out with broad steps or short terraces hemmed in between two houses.

Fig. 18.4: Málaga. Callejón de Aragoncillo, possibly part of medieval judería. View from top of bottleneck entrance. Street widens here, paved with pebbles in ancient traditional manner.

and the Paseo de Reding are located was reclaimed from the sea. If this tree-shaded area may be identified as the center of the medieval judería, it then follows that the Jewish quarter was once on the very seashore—an extinct beach on the Costa del Sol—in a remote corner away from the main body of the city. This location would place the judería on the farther side of the Alcazaba.

With this intuitive conjecture in mind, I traced a hypothetical route in an attempt to discover the physical limits of the judería with my footsteps. Beginning at the tree-shaded plaza, the *Subida de la Coracha* (Slope of the Leather Bag or Sack), a narrow street carved out of the hillside, rises toward the Alcazaba. If my guess that the synagogue might have been located at the bottom of the slope is factual, then it follows that Jewish houses surrounded it on all sides not only in the immediate vicinity, but also uphill on the very flanks of the hill up to the Alcazaba. These

Fig. 18.5: Málaga. Subida de la Coracha looking back to little tree-shaded plaza at foot of hill bordering Paseo de Reding. Street possibly part of medieval judería with houses huddled against steep slope of mountain surmounted on summit by Alcazaba at one end and Gibralfaro at other.

Fig. 18.6: Málaga. View from Gibralfaro toward Alcazaba. Walls and ruins of Alcazaba at top of picture. Subida de la Coracha at left. Jewish cemetery located somewhere on slope in area between Alcazaba and Gibralfaro, probably near/in wooded area at bottom of slope.

houses would have clung to the Subida de la Coracha, which afforded a splendid panorama of the harbor with ships at anchor or sailing about on the vast deep blue Mediterranean under a lighter blue sky. Off to the left and behind the rocky heights, the Gibralfaro beckoned.

The Jewish cemetery is said to have been located on the lower reaches of the slope, somewhere between the Alcazaba and the Gibralfaro, perhaps even near where I was standing. It was impossible to descend the slope through the dense stand of trees on foot and try to find the remains of the cemetery. I came down from the Subida de la Coracha and, in my automobile, circled around through the city and drove up to the Gibralfaro. From high up on the Gibralfaro, the area I

Fig. 18.7: Málaga. Harbor view from Gibralfaro. Judería at mountain foot to left, out of picture.

had identified as possibly the judería disappeared from view, hidden by the dense foliage. The Subida de la Coracha appeared as a thin line reaching up to the walls of the Alcazaba above and beyond. On the sharp slope to the left somewhere in the dense mass of vegetation, I looked for some token, some ancient sign of the Jewish cemetery. I found none. My eyes could not penetrate the opaque veil of trees to see if some broken tombstones had been embraced by the roots.

I stood there content in the thought that the cemetery, if it was there, afforded one of the most magnificent views in all Andalucía for both the living and the dead.

Fig. 19.1: Lucena. Plaza with Castillo. Relatively new part of town, dating from long after demise of Jewish community, in 1146.

19 Lucena

One morning in late February, when the cold winter rains had not quite ended and the bright Andalusian sun was still frequently hidden in the gray, damp overcast sky that often lasted for days on end, I drove from Málaga to Seville the long way around through Lucena. The first wild flowers of spring bloomed among the still green tall grasses by the roadside; they had not yet fallen victim to the blazing fire from heaven of summer. I left very early in the morning on a sunless day in a drizzle that left me wet and morose as I detoured slightly out of my way to drive by the conjectural judería and the Jewish burying ground hidden beneath the dense vegetation somewhere on the slope of the mountain of the Alcazaba and Gibralfaro. I looked up at the looming heights then burdened and bowed into soft contours by the mist. The winding, ever-climbing road went through clouds at Puerto del León and disheveled Colmenar.

Once past Antequera, after crossing the Guadalhorce River, the road rolled over a broad, slightly undulating plain divided between olive groves and newly plowed brown fields, muddy with the last rains of winter awaiting the proper moment to be sowed with wheat. It was deserted country; hardly a house intruded upon the horizon. In a distance of about sixty kilometers, I passed only three tiny villages, stranded, so it seemed, and isolated from the road. These three hamlets were not important enough to have the highway bisect them.

What had impelled me to go to Lucena was the hope that I might find some vestiges of the once-flourishing Jewish community that had existed there during the Moslem period. When Lucena was reconquered in 1236, it was described as being *una ciudad judía con un arrabal moro* (a Jewish city with a Moorish suburb). During the time of the caliphate of Córdoba and even during the troubled times after its fall and division into petty *taifas* (principalities), the Jews of Lucena formed an almost independent state within a state. What the Christian conquerors found, however, were not practicing Jews, but rather Moslems of Jewish ancestry.

Romans established the city of Lucena, and Jews are said to have been there from the very first. According to certain Arab chroniclers, Lucena contained some of the richest Jews in Moslem Spain. There they lived peaceably until the arrival of the Almoravids, who threatened to convert them to Islam. They escaped this fate only after paying a great sum of money to their oppressors. Unfortunately, the ransom bought but a short respite. A generation or so later the fanatic Almohads allowed no such alternative; the Jews of Lucena were given the choice of Islam or death.

Fig. 19.2: Lucena. Calle de Jalmín. Typical street in medieval section of town. Whole of town unlike medieval towns of Christian Spain, more in character with Arab towns in Near East/North Africa.

Fig. 19.3: Lucena. Calle de Zamora, typical street in medieval section of town. Street plan most irregular, more difficult to find one's way than in majority of medieval towns of northern Europe. Note traditional pebble paving of street.

In 1146, the Almohads attacked the city, destroying it along with Jewish property and the Jewish community itself.

The year 1146 is, then, a terminal date for Jewish history in Lucena—Lucena, a town famous for its scholars and its Talmudic academy. Here, the poet Ibn Gabirol was born, though he spent most of his life in Granada. Here, Judah ha-Levi studied under the great teacher Isaac al-Fasi, whose life spanned the greater part of the eleventh century, the heyday and zenith of Jewish life in Lucena. When the city fell to the Christians in 1236, they found no Jewish community in existence there. All the inhabitants were Moslem in religion, though the greater part of the population reputedly had been Jewish some ninety years before.

I arrived in Lucena in less than two hours after leaving Antequera, skirting the southern city limits before finding my way to the center. The town itself was not very large in area and most unprepossessing in appearance. It hardly caused the casual traveler to stop on impulse because some noteworthy object attracted his attention—an old church or some picturesque street scene. In fact, that day I was the only outsider in town and my automobile the only vehicle parked in the main plaza.

I spent most of the hours of the day before sunset wandering at random about the streets of old Lucena in order to get the *feel* of the town, allowing my instincts, for I had no other clue, to lead me like a hound dog searching for the scent of a rabbit that had passed hours before. The long-eared hound with nose close to the ground goes sniffing along until he finds even the faintest trace of the scent and then begins to bay and run in ever-widening circles, trying to pick up the track which the rabbit had taken. When he finds it, the dog spins off from his spiral path in the direction that the rabbit has gone. Unfortunately, I could not find a trace, not a scent to follow, and I seemed to be walking aimlessly. In fact, I was not walking aimlessly. I walked to the very edge of the town and out into the muddy fields and circled along the houses on the outskirts. I tried every opening and entered streets as if they might have been a "Jews' Street," an alley, or some high-walled court behind which a synagogue could have stood.

The town seemed so different from the many I had visited in Andalucía. Of one piece, the whole town looked like a judería. Or did it look like a typical Moorish town, with its labyrinth of narrow streets leading fortuitously nowhere in bends, zigzags, sharp-angled turns and, not infrequently, coming to a dead end? So I resorted to the written word of Cantera Burgos and followed him rather than my instincts. According to him, house No. 4 on the Calle de la Condesa Carmen Pizarro may have been the site of an ancient synagogue. I found the street and the house. When I stood before it, I had to agree that he was quite right in his uncertain identification.

My instincts led me nowhere, *nowhere*! Not a single spoor, not a single brick or a cobblestone came up to give me the scent to follow. Where was the house in which Ibn Gabirol was born? Where was the school in which Isaac al-Fasi taught Judah ha-Levi? Could the people of Lucena, who passed me in the streets with a simple and courteous greeting, have once been Jews, then Moslems, and now Christians?

Months later I bought a brass oil lamp, a *velón*, from a merchant of Lucena at the April fair in Seville. Since Moorish times, Lucena has been famous for its handcrafted brass work. The oil lamps of Lucena, until the coming of electricity, lit the homes of Andalucía for centuries. Cervantes in prison on the Calle de Sierpes in Seville wrote his masterpiece *Don Quixote* by the light of a brass velón from Lucena. The brass founders of Lucena find a ready market for their products in all

Fig. 19.4: Lucena. José Burgeño, a potter. Water jug, which he holds, made of porous clay that allows water to seep slowly to outer surface, allowing pot to sweat, thereby cooling water inside. Traditional shape of water jug—a double-handled amphora—harks back to Roman and Moslem eras.

the fairs of Andalucía. The velones of Lucena are sought after even by city dwellers, who nostalgically keep at least one, polished and shining, never stained by smoke from the olive-oil-soaked cotton wicks, on their dining room tables. The brass founders' craft was traditional among the Jews of Lucena, then among the Moslems of Lucena, and finally among the Christians of Lucena, and continues to be so to this day. Who then was the merchant of Lucena who sold me the velón that April morning during the Feria de Sevilla?

Thinking back to that rainy dark day in February when I walked the streets of Lucena looking for a Jewish sign, I realized that the Jewish stones and the bricks, and even the parchment of the Torahs and the linen paper of the pages of the Talmud have disappeared from Lucena, but the people and their brass wares have not, not even after almost eight hundred years. I still have the velón I bought at the Feria de Sevilla from the blue-eyed, round-faced, rosy-cheeked little man from Lucena. This memorial lamp serves the souls of Ibn Gabirol, Judah ha-Levi, Isaac al-Fasi, and the countless men of learning who once graced the Talmudical academies of Lucena and who walked the streets where I sought them but could not find them.

20 Cáceres

With the approach of Spring, wild flowers in the fields around Seville burst into blossom and the cold winter rains gave way to sunny days and blue cloudless skies. This time of year, the village women, with skirts tied up just below the knees, carried large buckets with whitewash and long-handled brushes to paint the fronts of their houses, in order to cover the dark streaks and stains caused by the winter rains. This scene presented itself in all the picturesque little towns in El Aljarafe. The El Aljarafe region extends from Seville to Palos de Moguer, Columbus' port of embarkation, as well as off the main road running south to Jerez de la Frontera, Sanlúcar de Barrameda, and the Mediterranean port of Cádiz. Along this scenic route, I decided to drive to Paris and, en route to France and back, visit some of the towns of Extremadura, Castile, and the Basque region. There, I had learned of the survival of some traces of medieval Jewish communities, especially in Cáceres, Plasencia, Béjar, Valladolid, Burgos, and Vitoria.

I left Seville via the Triana bridge over the Guadalquivir and swung into the street leading out of town. I paused for a moment to allow some pedestrians to cross the street as I was passing the Callejón de la Inquisición, with its iron gate. Behind this gate, I once again peered down the narrow slit of space between the high walls to the deadened black waters of the river, hardly discernible in the early morning light. Within a few moments I crossed another bridge, an ugly modern but practical structure, over the channel into which the mainstream of the river had been diverted to protect Seville from the constant flooding of the waters of the Guadalquivir every spring since time immemorial.

Once across the iron bridge, I soon came to a fork in the road at a spot, with the poetic name of La Pañoleta, on the outskirts of the small town of Camas. The left fork led to the west and through some of the most picturesque towns in all Andalucía and Spain. This region still preserves many vestiges of its Arabic and Moorish past, even to its very name, El Aljarafe. The road terminated in Huelva on the Atlantic just below the confluence of the Tinto and Odiel rivers. On the opposite shore from Huelva, the Franciscan monastery stands. This is the monastery in which Columbus took refuge for a while before convincing the Catholic kings to support his enterprise to sail to India by heading west. In the nearby village of Palos de Moguer, he recruited most of the members of his crew, including his pilots, the Pinzón brothers, who were probably of Jewish descent.

The view of the landscape and the villages, with their medieval churches and oriental street patterns, is not very different from that which filled Columbus' eyes when he traveled the road from Seville through El Aljarafe to that Franciscan monastery of La Rábida. The cloister of the Franciscan monastery of La Rábida, where he lived, and the fountain in Palos de Moguer, from which he watered his ships, the Pinta the Niña, and the Santa María, have remained unchanged since his day. Thus, the left fork in the road at La Pañoleta once led to America, to the discovery of the New World.

I was embarking, however, on a journey *back* into the Old World, the medieval Jewish world in Spain, and so I took the right fork of the road that led to the north and to Extremadura, the native homeland of the conquistadors, Hernán Cortés, Francisco Pizarro, and Pedro de Alvarado. They came down this road, turned west to the sea at La Pañoleta and on to the conquest of America, the Europeanization of the New World.

Just beyond La Pañoleta, a few kilometers distant to the north, the Roman city of Itálica lay on my left. This site, famous for its ruined architectural monuments and other wonders, birthed the Emperor Trajan, who ruled the Roman Empire from 98 to 117 c.e. The broad plain of the Guadalquivir lay ever on my right as I drove over the pot-holed road; I spied the town of Algaba off in the distance on the farther bank of the Guadalquivir. The road soon began to climb in gentle rises to Las Pajanosas, a nondescript one street village strung out along the highway. Las Pajanosas provides a popular halting place for travelers because of the local *venta* (roadhouse or inn) installed in an old stone barn with a slickly polished, uneven floor of earth mixed with cow dung.

Beyond Las Pajanosas and just before the village of El Garrobo with its mudéjar church sitting in a deep hollow, the road divides again; the left fork proceeds in the direction of Portugal, the right to Extremadura. The right fork soon brought me into the accidented country of the Sierra Morena, a brown, barren mountainous land covered by scrub and heather, blooming because of spring, and an occasional olive grove. More frequently, however, I encountered whole forests of *alcornoque* (evergreen oaks) trees, whose bark contributes the cork stoppers of the millions and millions of bottles of sherry in the wine cellars of Jerez de la Frontera, and whose acorns serve as fodder for the myriad droves of pigs destined to be converted into *jamón serrano* (mountain ham). Jamón serrano is considered a great delicacy, a table luxury much prized in all of Spain. Its flavor and excellence is derived from the diet of pigs that rely on the fruit of the *alcornoque* trees.

The road finally came down from the heights of the Sierra Morena, with its twisting and turnings, to level ground near Mérida on the right bank of the Guadiana River. The Romans founded *Emerita Augusta* (Mérida) in the first century before the common era. As the capital of the Roman Province of Lusitania, it was embellished with a number of magnificent architectural monuments, the remains of which are in various states of preservation. These include: a bridge over the river; a triumphal arch; an aqueduct; a temple; a circus; a theater; and an amphitheater. There are no remains, no traces of Jews in Mérida. Apparently, Mérida never had a Jewish community, neither in Roman, Visigoth, or Moslem times.

Extremadura is a hard land, a fit setting for the birthplace of conquistadors, who were iron-willed men of courage, resolute men of action, proud and ambitious men driven to seize every opportunity, no matter how slight, for their own betterment. The poor earth of their native homeland could not and still does not meet those needs that stem from ambition. Within the few hours it took to drive up from Seville in Andalucía, the whole ambiance changed. Gone were the white-walled houses with red tile roofs and gone were the windows gaily decked with red clay flower pots full of blossoms. The patios did not house songbirds in cages nor music produced by the crystalline tinkling of water falling in the fountains. Instead, in Extremadura all was cold, dark stone, the chief building material of the houses in the countryside. Cáceres, too, is a city of gray stone walls, harsh and hard. The blocks of the roughly cut stone are left with undressed faces and the walls are not softened with smooth whitewashed stucco, all in all a mien more appropriate to somber Gothic France than to bright Moorish Spain.

The history of Cáceres extends back to Roman times, as witnessed by the Roman walls of fortification still partly in evidence in the center of the city. After the Romans, the Visigoths appeared on the scene of Cáceres. The Visigoths always appear in the second act of the four-act drama plus prologue and epilogue into which the history of Spain may be divided. The Arian and Catholic Christians (ca. 585 C.E.) laid waste to the town in the bitter civil war between the opposing forces of King Leovigildo and his rebellious son Hermenegildo. When the Arabs occupied Cáceres in the eighth century, they rebuilt the city and renamed it Al-Cazires, from which the present Spanish name is derived. Al-Cazires fell into Christian hands in 1229 when Alfonso IX, the King of León drove out the Moors, the Cross triumphing over the Crescent.

Jews may have lived, or not lived, in Cáceres during the Moslem period or during the earlier Roman and Visgothic. However, one hundred and thirty Jewish families are known to have resided there in 1479, judging by a petition they signed appealing for tax relief. It seems that this small Jewish community carried a tax burden such as would be normally borne by two thousand people. This implies that the Jewish community must have been much larger prior to the persecutions, massacres, and forced baptisms beginning in the late fourteenth century and continuing into the fifteenth. The Cáceres Jews asked for relief, saying they were so few in number they could not meet their payments. The Crown, in the persons of Ferdinand and Isabella, gave them satisfaction. This may seem a strangely charitable act on the

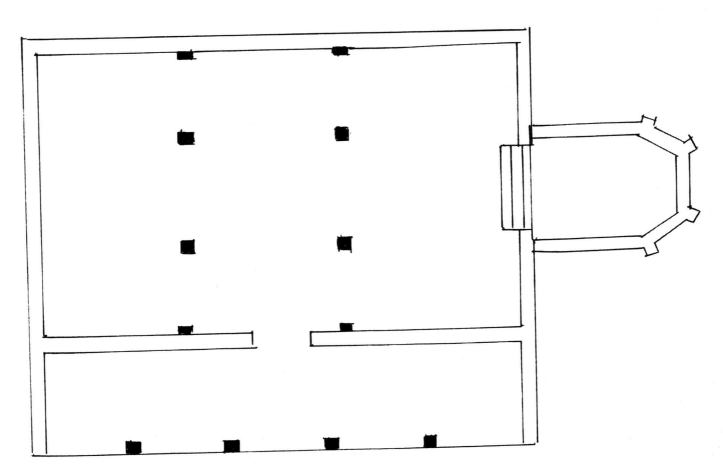

Fig. 20.1: Cáceres. Plan of Church of Espíritu Santo, formerly a synagogue. Building almost square in plan. Roof supported by two rows of columns supporting pointed arches, one horseshoe shaped. Porch and polygonal apse added when synagogue converted to church, probably after 1391.

part of these sovereigns who were to sign the Decree of Expulsion some thirteen years later, but paradoxical treatment of the Jews is the norm in Spanish history. In 1479 the Kingdom of Granada still remained to be added to the Christian crown, and the few professing Jews in Cáceres were still a source of income for the royal treasury.

Just where the medieval, post-Reconquest judería was located in the present limits of Cáceres is not certain. According to Cantera Burgos, a short distance from town about two kilometers or so, there is a neighborhood with a little church under the advocation of *El Espíritu Santo* (The Holy Ghost) that possibly may be the location of the medieval judería. The church is mudéjar in style, perhaps dating from the thirteenth or fourteenth centuries. That this building once could have been a synagogue is very possible judging by its plan, which is quite different from the usual church layout. Also, it remains in exceedingly good state of repair and is still in use as a Catholic Church.

The few leads concerning the location of the judería within the city limits encouraged me to go to the Barrio of El Espíritu Santo, isolated from the rest of the city by open country. The neighborhood consisted of a score or so of miserable houses grouped about the church in disarray, not following any definite street plan. Each house had a little yard in front or to one side. Few, if any, houses were built contiguous to one another, each standing on its own small plot of ground. This was unusual, indeed. An open arrangement of this sort with space between houses is rare in Spanish towns, where houses usually abut one on the other. The soil was sandy and rocky and bare of vegetation except for a few vines and some rachitic, undersized orange trees kept alive by hand-watering. Each tree trunk was encircled by a ring of rocks and earth; this ditch served as a receptacle for the water, ensuring that it went to the roots and did not run off to be wasted in the sterile soil all about.

The unusual manner in which the houses stood isolated from one another, in no concerted street plan, but arranged haphazardly about the area, seemed to indicate that they represented the remnants of a more densely built up village or neighborhood once far more populated than when I was there. The size of the church building attested to population density as well. It was out of proportion in size and monumental character when compared to the miserable condition of its present congregants and the few huts in the vicinity in which they lived.

During the troubles of 1391, as occurred in the rest of Spain, the Jewish community of Cáceres had been decimated. Yet, it continued to exist in straitened circumstances for almost a century, when it sought tax relief. Its original tax burden had not been readjusted and made commensurate with the reduced size of the community. Possibly the empty space surrounding the church today is a condition that may stem from 1391, when the Jewish houses were burned to the ground and never rebuilt because of the decrease in Jewish population through baptism and slaughter. The synagogue, however, remained more or less intact and very well may have escaped destruction during the pogrom. Like so many other Jewish houses of worship in late medieval Spain, it was converted to a church.

The one door giving access to the nave is located on one of the long sides, the south—that is, on the shorter tranverse axis rather than on the longitudinal as is to be expected in churches. The doors to the synagogues of El Tránsito in Toledo, Corpus Christi in Segova, and the ones in Córdoba and Bembibre also are not on the main west front or on the longitudinal axis, but on one of the long sides.

Furthermore, some changes or additions must have been effected on the south side here in Cáceres, for the door does not open directly to the street or a forecourt. Instead, a long, low portico or porch with very graceful slightly pointed arches supported on short piers lines the entire south side. A most unusual feature! This

Fig. 20.2: Cáceres. Church of Espíritu Santo. Porch or portico on south side later style than interior and probably added when converted to church from synagogue. Section to right with roof higher than main body of building forms apse that houses main altar of church, also added after conversion.

Fig. 20.3: Cáceres. Typical house of Barrio of Espíritu Santo, in proximity to Church of Espíritu Santo. No telltale vestiges exist in barrio to indicate characteristics of judería before extinction and conversion of synagogue.

porch along the south side of the building very likely represents an addition to the original plan when the synagogue was converted to a church. The shape of its arches, of mudéjar style, would seem to imply a fifteenth-century date at the latest for its construction.

The eastern end of the building is quite different in character from the main body of the structure; an apse in the Gothic style encloses the presbytery. This purely Christian element was probably added in the fifteenth century, after the pogroms of 1391 and the conversion of the synagogue into the Church of Espíritu Santo.

The west end also seems to have been altered. It is architecturally uninteresting and no longer preserves its original form. On close inspection, I found evidence of some changes and repairs, especially in the lower portions where a smoothly stuccoed reinforcing wall, out of concert with the rough stone masonry of the rest of the building, had been added at some unknown date. A high, stuccoed, stone fence, probably posterior in date to the date of the building, encloses an open square area in front of the west front, probably conforming to the shape of a former courtyard. The window high up in the gable is Gothic in style, also out of keeping with that of the mudéjar arches of the south portico. This window was probably altered at the same time the Gothic apse was added at the opposite end of the building. It is also quite possible that this Gothic window was originally a door that gave access to the women's gallery of the synagogue reached by an exterior stairway. This stairway may have disappeared as a result of the alterations carried out on the west wall after the conversion of the building to a church.

The north wall also has been changed. Its original appearance has been obscured by the addition of some later constructions abutting on it.

The interior is divided into three aisles of approximately equal width by four square piers with chamfered corners, two in each row. These support pointed, horseshoe-shaped arches of brick of mudéjar design. The central arches are higher than those over the side aisles. These, in turn, support the low cross walls on which the pitched roofs rests. The wooden ceiling of simple mudéjar joinery cannot be the original one. It is in very good condition and seemed relatively new to me. Therefore, I concluded that it probably was part of the recent restoration works that, according to Cantera Burgos, had been carried out earlier in the twentieth century. Its form corresponds to the type of roofing employed when the structure was first built, and fitted the overall scheme better than the Gothic apse. The whole building is but three bays long, the main door in the middle bay.

Unlike the churches of Andalucía resplendent with gilt and gaily colored retables and ornaments, the interior here is remarkable for its austerity and is in harmony with the hard, harsh, sterile soil the building stands upon. The main altar in the apse was but a rude stone table. Except for the crucifix on the altar and the cross on the peak of the roof of the apse outside, there was nothing to indicate that the

Fig. 20.4: Cáceres. Church of Espírtu Santo. Interior, north side aisle toward west. Side aisle arches lower in conformity with slope of pitched roof. Low or squat, side aisle arch mudéjar version of pointed arch, tending more to horizontal than vertical as in normal Gothic pointed arch.

Fig. 20.5: Cáceres. Church of Espíritu Santo. Interior, view to west. Door to prayer hall on left. Roof supported on two arcades of three pointed arches. Center arches higher than other two in each arcade, horseshoe shaped as well. Each arcade contains four columns with chamfered corners. Only center columns freestanding. Those at end of arcades embedded into walls. Middle arches higher in conformity with slope of pitched roof. Reader's table probably located in middle bay with higher pointed, horseshoe-shaped columns. In style, arches and piers typically mudéjar may date from fourteenth century.

Fig. 20.6: Cáceres. Church of Espíritu Santo. Apse at east end, added after synagogue converted to church. Neighborhood houses appear on right.

Fig. 20.7: Cáceres. Church of Espíritu Santo. West end of building, altered after conversion.

building was a church.

Except for the Gothic ribbed apse, the interior of the building easily could be re-converted to a synagogue. The platform where the Torah once was read doubtlessly stood in the middle bay of the central aisle, the space defined by the higher pointed horseshoe-shaped arches. In other words, the interior space was originally laid out with a central orientation, as is normal in the traditional synagogue plan. The spatial organization was changed to a longitudinal axial orientation by the addition of the Gothic apse when the building was converted to a church.

Before the conversion of the synagogue and the subsequent reorientation of the plan, the Torah Ark was located against the East Wall; this wall, in all likelihood, was demolished when the Christian apse was added. The other end of the building sustained changes as well. Probably located on a mezzanine floor built of wood, the women's gallery was entered from the door high up on the gable of the west end; its place is now occupied by the Gothic window.

I left the building, stared for a few moments at the monumental cross in front of me on a high, stepped pedestal in the rocky, unfenced courtyard to the south of building and went away.

21 Plasencia

From Cáceres I drove to Plasencia in a northeasterly direction, and within a short while snow-covered mountains, the Sierra de Gredos, came into view on the right. In Seville the orange crop had already been harvested, the wild flowers were still in bloom, and the bright cerulean blue sky was lighted by a gentle warming spring sun. In the distance, winter remained on the heights of the sierra. While still some distance away, I espied Plasencia on an eminence high above the right bank of the Jerte River. No more than a narrow creek, it is a remote tributary of the Alagón, which in turn empties into the Tagus. Thus, it adds its small and trifling treasure to the great stream as it winds its way through Spain and Spanish history to become one with the waters of the boundless ocean at Lisbon in Portugal. Plasencia, like the Jerte River, is also remote from the mainstream of Spanish history and at best

Fig. 21.1: Plasencia. Plazuela de Santa Isabel. View to north from Calle de Santa Isabel. Synagogue, once located on little plaza in heart of medieval judería, converted to church under advocation of Santa Isabel in honor of Queen after Expulsion. Synagogue-church no longer exists; plaza now surrounded by private homes.

Fig. 21.2: Plasencia. Calle de Santa Isabel from Plazuela de Santa Isabel. View downhill to west. One block long and so narrow that sun reaches street level only at midday, this street principal/only one of medieval judería.

Fig. 21.3: Plasencia. Calle de Santa Isabel. View uphill to Plazuela de Santa Isabel to east. Lower sections of walls on left, with semicircular arched openings, contemporary with time of judería. Upper sections house walls recent construction.

only a backwater of the Jewish past, offering nothing to compare with the opulent and learned community of Toledo downstream on the Tagus. Although no definite date suggests when the Jewish community was first established in Plasencia, at the time of the Expulsion (1492) it had a cemetery and a synagogue.

According to Cantera Burgos, after the Jews left Plasencia, under the advocation of Santa Isabel, the Church confiscated the synagogue and converted it to a church in honor of the queen. Early in the sixteenth century (1520-23), during a period of civil disturbance and revolt, the Comuneros accidentally destroyed the building when they set fire to some nearby houses. The synagogue had been located in the little plaza still known today as the Plazuela de Santa Isabel.

Houses of well-to-do people surrounded the quiet little square of Plazuela de Santa Isabel; a diminutive garden with some shrubs and one weeping willow tree occupied the center. Probably the principal street of the now vanished judería, the Calle de Santa Isabel presented a different character. High walls of adjacent houses hemmed in its long narrow passageway hardly wide enough for motorized vehicles.

The Calle de Santa Isabel opens from the plaza, descending in a westerly direction. It is a short one-block alley-like street of tenements, so narrow that only at midday does the sun enter for a few brief moments. Uncomfortably cool on the shady side of the street, I sought out the side where the sun already was warming the cold stone walls. Probably contemporary with the time when Jews still lived in these houses, some of the lower sections of the walls seemed to be very old indeed. Almost no windows exist at ground level. The heavy, massive walls are perforated here and there by semicircular arched openings. These openings have thick wooden doors held together by large iron nails with rosette-shaped heads forming a pattern of strength on the stout, weathered, vertical planks. The whole aspect of the walls at street level speaks of great age. The reaches of the walls in the upper stories present quite a different character. I concluded that these sections, laid up with smaller blocks of stone, must date from a time after the entire street was set afire in the early sixteenth century. The Jews no longer would have lived in the houses.

Not a single recognizable Jewish vestige remains; nor does even a spoor nor a sign indicate where exactly on the Plazuela de Santa Isabel the synagogue once stood. On the other hand, the community cemetery that the Jews had been forced to abandon (1492) has been located on the outskirts of town. The graves with the bones of the ancestors of the exiled Jews survived unmolested only briefly; the dean of the Cathedral of Plasencia soon purchased the cemetery. He resold it almost immediately (1496). Some buildings were erected on the site, but the area remains largely unexplored, awaiting the archaeologist's spade. I wandered about looking for the site but, lacking specific information from Cantera Burgos where the Jewish burying ground was to be found, I gave up the search and left Plasencia.

Fig. 22.1: Béjar. Calle del 29 de Agosto, formerly Calle de la Antigua and main street of medieval judería. Three houses on left, Nos. 3, 5, and 7, once synagogue. Cantilevered balcony of house in center, No. 5, torn down mid-twentieth century. Main entrance to synagogue, in this section of building, also dismantled. Original interior obliterated during alterations.

Fig. 22.2: Béjar. Calle del 29 de Agosto. Two women stand before destroyed section of medieval synagogue. Young woman with child in her arms related how her carpenter brother remodeled section of synagogue as a home for her and her family in late 1950s. One section of balcony, house No. 7, appears in photograph. Addition to house built on to projecting balcony, at some unknown date, obliterates medieval portions upper story section of synagogue.

22 Béjar

The countryside all the way from Cáceres to Béjar presents a desolate appearance; except for Plasencia, few villages or towns along the way interrupt the road. Though the Jewish community of Béjar had not figured among the prominent in medieval Spain, it achieved some measure of renown during the twentieth-century. This prominence did not come about because of its men of learning of yore, as in Toledo and Córdoba, but rather because, like Toledo and Córdoba, its synagogue was still standing. Little is known of the history of the Jewish community of Béjar, other than it was probably established in the early thirteenth century soon after the Reconquest. The whole aspect of the town of Béjar to one newly arrived from sunny and joyous Andalucía appeared rather dark and even nondescript. Nothing existed there to detain the tourist by way of architectural monuments worthy of note such as the magnificent Gothic cathedral in Burgos. This was the next pause in my journey in search of the tattered remnants the Jews left behind when they went into exile five hundred years ago.

Béjar manufactures woolen cloth as its principal industry, I learned. This seemed significant and led me to hypothesize that there may be some connection between the modern industry and the town's long-departed Jewish community; wool weaving and textile distribution was an occupation common among the Jews of medieval Spain as it also was in Italy. I mused, "Could the woolen cloth industry of twentieth-century Béjar have been introduced by the Jews who settled here in the thirteenth century bringing the craft of wool weaving with them?"

And the name of the town itself—Béjar! Could it be that the Jews carried the name of their native town along with them in their meager baggage when they were forced into exile in 1492? Béjar or Behar is not an uncommon family name among Sephardic Jews. And continuing this Sherlock-Holmes type of deductive reasoning, I asked myself, "Could it be that the family name Béjar or Behar originated here in Béjar, a cloth-weaving town?" After being baptized, Jews frequently took the names of their native towns as family names. Some common family names among some Spaniards, possibly but not always, of Jewish ancestry are also the names of towns: Cáceres; Toledo or Toledano; Segovia; Sevilla; Madrid; Tudela; and Burgos, among others. Do all the modern-day Sephardic Behars or Béjars then go back to the wool weavers and cloth merchants of medieval Béjar? This a question I only could answer by intuition rather than by verifiable facts, of which there were unfortunately none forthcoming.

Fig. 22.3: Béjar. Calle del 29 de Agosto. Street paving in bad state of repair, similar to condition of most houses in poor neighborhood. House No. 5, with roughly stuccoed front, once midsection of synagogue where main door located.

Aside from the question of whether the twentieth-century woolen cloth workers of Béjar descended from Jewish weavers, or whether the family name Behar or Béjar originated in this most unprepossessing town, there is, however, physical evidence that a Jewish community once flourished in Béjar. According to Cantera Burgos, the indisputable and verifiable testimony of the Jewish presence consists of the very striking remains of the facade of a synagogue probably dating from the thirteenth century, or the fourteenth at the latest.

I found the remains of the synagogue on the street known as Calle de 29 de Agosto, formerly the Calle de la Antigua, at houses Nos. 3, 5, and 7. The name of the street was probably changed again after the death of Generalissimo Francisco Franco and the return of the monarchy. I found the street to be no more than a narrow, irregular thoroughfare with a disarrayed, rundown paving of pebbles in need of repair. This street descended precipitously in a westerly direction toward the Church of la Antigua, which probably explains its former appellation.

When I first saw it in 1962, the building apparently had undergone a recent alteration. The center portion of the facade had been completely rebuilt and was flanked by houses with overhanging cantilevered wooden balconies of obvious medieval date. These balconies represented the remnants of the disemboweled synagogue. After the demise of Judaism in Béjar, the synagogue had been divided into

Fig. 22.4: Béjar. Calle del 29 de Agosto. View to east. Remains of front wall of medieval synagogue, now houses Nos. 3, 5, and 7. House No. 7 supported on the balcony by extension. House No. 5 remodeled, balcony and main door to synagogue destroyed. Last house, No. 3, preserves balcony in original form.

Fig. 22.5: Béjar. Calle del 29 de Agosto. Pebble pavement, laid down hundreds of years ago, in bad state of repair. House fronts, shabby and nondescript, repaired countless times so that patches have been patched. Children, many fair haired, play and run up and down street seeking warmth of sunny side.

three houses. A plain ugly house stood in the place of the center one. The main entrance of the synagogue had formerly been located in what was now the recently constructed facade between the two older parts. The synagogue entrance door was obliterated when the central part of the building was torn down to make room for the present dwelling. After remaining intact for so many centuries, this house of prayer finally succumbed to the materialistic needs of the twentieth century. I had arrived too late!

A young woman with a small child in her arms was standing nearby where I was silently lamenting the loss of this relic of the Jewish past in Béjar. I asked her what had happened. She told me that her brother was a carpenter and lived in house No. 3, one of the adjacent ones with the medieval wooden balcony. He had

Fig. 22.6: Béjar. Calle del 29 de Agosto. Cantilevered beam ends of balcony still extant on house No. 3. Three rows of wooden beams, cantilevered out one above other, support floor of balcony. Balcony once ran across front of synagogue, now divided into three houses, Nos. 3, 5, and 7. Ends of beams decorated with carved designs, some interpreted as rams' heads. Forty beam ends still preserved on two extant sections of balcony.

remodeled the center house as a dwelling for her family. Anxiously, I asked her to describe the interior before the alterations had been carried out. I had a photograph of the exterior, the one published by Cantera. Offhandedly and without any particular emphasis, she said that there had been large pillars inside, supporting pointed arches. Beyond this terse description, I could not learn any more from her. "But why did you tear this house down?" I asked. "Did you know that these three houses had once been a synagogue, and that had you not torn down the one where your new house stands, it could have been a museum?"

She replied, her gray-green eyes smiling behind her large gold-rimmed spectacles, "Oh, yes, we knew it once belonged to the Jews. Many foreigners used to come to see it. But what could we do? Where could we go? We had need of it to live in!"

The original building was some fifteen meters long. Its most interesting feature, an almost intact wooden balcony, was still extant on houses No. 3 and No. 7. The balcony, of Gothic style, was supported on three superimposed rows of cantilevered beams, the ends of which were carved, some with scrolls, others with flattened bulbous-like elements. The forty or so still preserved beam-ends varied in design. Some seemed to represent animal heads, perhaps rams, but were so badly weathered that only the general configuration could be made out. Simple moldings with a cavetto profile separated each row of beam-ends that stepped out progressively from bottom to top, thus providing the cantilevered support for the balcony floor. The balcony over house No. 7 had been enclosed with glazed panels, while that over house No. 3 probably preserved the original appearance of the open balcony that once ran across the entire building now divided into three parts.

It was still morning in Béjar that April day. The sun had not yet penetrated to ground level between the houses except where the Jewish street turned sharply eastward. The sun's light, hardly warm yet, came in as if by stealth. It was already *Semana Santa* (Holy Week for Catholics) and just a few days before had been Passover for Jews. Six hundred years ago or so on such an April morning the Jews of Béjar were getting ready for the great festival of liberation, their houses newly whitewashed, the floors scrubbed. The Passover tableware, pots, and pans had been taken from chest where they had been stored since Passover of the year before and were being cleansed and made ready for the Seder. Fathers and sons were leaving the synagogue (through the now non-existent door) after morning prayers and were hurrying down the street where on such an April morning I now saw some children playing in the Jewish street. A little boy ran with a gallop up and down carrying his laughing and shrieking blond-haired little brother on his shoulders. Did the Jewish children living on this Jewish street in Béjar six hundred years ago, only some eighteen generations ago, look any different or play any differently from those children playing in the Jewish street that April morning?

I walked to the end of the Jewish street near the Church of la Antigua coming out from the narrow sunless ravine of houses to open ground and saw the springtime snow on the Gredos Mountains to the east. Have the mountains and snow changed in eighteen generations? Have the Jews of Béjar changed?

Fig. 23.1: Burgos. Gate of San Martín with horseshoe-shaped arch of tenth-century date in city wall on western edge of city. Post-1391 judería, including synagogue, in immediate vicinity of gate. No vestige remains.

Fig. 23.2: Burgos. Gate of San Martín. View of west side of gate from outside with circular redoubt, one of many in wall. Synagogue of post-1391 judería just inside gate.

23 Burgos

I sped toward Burgos. Though it was supposedly spring already, the automobile swayed from side to side whipped by the cold winds that swept across the still, lifeless, muted-brown plains of Old Castile, scarred and pimply with the wheat stubble of last year's harvest. I forwent a visit to Valladolid, knowing that a search for Jewish vestiges there would be fruitless. The community had been extinguished long before the parlous days of the late fourteenth century. Decimated as far back as 1268, Jewish life probably had not revived there.

Once in Burgos, I walked along the street parallel to the Arlazón River and passed through the monumental gateway in the old medieval walls of Burgos, the Arco de Santa María, into the plaza in front of the Cathedral of Burgos, an outstanding monument of Gothic architecture. The crowd that had gathered there was watching some religious pageant as part of the Easter celebration.

Fig. 23.3: Burgos. City wall with redoubts descends down slope and turns corner to left. It continues in easterly direction along Paseo de los Cubos. Post-1391 judería confined to area just behind part of city wall of fortification.

Fig. 23.4: Burgos. Calle de Santa Agueda to east. Post-1391 judería, occupied by *new Christians* (forcibly converted Jews) on street just inside city walls. Ruined stone wall on left probably contemporary with judería and originally part of Jewish new Christian houses.

Fig. 23.5: Burgos. Calle de Santa Agueda to west. Location of post-1391 judería. Before 1391 massacres, judería located farther up slope of hill to right on summit where ruins of castle of El Cid was discovered.

While standing there in front of the cathedral, which seemed so un-Spanish to me and more akin to French Gothic cathedrals, I became aware of the Andalusian influence on my senses. I could not help but remember once again the adage that refers to Europe ending at the Pyrenees, or Africa beginning at the Pyrenees. Standing there before the imposing French-like, Gothic facade, the full implications of this aphorism dawned on me. In truth, Burgos and Old Castile were nearer to Europe, to France, than to North Africa, whose history was longer Christian than Moslem. Islam dominated Burgos for only a short while, only a moment in the long history of the Iberian Peninsula. Alfonso III, King of León, reconquered the city from the Arabs in 882. Begun in 1221 and not completed until three centuries later, the cathedral dominates the skyline and the history of Burgos. It is one of the finest examples of the Gothic architectural style, a style native to France. Burgos is Christian Spain; Andalucía is Moslem Spain. And the Jews, of which Spain are they?

Standing there shivering though bundled up in a heavy overcoat that cold April morning, watching the somber ceremony being enacted by celebrants clothed in medieval costumes in the plaza before the austere gray stone facade of the cathedral, I realized I preferred colorful, warm, sunny Moslem Spain to cold, gloomy Gothic Spain. The contrast between bright Andalucía with its whitewashed, red-roofed houses, its smiling people, its trickling fountains, and its flowers and singing birds in cool patios, is indeed a foreign land to the taciturn, somber people of Old Castile, a land of cold winters, gloomy stone castles dominating the barren, rocky forbidden landscape. Andalucía and Old Castile represent a contrast between two races, the Mediterranean and the Teutonic, a contrast as great as that between the blue waters of the Mediterranean Sea and the dark pine forests of northern Europe. Burgos had its El Cid, the medieval warrior, the man of action; Córboba had its Maimonides, the philosopher, the man of reason.

The site of the judería of Burgos was easy to locate following Cantera Burgos' directions, though nothing, absolutely nothing whatever, with a Jewish flavor could be found there. The judería once occupied a sizeable area on the northwestern outskirts of town on the south slope of the hill where the castle, now in ruins, the *solar* (family seat) or house of El Cid himself, stood.

Apparently, two juderías existed at one time, one high up the slope and the other down below, the two divided by a street running in a northwesterly direction. The street is a continuation of the Calle Fermín González. The farther limit, or boundary of the judería at the city wall, and the gate of San Martín, with its horseshoe-shaped arch of tenth-century date, still stand. In the fifteenth century, a synagogue stood somewhere in the vicinity of this gate. Some picturesque houses now abut on the city wall adjacent to the gate where the street widens a bit. This would be a likely location for a synagogue. However, there were no physical traces to be found anywhere to permit fixing a location with certainty.

The pre-1391 judería is said to have clambered up the slope toward the castle. All that I could see was an open field sown with grass. In the pogroms of that doleful year, most of the Jews of Burgos were either killed or baptized, and it is quite likely that their houses, built one above the other up the hill, were burned to the ground. The few hapless individuals who remained alive after the holocaust and who still clung to the faith of the fathers were herded together on the lower slope, but still within the city walls, down to the Calle de Santa Agueda. There I observed some remains of walls, possibly of medieval date, but the mute stones gave no indication that they were once part of Jewish houses.

The post-pogrom judería probably extended farther down the slope to the medieval city wall that runs along the *Paseo de los Cubos* (Promenade of the Redoubts). The whole area was desolate except for a few houses here and there. This was still an out-of-the-way part of town, far from the center and still considered a less than desirable neighborhood. Certainly, when the few Jewish survivors of the massacre were herded there in 1391, it was the least desirable neighborhood in town.

As is to be expected in a society where the folk heroes were warriors, men of action who lived by the sword and whose feats were written in blood on the battlefield, the outstanding members of the Jewish community of Burgos were men of wealth. They were merchants, entrepreneurs, traders, and bankers. The Jews of Burgos had been prosperous during the whole of the Christian medieval period, but they did not produce as many men of learning as had the communities of contemporary Moslem Spain, such as Toledo, Seville, Córdoba, Lucena, or Granada. The heros of these latter communities were men of learning who wielded the pen and whose feats were inscribed with ink on paper. There is a folktale still current relating how the Jews of Burgos extended a loan to El Cid himself (about 1070). The ironclad chest, supposedly filled with valuables, which he gave as a pledge for the loan, was actually filled with sand. This chest with the spurious collateral with which he duped the Jewish money-lenders is supposedly still to be seen in the chapel of Corpus Christi in the Cathedral of Burgos.

Judaism and Jews had been under constant and merciless attack in Burgos long before the wholesale massacres that drowned Spain in Jewish blood that fateful summer of 1391. The Jewish community was reduced time and time again like a sandy shoreline eroded by the relentless action of the ocean's waves. Finally, in 1391, the last of the steadfast remnant of professing Jews was converted. As New Christians, they continued to live in their judería on the same street where I was standing that cold Palm Sunday morning with the spires of the cathedral in the distance softened by the lingering winter's haze. I walked back to the plaza in front of the cathedral. The pageant was over, Christ had risen, and I could hear the singing of the Mass and the tinkling of bells inside.

24 Vitoria

I found Vitoria to be a modern, nineteenth-century, rather dreary-looking industrial town that, according to Cantera Burgos, once had a flourishing Jewish community whose cemetery figured in a most unusual happening. The celebration of the renewal of an ancient contract between the municipal authorities and the Jewish community of Bayonne across the border in nearby France took place because of and in the Jewish cemetery in Vitoria.

On June 27, 1492, the City Council of Vitoria had entered into and signed an agreement with the Jewish community on the eve of its departure from Spain, in compliance with the Decree of Expulsion emitted in Granada by the Catholic Kings, Ferdinand and Isabella. The City Council of Vitoria at that time agreed to maintain the Jewish cemetery and keep it inviolate and never build on it. This promise was given the reluctantly departing Jews as a token of gratitude for the humanitarian efforts of the Jewish physicians of Vitoria who had served the town well, saving many people during a plague. Almost four hundred years later the Jewish community of Bayonne sent a letter, dated April 30, 1851, to the City Council of Vitoria reminding it of the contract entered into with their forefathers and insisting that the agreement had never been abrogated, and therefore, was still in force.

Nothing was done at the time. A century passed between the date this communication was received and acted upon. In 1952 the Jewish community of Bayonne and the City Council of Vitoria met and took part in a solemn ceremony. During this ceremony, a commemorative plaque was affixed to mark the spot where the ancient *Campo Judizmendi* (Jewish cemetery in the Basque language) had been located so that the world would know that the mundane buildings there stand on hallowed ground.

Fig. 25.1: Gerona. View of medieval part of city along Onyar River. Main street of medieval judería, Calle de la Forza, short distance from river running parallel to it. One spire of cathedral surges above roofs of multi-storied houses. In museum or treasure room of cathedral cloister, some Hebrew inscriptions from synagogue and Jewish cemetery of Gerona found. Medieval judería literally in shadow of cathedral extending in southerly direction, marked on map in *Guide Michelin* as *Ciudad Antigua*.

25 Gerona

I drove into Gerona, stopped in a small plaza in the modern part of town, and went into a bakery to buy bread. I asked for directions to the cathedral whose towers I spied above the rooftops on the other bank of the Oñar River separating the medieval from the modern part of the town. The girl behind the counter did not understand a word I was saying in Spanish, for she spoke only Catalán, the language of the northeastern part of Spain. She called out and the baker came in from in back. He spoke *Castellano* (Spanish, that is Castilian) and in a few words directed me to a footbridge across the river, pointing out the way to me, the way to the medieval judería in the shadow of the cathedral.

The extinct judería, and also its cemetery still known as *Montjuich* (Jews' mountain in Catalán), still lingers in the local toponymy; many local people know exactly where it is located. The Castle of Geronella, where the Jewish community took refuge during the pogroms of 1391, lay in ruins at a distance, on a height overlooking the city. In the Romanesque-style cloisters adjacent to the cathedral at the north end of the judería, an historical museum has been installed where, among other items, some Hebrew inscriptions are exhibited. One inscription is from the Synagogue of Gerona; others are from tombstones and sarcophagi that had been found in the Jewish cemetery.

Gerona's beginning, like so many other cities on the east coast of Spain, goes back to the time when the ancient Greeks came there and established an emporium, a trading center. Little remains of the Greek presence now. The known history of the city begins during Roman times when it bore the name Gerunda. The Visigoths followed the Romans, and the Arabs followed the Visigoths, establishing themselves in Gerona in 713. Charlemagne, himself, reconquered Gerona from Islam in 785. The Franks remained in power, except for a ten year period when the Moslems retook the city. The Counts of Barcelona drove out the Franks for good in 1038. The first notices of the existence of the Jewish community in Gerona date from soon after the time when the city fell permanently into Christian hands in the eleventh century.

I had no difficulty finding the former Jewish quarter and the Jewish streets. The poverty of tangible Jewish remains, comprising the lay of the narrow dim streets I traversed, hardly was commensurate with the rich intangible legacy of piety and scholarship that the Jews of Gerona left behind. Gerona had been a seat of Jewish learning, counting among its scholars many whose "names are for a blessing," as,

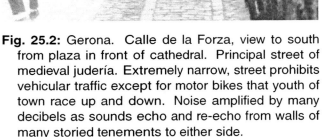

Fig. 25.2: Gerona. Calle de la Forza, view to south from plaza in front of cathedral. Principal street of medieval judería. Extremely narrow, street prohibits vehicular traffic except for motor bikes that youth of town race up and down. Noise amplified by many decibels as sounds echo and re-echo from walls of many storied tenements to either side.

Fig. 25.3: Gerona. Calle de la Forza, view to north near intersection of Calle de Cervantes. Jewish assembly or meeting hall probably located in open area in foreground.

for example, Nahmanides, a physician who wrote important commentaries on the Bible and the Talmud as well as works of purely philosophical import. In the Jewish communities over the whole of medieval Europe, the qualifying epithet *Gerondi* appended to a visitor's or teacher's name was sufficient to announce that he was a learned man and a scholar of worth.

Continual attacks and pogroms comprise the history of the Jews of Gerona. These attacks and pogroms began more than a century before the inflammatory preachments of Ferrand Martínez of Ecija that brought about the wholesale destruction of Spanish Jewry in the year of 1391. As far back as 1285 the rabble of Gerona destroyed the synagogue and laid waste the whole Jewish quarter; both were rebuilt soon after. In 1348 the scourge of the Black Death, which ravaged Europe, did not spare the Jews of Gerona. They were decimated; a pitiful remnant remained alive.

In addition to sudden outbreaks of violence or the inroads of epidemic diseases, the Jewish community was plagued by a rather brutal and savage custom. This custom, dating from the thirteenth century onwards, involved the riffraff and the lower social elements. These groups, inspired by the preaching and frenzy of the Easter season, made yearly forays into the judería, seeking to avenge the death of the Prince of Peace by committing acts of violence in His Name. The bishop's palace, which stood at one end of the judería on higher ground, became the vantage point where the hooligans would gather on the roof and throw stones and firebrands into

Fig. 25.4: Gerona. Calle de Cervantes, view to east from Calle de la Forza. Street at southern end of Calle de la Forza, paved with stairway as it ascends hill to main area of former judería. Left turn at top of stairs leads into Calle de Cervantes and then to Travesía de Cervantes, formerly Calle de la Sinagoga.

Fig. 25.5: Gerona. Calle de Cervantes, view to south. Very irregular street with many zigzags once center of judería on slope above Calle de la Forza. Buildings quite medieval in character; massive stone walls pierced by few doors/windows facing street, undoubtedly a means of defense.

the Jewish quarter. A letter from the king in 1278 made specific reference to this abominable practice and directed the bishop not to allow it any longer. The Jews constituted an important source of royal revenue; to hurt them was to hurt the king's purse.

Tragedy struck in the summer of 1391, as it did from one end of Spain to the other, when the Jewish community of Gerona was completely destroyed. The Jews that escaped slaughter fled the city. Some even committed suicide rather than allow themselves to be cleansed of their sins by the holy water of baptism. Others took refuge in the Castle of Geronella just outside the city, where they remained under siege for about a year. In 1392, some of the beleaguered Jews at last dared return to their homes. This handful of defenseless people, who had resisted escape through baptism, persisted in their ancestral faith. Few of the notables of the Jewish community of Gerona, men of both wealth and learning, converted; they chose death or exile instead. The few Jews left alive continued to preserve the tradition of learning and piety despite the holocaust. By 1431 the men of learning and piety all had died. The next generation of the few Jews still left slowly converted to the dominant religion so that the Jewish community of Gerona became extinct to all intents and purposes. Those individuals, who were still openly professing Jews at the time of the Decree of Expulsion, left their homes and the graves of their ancestors on August 3, 1492, still obdurate and unwilling to accept baptism.

I left the bakery and walked a short distance through the modern part of town, coming to the left bank of the Onyar River in a few minutes. There, the old medieval city with the judería loomed up on the other side. Some footbridges crossed the stream that was flanked by many-storied gray-walled tenements bearing glassed-in balconies that literally rose from the slow-moving water in which their facades were reflected. A tower of the cathedral stood out above the rooftops piercing the sky. It served as a beacon to guide me to the judería. The land rose sharply from the riverbank, the old city clambering up the slope; I was confronted by this beautiful sight in the pale light of the mid-morning sun. I crossed the bridge downstream, and found my way into a plaza with the cathedral rising high above on the opposite side. The facade, of eighteenth-century date, belied the Romanesque and Gothic interior. In fact, one tower of the cathedral may even date as far back as the time of Charlemagne himself.

The judería extended in a warren of alleys and narrow streets to the south of the cathedral and parallel to the river. The Calle de la Forza, which opened from the plaza, was originally the principal street of the judería of Gerona. It is now hardly more than a dark alley hemmed in by many-storied tenement buildings, an extremely sunless street.

The Calle de la Forza was full of pedestrians hurrying along and young men and boys riding up and down on their motorbikes. The deafening noise was amplified

Fig. 25.6: Gerona. Calle de Cúndaro, view to east from Calle de la Forza. Street no more than narrow passageway between buildings at either side. It ascends, opening at top on diminutive plaza in vicinity where synagogue stood.

Fig. 25.7: Gerona. *Travesía de Cervantes* (Passageway of Cervantes), view to east from head of Calle de Cúndaro. Little street, really passageway, once known as Calle de la Sinagoga, location of one of synagogues of medieval judería of Gerona.

by echoing and re-echoing in the stone sound box formed by the cobblestone pavement and the masonry walls. Somewhere along this street, at the very end perhaps, a Jewish assembly hall had once stood. Just where the synagogue had been located is not exactly known, perhaps on the site between the houses No. 2 and No. 6, according to some of Cantera's sources. It is likely that Gerona had more than one synagogue during the course of its long history, but where they were located will ever remain a mystery.

The size of the judería itself must have contracted in painful spasms and grown successively smaller with the vicissitudes suffered by the Jewish community from the thirteenth century onward. The Papal Bull of May 12, 1415, had ordered that all synagogues except one were to be closed in each of the towns of Spain with Jewish

Fig. 25.8: Gerona. Calle de Cervantes. View to west. One of the sections or zigzags of the street. This section on slope and paved with a stair. Defensive character of houses apparent in very small windows set high above street level. Heavy wooden door in massive semicircular arched doorway opening.

communities. The one selected to be spared was to be the least sumptuous and most humble of all, and also one that already had not been converted to a church. When this order finally reached Gerona on October 24, 1415, the one synagogue still left in the meantime had been expropriated and converted to a church under the advocation of San Lorenzo. It is an interesting coincidence that one of the former names of the Calle de la Forza was Calle de San Lorenzo, thus providing a possible clue to the fact that the last lone synagogue of the Jews of Gerona in the early fifteenth century was probably located somewhere along this street, also known sometimes in the Catalán language as the *Call Judaic* (Jews' Street).

Originally, before the onslaughts on the Jewish community, the judería itself was not confined to this one street. It extended further up the hill east of the Calle de la Forza. I walked a little way down the Calle de la Forza from the cathedral plaza and on my left found a narrow little opening of a street, the Calle de Cúndaro. This so-called street was really no more than a corridor with paved stone steps ascending uphill between the towering walls of the buildings to either side, which actually bridged it at the far end. The passageway was through a darkened tunnel ultimately ending at a diminutive plaza no bigger than a moderate-sized room in a private house. This open space at the top of the hill at the end of the tunnel-like Calle de Cúndaro has been identified by some investigators as the center of the judería. Not a trace of the synagogue that once stood somewhere in the vicinity still exists. Yet, it is a sad irony that the lost synagogue was still standing, more or less intact, at the beginning of the twentieth century. However, by the 1930s it already had been significantly remodeled; I could identify no vestiges of it among the walls pressing in on all sides along the narrow streets.

I decided to continue the search elsewhere in town for another synagogue of which I had been notified. I was urged to locate the street called Traversía de

Cervantes, once known as the Calle de la Sinagoga. I explored the judería from the other end to see if I could find my way there. I retraced my steps to the Calle de la Forza and walked its entire length and at the south end came to a rather wide street. This street was wide when compared with those on the hill above. It opened to the left and rose up a long flight of steps leading to the Calle de Cervantes.

I mounted the stairs and stopped on an intermediate landing. I stood a moment before a wide door with an iron grill over which a sign announced in large letters that the domicile of F. Sola was on the second floor, Apartment B. I read the sign as if it were a sacred document before continuing to wind my way up a series of zigzags in a northerly direction. To my great satisfaction, I was able to turn a corner where I expected the street would come to a dead end. Instead I found myself in the Traversía de Cervantes, formerly Synagogue Street. Following another zigzag, up more stairs, confronting more massive high walls with tiny window openings and doors with semicircular headers exuding Romanesque flavor, and I was once again in the tiny plaza at the opening of the tunnel of Calle de Cúndaro leading downhill back to the Calle de la Forza.

I found no traces, no visible traces, of the synagogues of Gerona. So I went back across the footbridge over the Onyar River and looked back on the Gerona of the Jews. The picturesque ensemble of the old city of Gerona reflected in the river was beautiful indeed.

Fig. 26.1: Barcelona. Map of medieval judería of Barcelona, in Barrio Gótico.

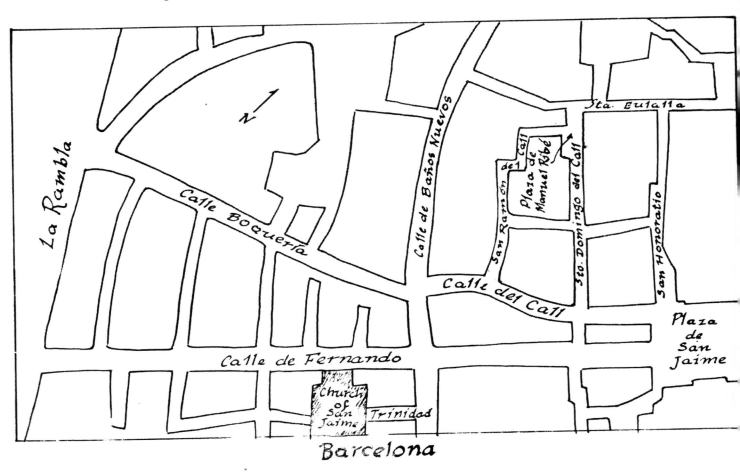

26 Barcelona

As I drove between Gerona and Barcelona, a distance of about one hundred kilometers, I observed that the slightly rolling countryside soon gave way to a flat uninterrupted plain reaching eastward toward the sea. Billboards advertising restaurants and hotels in such seaside resorts as San Feliú, Tossa, Lloret del Mar, Blanes, and others appeared alongside the road from time to time. These seaside resorts are popular among tourists from nearby France and the rest of Europe seeking a holiday in Spain on the *Costa Brava* (Wild Coast). At first I could only imagine what the coast was like, for it did not come into view until I reached Malgrat, where the road runs along the coastline. It is indeed a *costa brava* with mountains emerging from the sea in high cliffs and rocky promontories reaching far into the waves, all wild and barren with magnificent views at every turn.

Just a few miles before reaching Barcelona, the road turned inland once again and the tops of the buildings of the city appeared on the horizon as a serrated saw tooth outline cutting into the pale sky tinted a light, washed-out blue. The whole atmosphere changed from the natural environment of stark, rocky mountains dipping into the sea to one which had been altered by the hand of man. The sky lost its faint tint of color completely and the misty haze on the horizon became heavily laden with smoke from the many chimneys rising like so many sharp pickets above the rooftops.

Barcelona exemplifies the entrepreneurial spirit of modern Catalonia. Departing from other cities in Spain, it looks more to the future than to the past. Barcelona is a fast-paced city whose citizens express progressive attitudes. Many of its people appear overly concerned with the present and what presages for the future. In spite of the fact that the greater part of the physical city is almost wholly a product of the nineteenth and twentieth centuries, Barcelona does have a past, an ancient past, and a past in which the Jewish community figured prominently. Having left an ancient and enduring stamp on the town and its people, the Jewish community continues to set Barcelona apart from the rest of Spain to this very day.

In his discourse welcoming members of the Thirty-sixth International Congress of Americanists assembled in the Salón Tinell, a high-ranking provincial official remarked that the distinctiveness of Barcelona was in some part due to the medieval Jewish community that left an indelible mark, which still distinguishes Barcelona. In giving an account of the history of the city, he said that if Barcelona was industrious, efficient in manufacturing, and astute in commerce, it was doubtlessly due

Fig. 26.2: Barcelona. Calle del Call, view to east from corner of Calle de Baños Nuevos, principal street of medieval judería. Word *call*, Catalán pronunciation of Hebrew word *kahal* (community). Street of *Kahal* is Street of Jewish Community. Use of word *call* not unique to Barcelona; used to designate former Jewish streets elsewhere in Catalonia.

to an inheritance of these characteristics from the Jews whose blood still courses through the veins of so many of its inhabitants. He pointed out that just a few steps away from where we were sitting there was located the ancient judería that he invited us to visit.

The origins of the city go back to a Carthaginian colony or emporium founded, in the late third century B.C.E., on the site of an even older Celtiberian village. Not long after, the city fell into Roman hands, becoming a rather sizeable town during their rule. The Roman city covered the area in the vicinity of the cathedral, including the judería, immediately adjacent to the southwest. The Romans were followed by the Visigoths who remained there until 713 when the city was taken by the Arabs. Catalonia and its chief city, Barcelona, fell to the Franks and to Christianity in 801, becoming part of the Frankish kingdom. Catalonia separated itself from the French crown in 987 and became an independent principality.

In the fifteenth century when the Catalán king died without an heir, Ferdinand I of Castile was proclaimed king and only then was Catalonia united to the rest of Spain. By that time the destiny of the Jews of Barcelona already had unfolded completely and had come to an end; the Jewish community was extinct to all intents and purposes. The "evil decree" ordering the expulsion of the Jews from Spain emitted in 1492 in the Alhambra in Granada was moot; there were no professing Jews left to be expelled. Nor were there any Jews to welcome Christopher Columbus when he returned from the New World and was received by Ferdinand and Isabella in the same Salón Tinell where I was sitting and listening to the provincial official proudly relate something of the Jewish past in Barcelona.

Just when the first Jewish community was established in Barcelona is difficult to ascertain. History reveals that by the thirteenth century it already was flourishing.

The judería was located to the southwest of the cathedral in the center of the *Barrio Gótico* (Gothic Ward or neighborhood). This is the one part of town still preserving its medieval character, at least as regards its street plan. The Jewish quarter was populous and at one time had a number of synagogues. The principal one, known as the *Sinagoga Major* (Main Synagogue), was located somewhere on the Calle de Santo Domingo del Call. It was enlarged in 1267, implying that it had been in existence prior to this date. There were other synagogues as well, as attested to in contemporary documentary sources. However, no vestiges exist today.

The Calle del Call was once the southern boundary and principal street of the medieval judería. According to the speaker in the Salón Tinell, this street is still known by its Jewish name. I wondered what the word *call* (pronounced with a broad *a*, *cahl*) could possibly mean. The Street of the Call! Apparently the Catalán word *call* is a corruption of the Hebrew word *Kahal*, meaning congregation or community. In fact, all through Catalonia the Jews' streets are frequently named Calle del Call just as in Andalucía Jews' streets are known as Calle de la Judería, or Calle de Judíos.

Just as the Jewish past of Barcelona is no secret to the lettered among its inhabitants, so the extent and the boundaries of the judería are also known. Without difficulty, I located

Fig. 26.3: Barcelona. Calle del Call, view to east at intersection of Calle del Arco de San Ramón del Call. Street principal one of medieval judería, now main commercial street in Barrio Gótico. During work-a-day week, Calle del Call, and others, teem with crowds of shoppers. Photograph taken early one Sunday morning when all business establishments closed. Atmosphere probably not far different from earlier Sabbath mornings when Jewish community existed in Barcelona hundreds of years ago.

the Jewish streets enmeshed in the maze of crooked, winding, narrow alleys of the Barrio Gótico. Beginning at the corner of the Plaza de San Jaime and the Calle de San Honoratio, the eastern boundary of the judería once ran in a northerly direction along the Calle de San Honoratio as far as the Calle de Santa Eualia two blocks away. From there it continued in a westerly direction, past the first intersection, the *Calle de Santo Domingo del Call* (Street of Saint Dominick of the Jewish Congregation or Community) and extended one more block to where the Calle de

Santa Eualia terminates at the *Calle de los Baños Nuevos* (Street of the New Baths). The curve described by the Calle de los Baños Nuevos still preserves the outline of the medieval judería wall and its western limit. This street arches in a southerly direction from the Calle de Santa Eualia down to the intersection of the Calle del Call, the main street of the Jewish quarter.

Fig. 26.4: Barcelona. Calle del Call, view to west from Calle de San Honoratio and Plaza de San Jaime. Synagogue once stood on plaza in medieval times.

On weekdays, the winding path of the Calle de los Baños Nuevos teemed with people going in and out of the many tiny workshops of carpenters, tinsmiths, tailors, metal workers, and even a shop devoted to motorbike repair. Some stores sold odd bits of clothing, camping equipment, and miscellaneous merchandise. The buildings were modern, but the small shops combining both workshop and sales in the same establishment, preserved a medieval craft tradition remote from the smokestacks of the factories ringing the outskirts of the modern city.

The Calle de los Baños Nuevos ends at the corner of the Calle del Call, the southern boundary of the judería. At the corner, just one block away to the east, an alley-like street opens to the left or north. This street bears the romantic-sounding name, *Calle del Arco de San Ramón del Call* (Street of the Arch of Saint Raymond of the Jewish Congregation). Sometimes I would linger in this Jewish street, whose plan is almost impossible to describe. It curves slightly to the right and seems to come to a dead end, then zigzags in short stretches before emerging into the Calle de Santo Domingo del Call and the tiny little Plaza de Manuel Ribé. The Calle del Arco de San Ramón del Call is narrow; little light enters between the walls of the modern four- and five-story tenements to either side. Nothing remains there of the Jewish past; in fact nothing remains even of the medieval Christian past, except the lay of the street itself.

The next intersection along the Calle del Call on the perimeter of the judería is that of Santo Domingo del Call. This was once an important street in the Jewish quarter and the location of one of its synagogues. The width of the street is so constricted that the tall tenement houses on either side seem to incline toward each other and the space between them to narrow to a mere arm's length at roof level so that the vast sky above is reduced to a narrow ribbon filling the slit. The third and last intersection along the Calle del Call, the southern boundary of the judería, is at the corner of the Plaza de San Jaime and the Calle de San Honoratio. From this point, I started my circumperambulation around the judería's outer limits. The whole of the judería is about two blocks by three in area, and the circuit around its periphery takes less than a half-hour to cover, even walking at a slow place. Here the Jews of Barcelona lived until the end of the fourteenth century.

Montjuich, the cemetery where the Jews were housed in their eternal homes, provides another place in Barcelona replete with Jewish memories. Though the graves of the Jews have been violated a thousand times, and not a single bone remains, nor even the exact location of the cemetery itself is known, the high hill still bears its Jewish name. Montjuich is a butte or isolated mountain that seems to rise from the waters of the harbor. From the summit, a bird's-eye view reveals the vast city extending to the north, its outskirts lost in the misty light even at midday. A large fortress sits on the crown of the mountain, and further to the west and downhill is a museum with one of the most outstanding collections of Romanesque paint-

Fig. 26.5: Barcelona. Calle del Call, view to west from Calle de Santo Domingo del Call. Street sign affixed to corner of building on right in sense a memorial to *Kahal*, obliterated six hundred years ago. Name joined to that of Christian saint, Santo Domingo. Young husband and wife and two children on way to outing in country as morning advances and sun begins to penetrate some streets of judería.

ing and sculpture. The view from the broad-stepped esplanade in front of the museum delights the eye. Unfortunately, the Jewish burying ground is lost; its exact location on the mountain named for the Jews is known no longer. The northeast side has been converted into a beautiful park. "On which side did the Jews bury their dead?" is a question that may never be answered. The answer matters little, for the vistas from all sides must have been as splendid and breathtakingly beautiful in the centuries long past, when the Jews buried their dead there, as these views are to this very day.

Beginning in the fourteenth century, the Jewish community began to succumb to its doomed fate, though shortly before it had been augmented by an influx of some sixty families who had been expelled from some nearby towns in France. The sixty new families probably represented one-third at most, or one-fifth at least of the total Jewish population. That is to say, in 1306 there were neither less than 180 nor more than 300 Jewish households in the judería of Barcelona, whose perimeter it now takes less than one half-hour to traverse on foot. Allowing five persons per family, the Jewish population of Barcelona may have numbered from about 900 at least to about 1,500 individuals at most in the early fourteenth century.

During the course of the fourteenth century, the general population of the city as a whole grew as did the Jewish community. Though the physical boundaries of the city, it is believed, were extended to accommodate the 30 to 40,000 inhabitants estimated there at the end of the fourteenth century, the space occupied by the judería remained the same as it had been as far back as in the twelfth and thirteenth centuries. Several hundred families were squeezed into an area previously inhabited by between 180 and 300 families at the end of the thirteenth and beginning of the fourteenth century.

Exactly how many individuals comprised the population of the Jewish community at any given time during its existence may never be known. Estimates of the total population of Barcelona, Jewish and Christian, are almost impossible to arrive at except impressionistically; accurate and objective statistical data, in the modern sense, are wanting. Also, the ratio between space and the number of individuals occupying that space must also be qualified by social, economic, and other factors. In other words, neither is possible to arrive at a realistic estimate of how many Jews lived in this area of about five or six city blocks, nor is it possible to compute accurately the total general population of Barcelona at any given time during the Middle Ages and then extrapolate what percentage of that population was Jewish. Nor is the criterion of the number of synagogues and their size or architectural quality, that is, their cost, a reliable measure of how many individuals and/or families comprised the Jewish community of Barcelona, nor for that matter of any other community in Spain as well as the whole of medieval Europe.

About half the Jews of Barcelona were manual workers, counting among their numbers weavers, tailors, dyers, shoemakers, engravers, blacksmiths, bookbinders, silversmiths, and porters. Some were also physicians and many were merchants and scholars. The Jewish community also maintained a rabbinical school. Barcelona had a flourishing port during most of the fourteenth century. Although the judería was a short distance from the docks, the Jews were not permitted to share in the maritime commerce that flowed into the city.

The century ended with the knell of a violent death for the Jewish community. On August 5, 1391, on the Sabbath, the rabble of Barcelona ringed the judería demanding vengeance for the death of the Prince of Peace. Ostensibly inflamed with religious passion to punish the still-responsible descendants of the deicides, the hooligans were in fact motivated even more by a rampant covetousness for Jewish property and the opportunity to take by force, and even murder, the goods that the hated Christ-killers had accumulated. The slaughter and destruction was appalling even to contemporary Christian witnesses. Those Jews who had the most to lose in *ha olam ha ze* (this world) lost heart and rather than receive the rewards of *ha olam ha bah* (the world to come) as dead Jews, chose to remain in *ha olam ha ze* and to survive as live Christians. They were the notables, the wealthiest and most socially prominent, among whom were also men of learning—the natural leaders of the community.

Yet, a steadfast remnant of Jews had escaped baptism and were still alive when the authorities formally abolished Jewish community life on September 10, 1392. The cemetery on Montjuich was suppressed and Jews could no longer join their ancestors, even after death. Less than a month later, however, the matter was given more thought and a new Jewish community was licensed. The new judería, specifically ordered not to be located in its former quarter around the Calle del Call, was established in a reduced area two blocks below the Calle del Call on the Calle de Trinidad where a synagogue had existed previously. The number of people allowed to reside in the new judería was limited to two hundred; the cemetery on Montjuich was returned to the Jewish community.

Nevertheless, the Christian population continued to oppose the Jews. Those few professing Jews remaining were unable to live in Barcelona any longer. Most of the wealthy and prominent Jews already had been converted in 1391 and so continued to live there as Christians. Finally, by 1395 the pitiful congregation of the new synagogue had diminished in size to five families. Against such great odds they could hold out no longer; they too submitted and kneeled with bowed heads to accept baptism. Their synagogue was converted to a church under the advocation of La Trinidad. The synagogue building no longer exists; on its site now stands the Church of San Jaime. The last few remaining stiff-necked Jews, who still resisted baptism, left Barcelona. No Jewish community existed in Barcelona until the middle of the twentieth century. In 1953 a Sephardic synagogue opened its doors in a flat on one floor of an apartment house. An Ashkenazic congregation established itself in another flat in the same building a few years later.

I often returned to the judería and tried to visualize in my mind's eye what it was like before Jewish life was extinguished there. On weekdays the Calle del Call teemed with upwards to thousands of people. The crush was so great that in order to move along more quickly I frequently had to step down from and immediately step back up to the narrow sidewalks, hardly wide enough for two people walking abreast. This was a procedure not without some hazards, for the roadway was

Fig. 26.6: Barcelona. Calle de Santo Domingo del Call, view to north from Calle del Call. During time of Jewish community in Barcelona, street known as Calle de la Sinagoga Major. Synagogue probably located at head of street further up from Calle del Call. Two women sit in front of door to tenement house; young woman dressed in Sunday best moves with deliberate, even-stepped paces, her high heeled shoes click-clacking down street.

Fig. 26.7: Barcelona. Calle de Santo Domingo del Call, view to north and Plaza de Manuel Ribé. Tall tenements seem to lean toward one another, almost touching roofs. Main synagogue of Jewish community located up ahead, probably in little Plaza de Manuel Ribé. Sun never enters narrow street, except for short moment at midday in midsummer.

constantly choked with vehicles. I had to keep an eye on the oncoming motorized traffic behind me as I sought to overtake the slow-moving pedestrian flow. The three short blocks of the Calle del Call continue as an important shopping area, not for the fashionable people of present-day Barcelona, but for the working classes. The street must also have been a teeming place when it was lined with Jewish-owned shops, but hardly packed with the multitudes that frequent the street today.

On Sundays the whole atmosphere of the Barrio Gótico and its section of the judería changed. The Calle del Call was deserted, especially in the early morning. The stores were all shuttered and a scant few passers-by, carrying small baskets with picnic lunches and bathing suits on their way to the beach, walked here and there right down the very center of the street, eschewing the narrow sidewalks without peril. Most pedestrians chose to walk in the middle of the street, especially in the early morning hours, savoring and enjoying the safety and freedom afforded by the absence of automobiles that preempted the roadway all week.

The side streets of the old judería were even more silent on Sunday mornings. The Calle de Santo Domingo del Call, which even during the week was relatively quiet and out of the main flow of traffic that surged down the Calle del Call, was then altogether devoid of life. The narrowness and the darkness of the crooked slit of open space between the towering walls of the tenements to either side appeared foreboding. Closed and shuttered, the windows emanated few sounds.

I stood on the corner of the Calle de Santo Domingo del Call looking up the dark corridor running in a northerly direction from the Calle del Call. During the times the Jews lived there it was known as the Calle de la Sinagoga Major or *Scola Major* (Street of the Chief Synagogue of Chief School). Suddenly a young woman, nattily dressed, appeared. I heard her a few moments before I could see her. She came into view as she hurried, click-clacking on her high heels on the cobblestones, a twentieth-century anachronism in a fourteenth century alley. I could not see the end of the street because it twisted slightly to the left where the buildings were so close together that they were hardly an arm's reach away from balcony to balcony on opposite sides.

I walked up the street and soon came to a slight widening and a small plaza, Plaza de Manuel Ribé. I noticed a plaque high on the wall of a house there and read the inscription. The plaque marked the site where the monastery of Santo Domingo once stood and gave its founding date as 1219. It mentioned not a word that this previously had been the site of a synagogue. It is safe to assume that a Dominican monastery had not been located in the heart of the judería in the early thirteenth century. A more likely ex-

Fig. 26.8: Barcelona. Plaza de Manuel Ribé to right and end of Calle de Santo Domingo del Call in background. Main synagogue of medieval judería located here.

planation would be that the monastery indeed had been founded in 1219, but that it had been located elsewhere first.

However, after the massacres of 1391 and the subsequent suppression of the Jewish community, the Dominicans took control of the main synagogue. They converted it to a church when they moved to this location. The main synagogue of the Barcelona Jewish community, then, most likely once was located right here in the little plaza where I was standing; the plaza was no bigger than a synagogue courtyard. There were no Dominican friars walking about, nor were there any Jews in the plaza taking a short respite from services in the obliterated synagogue. The synagogue court, the Plaza de Manuel Ribé, served the irreverent needs of today's world, a convenient place to park automobiles.

There were a few people standing or sitting about in front of a *bodega* (wine and grocery shop) getting ready to go on an outing. A dog came out of the shop and smelled the ground paved with large cobblestones. A woman gesticulated as she berated her husband who was indifferent to her reproaches.

Leaving the synagogue court-parking lot, the Plaza de Manuel Ribé, I wandered down the zigzags of the Calle del Arco de San Ramón del Call back to the Calle del Call. The Calle del Call was empty; Sunday morning had become Sunday afternoon. The streets of the judería were even emptier than in the morning. The sun, overhead by then, timidly reached down to light up the dark gray stone walls of the tenements of the Calle de Santo Domingo del Call. The noise of the city was stilled just as the life of the Jewish community had been stilled almost six hundred years ago.

27 Lérida

I found my way out of Barcelona and drove off on the Madrid highway, relieved from the tensions of city traffic. At first the road went south but soon turned in a northwesterly direction toward Cervera and traversed a mountainous region ever twisting, climbing and descending, especially between Martorell and Igualada, a distance of about seventy-five kilometers or forty-five miles. The seemingly never-ending sinuous ups and downs demanded complete attention. Once beyond Cervera, the road passed over level ground until reaching Lérida, situated on the right bank of the Segre River and the western limits of Catalonia.

A Jewish community, rather small and undistinguished, had existed in Lérida during the Middle Ages. Despite its size, it had, nevertheless, experienced vicissitudes and tortures to no less a degree than those suffered by the Jews of Barcelona. In the massacre of August 13, 1391, seventy-eight people were slain and the majority of the survivors baptized. Their synagogue was converted to a church under the advocation of Santa María del Miracle; the miracle being the conversion of the few Jews left alive.

The New Christians apparently continued to attend their former synagogue, not for the reading of the Torah, but rather for hearing Mass and taking communion. Both the congregation and its synagogue had been converted! Apparently, the Jewish community was not totally obliterated in 1391, for there were still some Jews left in the early fifteenth century who petitioned to have their synagogue returned, claiming it had been illegally [sic] expropriated. The records are mute as to what disposition was made regarding their request, and the Jews of Lérida never were heard from again. To all intents and purposes, the community thus was finally extinguished by the early fifteenth century. According to the documentary evidence available to Cantera Burgos, the judería had been located in the parish of San Andrés and had been there since some time in the twelfth century, if not earlier.

After securing a room for the night in a local hostelry, I went out to explore the town. It was still light and at least two or three hours before sundown. Asking a number of passers-by and even a policeman for directions, I soon found the street of San Andrés. I reasoned that, though I could find no church under this advocation still existing, it seemed logical that the Calle de San Andrés got its name because the Church of San Andrés had been located somewhere along its trajectory. The street must have been in the parish of San Andrés where the judería had been located.

The area of the town I tentatively identified as having once been the parish of San Andrés was located on a steep hill rising up from the riverbank. The neighborhood appeared to be extremely poor and almost ragged looking. Finding the Calle de San Andrés near the top of the hill, I entered many of the streets in the immediate vicinity to see if I might discern some vestige of the past when Jews lived there. Nothing of the kind occurred. Modern Lérida, it seemed, was largely of late nineteenth- and early twentieth-century confection. Its narrow streets were lined with ugly many-storied, nondescript tenement houses all uniformly pockmarked with small, iron-railed balconies timidly projecting from the facades in front of the long floor-length windows. Judging by the items with which they were bedecked, these balconies principal function was not, so it seemed, a place for the tenants to enjoy a brief respite from their dark and stuffy flats, but rather as a place for hanging their freshly washed gray-white bed sheets, undergarments, dresses, shirts, and sundry pieces of laundry for drying in the open air of the dim streets, where the sun hardly penetrated except at midday.

The most likely candidate for a Jewish street, so I thought, was a narrow alley, *Calle de la Compañía* (Street of the Company, the Company of Jesus or the Jesuit Order) that opened off the Calle de San Andrés. It divided into a sharp left and a slight right fork about twenty yards from the corner, seeming to terminate in a cul-de-sac formed by an ugly brick building with a blind chamfered wall. The dreary prospect of this street and the others in the immediate vicinity created a depressing atmosphere. The unsmiling people, the women all uniformly dressed in black with whom I could not converse because they did not speak Spanish and I spoke no Catalán, contributed to the gloom. I was glad to abandon my search and return to the hotel to spend what was left of the afternoon on the terrace of the hotel café near the riverbank. There it dawned on me that the judería could not have been on high ground above the center of town, but rather somewhere down below on the outskirts near the river where I was sitting and in a location not too far different from that of the judería of Bembibre where I had been a year before.

28 Zaragoza

The highway leaving Lérida was an execrable, potholed, narrow road beset with a never-ending stream of traffic of heavily overloaded, evil-smelling, diesel-engine trucks and all sorts of swaying, bumping buses crammed with people and mountainous heaps of bundles, suitcases, and packages toppling about on the roofs. Within a short while after leaving Lérida, I also left Catalonia behind. After crossing the Cinca River, I noticed the landscape abruptly changed. In a moment, so it seemed, I passed from a relatively rich agricultural region of Catalonia with freshly plowed fields, still damp from the last of the spring rains, with winter wheat either ripe or already harvested and stacked in the warming sun to dry, to a scene that looked like a dead desert, the region known as Los Monegros. Not only the people and the language changed instantaneously from Catalonia to Aragón, so it seemed, but also the very earth itself. I had crossed the river into Aragón and I was heading for its principal city, Zaragoza.

Without warning, Europe had become a North African desert. The land was barren, flat, and arid. Vegetation was scant and human settlements were far from one another as I sped down the road bouncingly and joltingly maneuvering the automobile around the larger crater-like potholes. Even though it was early spring and not long after the recent rains, that is in Catalonia but apparently not here, the land here in Aragón was as dry and as parched as in Castile in the middle of a hot, rainless summer. All the way from Lérida, the last town in Catalonia, the road to Zaragoza passed through but three hapless villages, each looking more forlorn and thirsty than the other. Though Aragón is one of the poorest agricultural regions of Spain because of the aridity of the soil due to the lack of sufficient rainfall, the majority of its people eke out an impoverished livelihood from the sterile ground through farming. A constant flow of people leave, the majority emigrating to Barcelona or Madrid to locate employment mainly in factories.

Contrasted with Catalonia, Aragón is also culturally nearer to North Africa than to Europe. In fact, Moslem—that is Arab and Moorish—vestiges have not altogether disappeared, neither from the physiognomy of the people themselves nor from the architecture of so many centuries ago in which Islamic building traditions persisted long after the departure of its creators. The buildings possess an afterlife in the late medieval mudéjar architectural style of Aragón. The *mudéjar* style or building tradition is one in which Christian, that is, Gothic, and Islamic elements blend. This style was developed during the thirteenth, fourteenth, and fifteenth centuries

Fig. 28.1: Zaragoza. Map of judería of Zaragoza. Judería occupied southeastern quadrant of area of ancient Roman city on right bank of Ebro River.

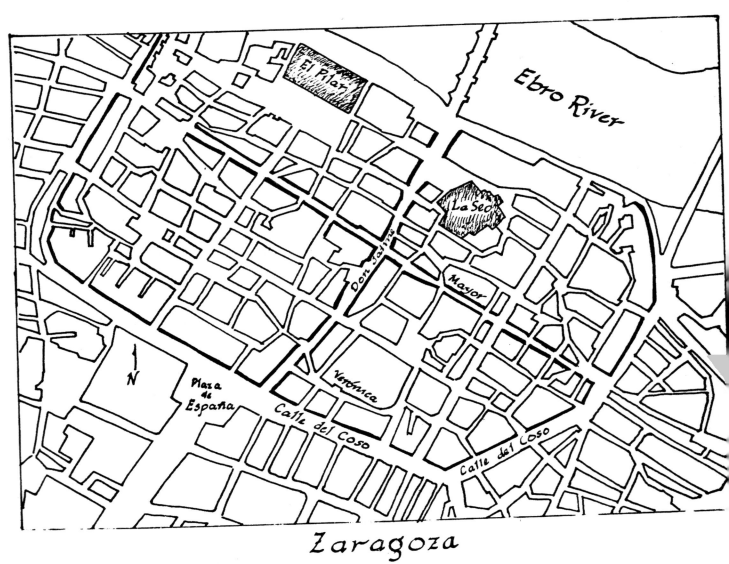

in those parts of Spain that had been under Moslem domination before once again succumbing to Christian domination.

Mudéjar architecture directly reflects the social and historical phenomena that developed as the Christians wrested the Iberian Peninsula, piece by piece, from the Moors. It is, therefore, understandable why the still-extant synagogues of Toledo, Segovia, Córdoba, and Cáceres are mudéjar in style; they all date from the same period of the Reconquest of Spain from the Moors. The Aragonese, because of their inheritance of an all-pervading Moslem past of centuries, have much in common with the Andalusians: music, dance, folklore, and even Semitic and Berber (Moorish) racial antecedents, possibly including a minor degree of Jewish strains.

An axiom of Spanish history suggests that where one finds Moors one also finds Jews. Zaragoza did, indeed, have one of the larger and more flourishing Jewish communities of medieval Spain. Jews probably represented a considerable proportion of the total population of Zaragoza, judging by the fact the judería covered approximately one-quarter of the area within the perimeter of the walls of the original city first laid out and built by the Romans. Whether Jews were already living in Roman Zaragoza in appreciable numbers is not known. There is ample evidence, however, that a Jewish community had been in existence in Zaragoza long before the Visigoth conquest at the beginning of the fifth century c.e., though its size cannot be ascertained. Throughout its long history of well over one thousand years and until its extinction in the fifteenth century, the judería, in all likelihood, always was located in the same area of the original Roman city plan.

When first founded by the Romans, the city of Zaragoza was a small and insignificant town. It became important, however, after the time of the Emperor Augustus, whose name the city still bears in altered form. In the course of the millennia *Caesar Augusta* became Zaragoza. The Visigoths conquered Zaragoza in the fifth century only to be dislodged by the Arabs in the early eighth. Charlemagne himself tried to take the place in 777, but the Arabs soon returned. The city fell into Christian hands permanently in 1118. It then became the capital of the kingdom of Aragón. Because of the absence of supporting data from literary and documentary sources, the history of the Zaragoza Jews during Roman, Visigoth, and Moslem times can be only conjectured. Quite the contrary is the case with regard to the Christian period beginning in the early twelfth century when Jewish history in Zaragoza is amply and painfully well documented. The step-by-step dismemberment of the judería is relatively well known. History records its demise from an area originally occupying almost one-fourth of the space within the ancient Roman city walls with its many synagogues and other communal buildings to the time of its total extinction by violence and forced baptisms.

I had my first view of Zaragoza, a view of the towers and domes of its many churches, while still at a distance where the road neared the Ebro River. The road

Fig. 28.2: Zaragoza. The Church of San Gil. Located in former judería, church typical of architecture of Zaragoza, with stylistic remembrances of Islamic past. Tower, with beautiful surface decoration in brick, really minaret similar to those adjacent to mosque. All synagogues and other Jewish communal buildings disappeared, probably same architectural style as tower of San Gil.

ended abruptly at a bridge over the river that led directly to the very gates of the city, or at least to where the Romans had built one of the main gates. This gate gave access to one of the two main streets, which crossed at right angles and divided the original gridiron city plan into four quadrants.

The many-domed, seventeenth-century Basilica of Nuestra Señora del Pilar, reflected in the water, dominated the skyline to my right. Partially hidden by the buildings that crowded the riverbank, the towers of the Cathedral La Seo appeared. They testified to the historical fact that Zaragoza is the product of the blending of Christian and Islamic elements. First built as a mosque, La Seo still preserves some of its original Arab architectural details. Just to the south and east of La Seo, and out of sight, lay the judería.

I walked back to the bridge where I had parked the automobile and entered the first of the two principal streets of the reticulated or gridiron town plan, the *cardo* of the ancient Roman city plan now called the Calle de Don Jaime de Aragón. The other principal cross street, the *decumanus*, which bisected the ancient Roman city plan, was a few blocks farther down to the south. The section of the decumanus, which once marked the northern boundary of the medieval judería was simply named Calle Mayor.

In medieval Christian times the judería lay, as it probably had since the remote past, in the southeast quadrant of the city between the two main cross streets, the cardo and the decumanus. Originally, the judería comprised almost one-quarter of the total area of the city within the ancient Roman walls; it was physically reduced in size as the Jewish population diminished in number. Bounded by part of the city wall along the south and east sides, the judería's original southeastern perimeter is possible to trace by following the Calle del Coso. First it runs approximately east-west and then turns in a direction approximately north-south. Without difficulty, one can see the rest of the boundaries of the judería: beginning on the opposite side of the Calle de Don Jaime de Aragón near the Church of San Gil with its Moorish minaret still intact as a reminder of ages past; then in a northerly direction back to the Calle Mayor, formerly the Roman decumanus; and finally along this street to the east as far as the Calle del Coso.

By the end of the fifteenth century, just prior to the final dismemberment of the already minuscule-sized judería, all that was left of the Jewish section of the city lay in the vicinity of the Plaza de la Verónica and the street of the same name, parallel to the Calle del Coso one block to the north. Both may also be entered from the Calle de Don Jaime de Aragón.

I found the little street and the Plaza de la Verónica, an ugly, disheveled area. At the time I was there, it was in the process of "urban renewal." Buildings were being dismantled, the pavement broken up, and the narrow sidewalks were heaped with not only construction debris, but also with domestic refuse, garbage. One or two buildings had been torn down and their sites screened from view by massive ten-feet-high brick walls. This area was the last remnant of left of the moribund Jewish quarter at the end of the fifteenth century. The old street names, changed long ago, have been rescued from oblivion only because they are mentioned in contemporary records. These street names described the trades and commerce engaged in by the Jews living there: *Cuchillería*, *Pellicería*, *Platería*, *Tenería*, and *Frenería*. In English, these were streets named for Cutlers, Furriers, Silversmiths, Tanners, and Saddlers. The present street signs bear names such as San Andrés, San Pedro Nolasco, San Jorge, San Lorenzo, and the like.

By the time of the Expulsion in 1492, there were still perhaps five synagogues left in Zaragoza, despite the persecutions that the community, along with the others of Christian Spain, had endured during the fifteenth century. The main synagogue at that time was located near or adjacent to the Church of San Carlos which may occupy the very same plot of ground. The site where the Church of San Andrés now stands may possibly have been the location of another synagogue. Mention is also made of a *Casa del Talmud* (Talmudic School), sold in 1410, located somewhere in the judería. The Zaragozan Jews also had a *khevra* (an organized brotherhood) for visiting the sick, to judge by the fact that one of the synagogues bore the name *vicorholim*, as written in the local dialect in contemporary documents and obviously a transliteration of *Bikur Kholim* from the Hebrew.

After the Expulsion, the synagogues fell into ruin; not all had been converted to churches. Cantera Burgos assembled some data concerning the main synagogue, which, as mentioned above, probably stood on the site of the present Church of San Carlos. After the Jews left in 1492, it fell into a state of disrepair, used as a pigsty. Sixty years later (in 1557) the Jesuits took it over and remodeled it as a church under the advocation of Nuestra Señora de Belén. Seventeen years later (ca. 1574) they tore it down as they considered it too small for their purposes.

In plan it was divided into three aisles separated by two rows of marble pillars, with the central aisle, or nave, the highest. The synagogue was roofed with an

Fig. 28.3: Zaragoza. Calle de la Verónica. Street formerly in medieval judería, of which not a trace remains. In 1960s, area was razed, new buildings under construction.

Fig. 28.4: Zaragoza. Plazuela de la Verónica, center of medieval judería. Unknown if anything of judería extant in area before 1960s; modernization in process at time.

artesón (carpentry-work ceiling), probably comparable to that of the Synagogue of Segovia. The building had seven doors, three on each long side and the main door on the front. There were also some paintings as well as some mosaics still visible when the Jesuits took possession. Even the Ark of the Torah was still intact. Like the Synagogue of El Tránsito in Toledo, Hebrew inscriptions in modeled plaster, by way of decoration, ran along the top of the walls on the interior.

Though the Jewish population had grown and was greater in size than during the thirteenth century, the judería was not allowed to expand beyond its old limits. The onslaughts against the Jewish community of Zaragoza had begun in the early fourteenth century and long before the consuming fires from Seville had spread to the whole of Spain. For a century or more after the Reconquest of the city from the Moors, Jews lived in peace side by side with the Christian conquerors. Alfonso I of Aragón, who took Zaragoza in 1118, recognized the importance of the Jews for the wellbeing of the city as a whole and granted them certain privileges ensuring the continuance of Jewish communal life, both religious and secular, they had enjoyed under Moslem rule. All changed in the fourteenth century. The Jews and their religion were no longer tolerated, let alone protected.

The rabid prejudices of the church outweighed the lukewarm defense rendered by the civil authorities; the Jews were only of economic interest. The Holy Office of the Inquisition held some trials in Zaragoza early in the fourteenth century, striking fear into the hearts of all Jews, especially those who had ostensibly converted to Christianity but had continued practicing Judaism in secret. A number of them were accused of having encouraged some of the converts to return to their ancestral faith. In fact, one synagogue was closed and destroyed as a result of the trials. Furthermore, because of rampant racial hatred on the part of the populace coupled with economic liabilities, the Jewish community of Zaragoza was ultimately reduced to a poverty-stricken state.

In that same year (1335), during and after the trials, the mob stole or pillaged much Jewish communal property. Three years later the Black Plague did not spare the Jews either. They died suffering the same agonies side by side with their Christian neighbors and tormentors. When the plague abated, only one-fifth of the professing Jews of Zaragoza were still alive. The flames of the conflagrations and the fury of the massacres of 1391 also reached Zaragoza. Nor did it all end then, for violent riots continued on into the fifteenth century. The worst blow dealt the Jewish community in Zaragoza was not physical but rather moral and mental, to the extent that nothing was left to live for, not even the hope in the coming of the Messiah. A crushing wave of despondency that He would never come at all overtook the terrorized and terrified Jews after the defeat at the Disputation of Tortosa in 1414 in which Judaism was supposedly proven to be in grievous error. The Jewish community of Zaragoza lost all; it lost its faith in the Law of Moses.

A rash of mass conversions ensued, some doubtlessly out of conviction, but most out of desperation. During the fourteenth century, it was mainly the rich, the learned, and the influential people who had accepted baptism, frequently more for convenience rather than out of conviction. Thus it was the undistinguished, the small people, those of limited means, the artisans, and the unlettered that filled the vacuum and became the leaders of the Jewish community, which by the early fifteenth century had been reduced to about two hundred families in all. After the defeat of Judaism at Tortosa in 1414, these humble people, despondent and without hope for surcease from their suffering, were finally driven to the baptismal font.

By 1492, only a miserable but still steadfast and heroic remnant of Israel was left to go into exile. Not a single stone of a single house of prayer remains as physical testimony that at one time a considerable portion of the total population of medieval Zaragoza had been Jewish.

Who then in Zaragoza does not have some trace of Jewish blood coursing through their veins?

29 Gibraltar

After wandering the countryside of Spain in search of the Jewish past, frequently in out of the way and long forgotten extinct juderías, I inadvertently found a living Jewish community, one founded about the mid-eighteenth century, but whose roots extend deep into the Spanish past—Gibraltar. In a sense the modern community of Gibraltar is unique, for after a period of about two hundred and fifty years, its members returned from exile to a tiny iota of their native land on the southern tip of Spain. The community of Gibraltar, therefore, has the distinction of being the first to have been revived on Spanish soil after the Expulsion in 1492.

The establishment of the contemporary Jewish communities in Madrid, Barcelona, and latterly Seville are not to be interpreted as representing the "return from exile" of its members, but rather as the effects of the social, political, and economic discontinuities and disjunctions that characterized so much of twentieth-century European history. These effects had an especially disastrous impact on the Jews of Germany and eastern Europe as well as on those in the Arab lands of the Middle East and North Africa. No viable Jewish communities existed in Spain at all until the mid-twentieth century except that of Gibraltar, a British crown colony and Spanish only by reasons of geography. Uniquely, the Jewish community of Gibraltar, whose native speech is Spanish, is located in a far-flung corner of Britain though less than three kilometers from Spain.

I once visited a German Jewish family in Madrid who had been living there since the end of World War One and to whom I had a letter of introduction from friends in Guatemala. I wished to know something of the Jewish community in Seville where I was to spend a year. I learned that at the time, 1961, there was but one single Jewish family living in Seville, also German Jews. They had a cork export business, doubtlessly the cork from the evergreen oak trees of the Sierra Morena on whose acorns the pigs destined for conversion to *jamón serrano* (mountain ham) were fed.

When I arrived in Seville, the Jewish New Year already was approaching. I called this family on the telephone to learn if, by some chance, synagogue services would be held there. A servant girl answered the telephone and told me that the family was not at home and would remain away for at least two weeks. I conjectured that they had probably gone to either Madrid or Barcelona for the holidays.

On the chance that he was organizing services for the Jewish military personnel there, I called the chaplain at the nearby U.S. air base. He informed me that there were fewer than ten Jews, including women and children, on the base and they had all been furloughed to Madrid where services for all U.S. military personnel in Spain would be held. He then suggested that I try the British base in Gibraltar where they might be conducting High Holy Day services.

I thereupon called the British consul in Seville. He informed me that specially organized Jewish religious services for the military in Gibraltar were not necessary, for there were three, perhaps, four synagogues in operation there. He forewarned me that the Jews of Gibraltar were all Sephardim and that services are held according to their custom. According to him, as an American Jew, probably an Ashkenazi, I might find this type of service strange and unfamiliar.

Two days before the holidays, accompanied by my family, I drove to Gibraltar. Leaving Seville, the road runs directly south over a flat alluvial plain laid down by the waters of the Guadalquivir over the millennia with fields of ripening wheat and countless olive groves on the slight rises of land. Though it was still forenoon, the brilliant sun in the cloudless cerulean blue sky was like a fiery furnace. A brief stop at the *venta* (roadside inn) in Los Palacios for a second breakfast of fresh bread and coffee provided a welcome respite.

Then on to Jerez de la Frontera, one of the most charming and congenial towns in all Andalucía, with its easy going smiling people and famous, especially among tourists, for its bodegas. There sherry, the best in the world, may be sampled without limit and without cost. Avoiding the turn in the road to Sanlúcar de Barrameda, a town also associated with the voyages of Christopher Columbus, I continued on in the direction of Cádiz, which I by-passed by taking the fork to the east. This road runs parallel to the Mediterranean, passing small, picturesque villages dotting the flat landscape. Suddenly the terrain changed to hilly ground where the magnificent white-walled and red-roofed Véjer de la Frontera, high on a pinnacle to the right, dominates the landscape to the north and the sea to the south. Here the waters of the Atlantic and Mediterranean crowd together, one leaving and the other entering the narrows between Europe and Africa.

It is here that one senses that the already vague distinction between Europe and Africa is completely blotted out, for here both sides of the Mediterranean seem very much the same. The town of Tarifa just a few miles further east from Véjer de la Frontera is actually on the southernmost tip of Spain, even further south and nearer Africa than Gibraltar. Tarifa is still quite Moorish in aspect and is akin to that of an Arab town in the Near East. Tarifa would not be out of place in far-off Lebanon or in nearby Morocco just across the strait. The English word *tariff* is derived from the name of this town, for it was here that the Moors exacted tolls from ships passing through this narrow funnel-like stretch of the Straits of Gibraltar.

It was in Tarifa that I saw Africa for the first time looming out of afternoon haze so near it seemed only a stone's throw away from where I was standing. High above the narrow waterway on the opposite shore arose the majestic *Jebel Musa* (Mountain of Moses). Musa was the African viceroy of the caliph of Damascus whose forces were the first to invade the Iberian Peninsula in 711 and begin the conquest and domination of Spain that was to last more than seven hundred years.

Leaving Tarifa and driving further east with many views of the Mediterranean to delight the eye, from a great height in the road, and without warning, I came upon a bird's-eye-view of *Jebel al Tarik* (Mountain of Tarik), Gibraltar. There it was in fact and not in legend or in metaphor, not as a figure of speech or an abstraction, and not as the logo of an American life insurance company. The Rock of Gibraltar rose up on the horizon like a recumbent lion emerging from the sea, connected by its tail to the mainland, a narrow strip of flat land, the no-man's-land between Spain and that indomitable corner of Britain.

It is most unlikely that a Jewish community of any appreciable size ever existed in Gibraltar prior to the British conquest in the early eighteenth century. The Arabs invading from across the strait took Gibraltar in 711 and held it until 1309 when it was reconquered by the Christians. The latter were able to hold it for but a short time until it was recaptured by the Moors in 1333. Finally it fell once again into Christian hands in 1469, only a few years before the fall of Granada, the last Moorish kingdom in Spain, and the Expulsion of the Jews as well as the discovery of the New World in 1492.

A few brief references to Jews in Gibraltar exist dating from pre-Expulsion. In 1356 the Jews of Gibraltar appealed for help to ransom some Jews who had been captured by pirates. Also in 1473, a group of marranos requested permission to settle in Gibraltar. The outcome of this request is not known. Nevertheless, in no case is there evidence that a permanent Jewish community existed in Gibraltar until about 1729 when the British entered into an agreement with the sultan of Morocco. This agreement permitted the sultan's Jewish subjects to travel to Gibraltar for trade. Not long after this agreement went into effect, the British authorities gave legal sanction for a permanent settlement of Jews in 1749.

Approximately six hundred Jews lived in the community at that time. They comprised perhaps as much as one-third of the civil population of Gibraltar as a whole. By mid-nineteenth century, there about two thousand Jews in Gibraltar; the majority engaged in retail trade. The Jewish community grew apace during the rest of the nineteenth century and well into the twentieth. The Jews were an important element in the general population just before the World War One. They constituted a tightly knit community, which kept itself apart both socially and religiously from the other elements of the general population. That the Jewish community did not intermingle with the other *racial* elements of the population was judged to be a characteristic worthy of special note in the article on Gibraltar that appeared in the 11th edition of the *Encyclopaedia Britannica* about 1909:

The inhabitants of Gibraltar are of mixed race; after the capture of the town by the British nearly the whole of the former Spanish population emigrated in a body and founded, 6 m. away, the little town of San Roque. Most of the native inhabitants are of Italian or Genoese descent; there are also a number of Maltese, and between two and three thousand Jews. The Jews never intermarry with the other races and form a distinct society of their own. (vol. XI:939)

When I first came to Gibraltar in the early 1960s, the Jews were just recovering from the most recent disjunction in its community life, the evacuation of the civilian population of Gibraltar during World War Two. Originally, the community had supported four synagogues and a yeshiva. Not all the evacuees had returned and so the yeshiva and one of the synagogues did not reopen. The community sustained a further blow, an economic one, when (in 1965) Franco shut down the frontier between Spain and Gibraltar. The majority of the retail trade was in the hands of the Jewish community when I arrived there for the first time. This fact revealed itself to me when I discovered that on Saturday the majority of the stores in the main street were shut and the three remaining synagogues were all full.

Before the advent of widespread air travel, many steamships would stop for a spell, sometimes only a few hours, to allow the passengers to shop in Gibraltar, a duty-free port. Also, it was customary for many Spaniards and tourists, too, to make excursions to Gibraltar for the express purpose of purchasing radios, binoculars, stereo and electronic equipment, cameras, English woolens, china, and other high-quality items that cost much more in Spain. With the decline in passenger steamship travel and later the closing of the frontier, the duty-free goods languished on the shelves of the shops for want of buyers. Twenty-two years later (in 1987) when the new Spanish government opened the frontier, the Jewish community numbered a fraction of what it had been before the closing, perhaps less than one thousand individuals out of a total population of about 25,000.

Gibraltar is no bigger in size than a village, its total area being some two and one-half square miles, only a fraction of which, the west side, is reserved for the civilian population. Despite the recent decline in the Jewish population, within that tiny compass three synagogues function. The smallest of the three synagogues is the one referred to as being "the Synagogue behind Barclay's Bank." I would never have found it if a border policeman had not directed me to it. On the day I first came to Gibraltar, I inquired of him how I might find the synagogue, he answered, "Synagogue. Which one? We have three," and he directed me to all three. I thought I did not quite understand him when he responded that there was one behind Barclay's Bank.

A synagogue behind Barclay's Bank seemed rather strange, but I found it exactly so, behind Barclay's Bank on a narrow street and totally hidden from view. I entered through a passageway to one side of the bank and came into a small paved courtyard with a building at the far end with two flights of stairs rising to the second. One led to the prayer hall reserved for men. The other stair led to the women's section in a small room projecting at right angles from the main prayer hall. After I entered, I noted that the women's section was physically separated from the men's prayer hall by a low wall with an iron grill. This wall arrangement allowed the women a side view of the Ark on the East Wall and an oblique view of the reading desk in the center. I was somewhat disquieted at first; I knew this to be an arrangement common in churches attached to cloistered convents. Here, the nuns attend Mass in a chapel or section to one side of the main altar separated from it by a grill, sometimes of iron sometimes of wood. The women in the synagogue behind Barclay's Bank were separated from the main prayer hall in the same fashion as are nuns from the lay worshippers in a conventional church. This arrangement was probably chosen here because the synagogue occupied the second story of the building and there was no third story where a women's gallery might be placed. The congregation, perhaps unwittingly, chose an arrangement that seemed to me so out of concert with a synagogue. They just as easily could have seated the women in a section on the same floor behind the men and separated by a curtain; but then both sexes would have had to enter the prayer hall by the same door, which was apparently deemed improper.

The synagogue glistened with crystal chandeliers and shining crystal olive-oil lamps hung from the ceiling with bright newly-polished silver chains. The Ark was covered with a rich, dark blue velvet cloth embroidered with a seven-branched candelabrum and appropriate biblical verses. The pews, arranged around three sides of the reader's desk, were of smoothly polished mahogany, and shone like mirrors. The wooden floor was highly waxed so that it reflected light and the grain of the wood was clear and beautifully smooth with a patina that only time and countless footsteps could have created. No more than thirty men and boys assembled there, dressed in well-cut, new clothes, all wearing felt hats.

An ancient man, very short of stature, clean shaven, in a top hat and formal morning coat led the New Year prayers in a high-pitched, solemn chant that sounded like crunching crystal, yet one which signaled a loud, deafening response in unison from the congregation. The enthusiasm for the prayers and the exultation felt was revealed in each individual's face. Each individual became one with the congregation, all praying as if with one mouth and one heart. Here in Gibraltar, in the synagogue behind Barclay's Bank, all thirty men and boys prayed as one, like an organized cheering section at a college football game, the only individuality expressed was that of the power of each man's voice. Each tried to out shout, to out pray his neighbors as the soprano of the young boys' voices rose piercingly high above the baritone and bass registers of the men.

At the end of the service, a rather corpulent man dressed in a dark suit and wearing a Homburg felt hat, who had invited me to share his pew when I entered, informed me that this little synagogue was the oldest in Gibraltar, its congregation organizing soon after the "Rock" fell to British forces in 1704. The Jewish community of Gibraltar was the first to have been re-established on Spanish soil since the Expulsion. The British, in need of interpreters, invited Jews from North Africa to serve in that capacity. They subsequently founded this synagogue.

He went on to relate that the majority of the Jews of Gibraltar are merchants, though some have entered the liberal professions, going to England for their university training, and also that an appreciable number are on the local police force. All are bilingual, speaking Spanish and English; Spanish is spoken at home and with the rest of the Gibraltarian population and English with the British authorities.

The Sabbath is strictly kept by all. He related an incident illustrating that even the non-Jewish population respects the Jewish traditions regarding the observance of the Sabbath. A well-known and popular American singer and movie star, a

Fig. 29.1: Gibraltar. Synagogue in Engineers Lane also known as Synagogue Shar ha Shamayim. Synagogue actually behind house that fronts street. Arched doorway accesses passage through house to synagogue courtyard in back. Chief rabbi of Gibraltar occupies house in front of synagogue.

Jew, once came to Gibraltar and with pleasure he showed the visitor around the town. It was Sabbath afternoon and the streets were filled with people, both Jews and gentiles. A crowd of young people, admirers of the world-renowned popular entertainer, gathered around the two men. A boy handed the American crooner a bit of paper and a fountain pen asking for an autograph, then in a flash drew them back, apologizing that he had momentarily forgotten that it was the Sabbath. The singer asked my informant if the boy was Jewish and was aware that writing on the Sabbath was not permitted. When he heard that the boy was not, tears filled his eyes for it suddenly dawned on him that Gibraltarian gentiles knew and were respectful of Jewish traditions with regard to the sanctity of the Sabbath.

The policeman at the border had given me directions to a second synagogue when I first came to Gibraltar. He called it the "Synagogue in Engineers Lane," and after inquiring of some passersby, I did find it En- gineers Lane a short distance uphill from the main street. Unlike the little synagogue be- hind Barclay's Bank, this one was easy to lo- cate; in a lunette over a window of an other- wise undistinguished two-story building, there was inscribed the word *Synagogue* in English. Immediately above this terse announcement, another inscription, this one in Hebrew, read *Shar Hashamayim* (Gate of Heaven).

I saw no synagogue, even though I was standing there before the Gate of Heaven. Only after I entered a door to one side open- ing on a narrow passageway did I realize that this synagogue, like the one behind Barclay's Bank, did not front directly on the street. The corridor gave access to a small courtyard in the rear where the actual synagogue rose at the far side. A broad, arched door at the head of a short flight of stairs was the entrance to the main prayer hall, reserved for men. The women, as in many traditional synagogues, worshipped in the gallery, which ran around three sides of first floor prayer hall. A long flight of stairs in the courtyard, abutting on one wall of the synagogue, allowed access to the women's gallery.

Fig. 29.2: Gibraltar. Synagogue in Engineers Lane. Main entrance to prayer hall. Stairway (not in photo- graph) abuts on building to right, accesses women's gallery inside prayer hall. Building dates from late eighteenth/early nineteenth century.

I went into the men's section and found a place in a pew under the gallery on one of the long sides of the building. The services were being conducted in a manner quite different from those in the synagogue behind Barclay's Bank. They were more reserved, seemingly more cerebral than emotional. A bearded man, the rabbi, chanted the prayers not unlike a cantor in an Ashkenazi synagogue.

He was actually the chief rabbi of the Jewish community of Gibraltar, and the only one in town. He and his family lived in the house fronting the street and thereby shielding the synagogue from public view. His is an official position to which he is elected by the Jewish community as a whole. All problems and questions related to community life as well as religious matters are all referred to him for judgment or advice.

Fig. 29.3: Gibraltar. Synagogue in Bomb House Lane, main facade behind synagogue courtyard wall. Synagogue also known in Spanish as *La Sinagoga de la Muralla*; in Hebrew as *Kahal Kadosh Nefutsot Yehudah* (Holy Congregation of dispersed of Judah).

The congregation of the Synagogue in Engineers Lane, or Har Hashamayim, was founded in the eighteenth century not long after the British takeover of Gibraltar. However, the synagogue building must have been constructed much later; its architectural style, Georgian and with semicircular Palladian windows, may date from late in the eighteenth century or even in the first part of the nineteenth. Inside there were a great number of large crystal chandeliers and silver olive-oil lamps hung by silver chains from the ceiling. In addition to the reading platform in the center of the hall, occupying the entire width of the East wall, there was a monumental Torah Ark with paneled wooden doors and velvet curtains with appropriate Biblical verses embroidered with gold and silver thread.

The third synagogue mentioned by the policeman at the border had various names according to the language I spoke when asking directions. In English, both Jews and gentiles referred to it as "the Synagogue in Bomb House Lane." In Spanish it was referred to as *La Sinagoga de la Muralla* (the Synagogue of the Rampart). One or two other Spanish-speaking informants called it *La Sinagoga Flamenca* (the Flemish Synagogue). Flemish Synagogue, why this name? I never found out, but conjectured that it got this name from the architectural style of its main facade with a quasi-baroque gable of Netherlands inspiration. The synagogue, that is the La Sinagoga Flamenca, I learned also had a Hebrew name, *Kahal Kadosh Nefutsot Yehudah* (Holy Congregation of the Dispersed of Judah), which no one used.

I found the Sinagoga de la Muralla or the Synagogue in Bomb House Lane located on Bomb House Lane and just behind the massive rampart or wall of fortification which lines most of the west side of Gibraltar, thus explaining both its Spanish and English identifications. The synagogue is a freestanding building on a large lot fenced with a high masonry wall. I went through a gate in the wall and found a group of children playing, under the care of a young man. He told me he was the Hebrew teacher and a native from across the strait in Morocco from which he had had to flee because of the recent Jewish persecutions. He graciously offered to show me the interior of the synagogue.

We entered and he turned on all the lights. The interior of this synagogue was even more sumptuously furnished than the Synagogue in Engineers Lane. It was also considerably larger and had a women's gallery on three sides supported on graceful and well-proportioned Tuscan columns of dark marble. It was lighted by the traditional silver olive-oil lamps hung from the ceiling with silver chains as well as crystal chandeliers with electric lights.

The Ark of the Torah at the east end of the hall was of simple neo-classic design. The reader's desk was not in the center of the hall as in more traditional synagogues, but at the east end near the Ark of the Torah. The seating arrangement was also not the traditional one with the pews ranging around three sides facing the reading desk in the center. In modern fashion, the pews were arranged on the longitudinal axis of the hall and faced toward the Ark of the Torah on the East Wall.

As already noted above, this synagogue is also unlike the other two synagogues in that it does not abut on adjacent structures; rather it is located on its own plot of ground surrounded by a high wall enclosing the synagogue courtyard. Except for the west gable, of Flemish neo-Baroque style, the building is not visible from the street. It can best be seen from *la muralla* (rampart wall).

The circumspect or guarded manner in which the synagogues of Gibraltar are shielded from the everyday urban world represents the preservation of medieval Spanish synagogue tradition. Characteristics of this shielding are the separation by a courtyard, an intermediary space between the temporal realm of the city and the spiritual realm of the synagogue, and no direct location on city streets. The Christian authorities, seconded by the secular, would not brook the presence of a synagogue directly on the street as was customary for churches. By decree, synagogues had to be self-effacing, inconspicuous, and never taller than any nearby church. The Jews from North Africa, that is, from Morocco, invited by the British in the eighteenth century to settle there, brought this tradition with them when they re-established Jewish community life in Gibraltar.

How close to this old tradition, then, are the three synagogues of Gibraltar, which, though in a place where Jews are respected British subjects, are still hidden behind houses or surrounded by high walls. Another reason why this tradition has survived in Gibraltar is that of shielding the house of worship from the every-day life of the street on the Sabbath and holidays. Still another reason exists that is rather mundane. The building in front of the synagogue behind Barclay's Bank houses a respectable and venerable British financial institution and belongs to the congregation, so I was informed. The rent the bank pays the congregation is an important source of income for the support of the house of prayer. The house in front of the Synagogue in Engineers Lane is the residence of the official rabbi of the whole Jewish community.

The most important reason for preserving the age-old and traditional setting of the synagogue in the twentieth century, however, is that of propriety. Jews keep the Sabbath on Saturday, and Jewish holidays fall where they will in the civil calendar. With the house of prayer removed from the bustle and noise of the street, away from the work-a-day milieu of the non-Jewish Gibraltarian population, the spirit of the Sabbath or of the holy day is not disturbed by intrusions from the non-Jewish and temporal world outside. Therefore, one can leave the profane world behind for a while and enter the hallowed realm of the spirit on the other side of the wall and there celebrate the Sabbath as if in Zion itself.

Books for Further Reading

This bibliography is intended for the general reader as well as for those who may wish to visit places of Jewish interest in Spain. Some of the works listed are in Spanish and are included because of their importance.

Amador de los Ríos, José. 1960. *Historia social, política, y religiosa de los judíos de España y Portugal* (Social, political, and religious history of the Jews of Spain and Portugal). Madrid and Barcelona: Aguilar.
    Originally published in 1875, this book is one of the first on the subject by a Spaniard. Published also in later editions, particularly in Buenos Aires.

Ashtor, Eliyahu. 1973, 1979, 1984. *The Jews of Moslem Spain*. Philadelphia: The Jewish Publication Society. 3 volumes.
    Scholarly book on a rather obscure period of Jewish history in Spain, based almost entirely on contemporary literary and documentary sources.

Baer, Yitzhak. 1961, 1966. *A History of the Jews of Christian Spain*. Philadelphia: The Jewish Publication Society. 2 volumes.
    Excellent scholarly treatment of Jewish history in medieval Christian Spain. It is based on Baer's book on the same subject, *Die Juden im christlichen Spanien*, Berlin, 1929. 2 volumes.

Baron, Salo W. 1958 to 1983. *A Social and Religious History of the Jews*. Philadelphia and New York: The Jewish Publication Society and the Columbia University Press. 18 volumes.
    See volumes III, pp. 33-46, 244-50 and IV, pp. 27-43, 245-55, for general matters on Spanish Jewish history.

Cantera Burgos, Francisco. 1955. *Sinagogas españolas* (Spanish synagogues). Madrid: Instituto Arias Montano.
    Invaluable guide for the location of medieval synagogues and Jewish communities. Abundant data included on Hebrew inscriptions in synagogues and elsewhere as well as sketch maps of some of the more important *juderías* (Jewish quarters).

Caro Baroja, Julio. 1961. *Los judíos en la España moderna y contemporanea* (The Jews in modern and contemporary Spain). Madrid: Ediciones Arión. 3 volumes.
    Work deals with the post-Expulsion history of the Jews of Spain, both the *marranos* (secret) as well as the sincerely baptized. Replete with illustrative materials, including maps and photographs of Jewish import.

Castro, Américo. 1948. *España en su historia: cristianos, moros, y judíos* (Spain in its history: Christians, Moors, and Jews). Buenos Aires: Editorial Losada.
Author advances some provocative hypotheses concerning the nature of modern Spanish society and the Spanish people in whose history the Jews played a prominent, if not illustrious, part.

Czekelius, Otto. 1931. "Antiguas sinagogas de España" (Ancient Synagogues of Spain) published in *Arquitectura*, Madrid, vol. 13, October.
One of the earliest and one of the few works considering specifically the architecture of the medieval Spanish synagogue. Author deals with the synagogues of El Tránsito and Santa María La Blanca in Toledo, San Pedro in Bembibre, that in Córdoba, the one in Lorca, and also the Synagogue of Santa María La Blanca in Seville.

Grayzel, Solomon. 1965 and later editions. *A History of the Jews*. Philadelphia: The Jewish Publication Society.
See Book Three, chapter III, "The Golden Age in Spain," and also chapter VIII, "Tragedy in Spain," for a succinct account of the history of the Jews in Spain.

Guias Afrodisio Aguada. España (Afrodisio Aguado Guides. Spain). Madrid: Afrodisio Aguada, S.A.
Perhaps the best guide book to Spain. Though written in Spanish, it will be still be useful for those who do not read that language because of the abundance of city maps as well as descriptions of the monuments including the synagogues of Toledo, Córdoba, and Seville.

Guide Michelin. Spain. Published annually in Paris. Good, though small, city maps as well as important information for the tourist traveling by automobile. Little information relative to Jewish monuments or places.

Halperin, Don A. 1969. *The Ancient Synagogues of the Iberian Peninsula*. Gainesville: University of Florida Press.
Short monograph treating the architecture of the medieval Spanish synagogue. Author recapitulates much of the information given by Czekelius (see above) and includes some new renditions of the latter's drawings. Illustrations are from photographs taken by the author.

Jewish Encyclopaedia. 1970 and later. New York and Jerusalem: *Encyclopaedia Judaica* and Macmillan Company, 16 volumes.
See articles listed under various subjects of Spanish Jewish import as well as those for the different cities where Jewish communities existed. See especially the article "Spain" for a concise history of the Jews in Spain down to the present day.

Lowenthal, Marvin. 1938. *A World Passed By*. New York: Behrman's Jewish Book House.

Though written about sixty years ago and dealing with the traces of Jews in Europe as a whole, the chapter on Spain is still useful, in a general way.

Newman, Abraham. 1944. *The Jews in Spain*. Philadelphia: The Jewish Publication Society. 2 volumes.
Scholarly history of the culture and religion of the Jews of Spain.

Postal, Bernard and Samuel H. Abramson. 1973. *The Traveler's Guide to the Jewish Landmarks of Europe*. New York: Fleet Press Corp.
This is a concise guidebook dealing with Jewish landmarks in all of Europe including a chapter on Spain. Includes some data on the contemporary Jewish communities in Madrid, Barcelona, Málaga, and Seville.

Roth, Cecil. 1959. *A History of the Marranos*. Philadelphia: The Jewish Publication Society.
Well-written account of the forcibly baptized secret Jews of Spain and Portugal.

Roth, Cecil. 1960. "The European Age in Jewish History," in Louis Finkelstein, editor, *The Jews: Their History, Culture, and Religion*, 3rd edition. Philadelphia: The Jewish Publication Society, vol. I, pp. 221 ff.
Brief account of Spanish Jewish history.

Sachar, Abram Leon. 1965. *A History of the Jews*, 5th edition. New York: Alfred Knopf.
See chapters XIV, "The Golden Age in Spain," and chapter XVI, "The Decline of Jewish Life in Spain."

Torroba Bernaldo de Quiros, Felipe. 1961. *The Spanish Jews*. Madrid: Rivadeynera, S.A.
Small book of extremely popular character written by a Spanish journalist. Sometimes inaccurate, but always sympathetic to Jews.

Wischnitzer, Rachel. *The Architecture of the European Synagogue*. Philadelphia: The Jewish Publication Society.
Very well-written and profusely illustrated architectural history of the development of the synagogue building in Europe. See chapter 2, "Ark and Bimah: Spain, Italy, Portugal, 12th to 15th centuries."

MAPS: Excellent road maps for the motorist are those published by Firestone Hispania. Best city maps are *Planos Foldex*, published by Editorial Almax, in Madrid: Available only for the major cities of Spain.

Index

Abd-er-Rahman III, 7
    caliphate in Córdoba, 7
advocation of
    La Trinidad, 199
    Nuestra Señora de Belén, 209
    Our Lady of the Transit, 66
    San Lorenzo, 190
    San Miguel, 107
    Santa Isabel, 169, 170
    Santa María del Miracle, 203
    The Holy Cross, 127
    The Holy Ghost, 162
Africa, North, *see* North Africa
Albeneh, Jacob, 61
    and massacre of June 20, 1391, *see*
        massacres, June 20, 1391
Alcazar of
    Alcalá de Guadaire, 104, 106, 108
    Córdoba, 77
    Carmona, 95
    Segovia, 49
    Seville, 113–117, 122, 123
Algeciras, 4
Almohad, 7, 8, 60, 78, 81, 104, 111, 123,
    145, 155, 156
Almoravids, 7, 8, 60, 111, 155
Andalucía, 7, 75, 78, 100, 111, 123, 155,
    181, 207
antisemitism, 59
apocryphal, 5, 30, 61
Aragonese, 207
architectural style elements
    alfarfe (pattern of interlaced moldings),
        53
    alfarje (wood-paneled ceiling), 88
    alfiz, 100
    apse, 14, 85, 118, 120, 162, 164, 165,
        167, 168
    cantilevered, 172, 174, 176

    chamfered, 165, 166, 204
    chancel arch, 52
    clerestory, 52, 53, 62, 64–66, 69, 71
    coffered, 67
    corbel table, 66, 100
    Corinthian capital, 64, 128
    cornice, 66, 100
    lintel, 82, 126
    lobulated, 65, 68, 69, 71, 87, 88
    minaret, 77, 80, 123, 208
    Palladian windows, 220
    pillars, 176, 209
architecture, 1, 2, 29, 46, 57, 65, 79, 85, 109,
    125, 139, 145, 160, 161, 173, 179,
    181, 205, 207, 208, 220, 221
    baroque, 1, 92, 109, 125, 128, 130, 139,
        221
    Burgos, 173, 179, 181
    Córdoba, 79
    Carmona, 96
    Georgian, 220
    Gibraltar, 220, 221
    Gothic, 2, 50, 114, 128, 161, 165, 166,
        168, 173, 176, 179, 181, 188, 195,
        205
    Madrid, 46
    mudéjar, 2, 52, 61, 64–66, 86, 88, 100,
        107, 128–130, 133, 160, 162, 165,
        166, 205, 207
    Romanesque, 185, 188, 191, 197
    Salamanca, 29
    Segovia, 48
    Seville, 92, 109, 125, 128, 131
    Toledo, 57
    Zaragoza, 208
Arco
    Arco de Santa María, 179
    Arco del Mariscal, 38
Arian form of Christianity, 6, 78, 161

Jewish Remnants

Arks
>of the Law, 131
>of the Torah, 2, 15, 52, 53, 62, 67, 68,
>>86–88, 107, 130, 168, 211, 217,
>>220, 221
Asociación Judeo-Cristiana, 3
Averroes the Moslem (1126–1198), 77, 78

Barrio de la, de las; del, de los...
>Espíritu Santo, 163
>Gótico, 192, 195, 200
>Judería, 79
>La Luna, 24
>San Miguel, 104, 108
>Santa Cruz, 8, 109, 110, 112, 113, 120,
>>123
>Triana, 136
Basilica of Nuestra Señora del Pilar, 208
Basque, 5, 159, 183
Bible, 84, 186
Bikur Kholim, 209
Bishop Isidor of Seville, 7
burning of synagogues in, 114

Cabala, 60
Calatrava, 66, 69
Call Judaic (Jews' Street), 190
Calle de la, de las; del, de los...
>29 de Agosto (Béjar), 174
>Abades (Seville), 117
>Aguilas (Seville), 117
>Almuzara (Segovia), 54–56
>Antigua (Béjar), 172, 174
>Archeros (Seville), 128–132
>Arco (Astorga), 11
>Arco de San Ramón del Call
>>(Barcelona), 195, 196, 202
>Argumosa (Madrid), 43
>Baños Nuevos (Barcelona), 20, 21, 196
>Balborraz (Zamora), 19
>Baltasar Bachero (Madrid), 41, 43
>Cúndaro (Gerona), 189–191
>Cabeza del Rey Don Pedro (Seville),
>>117
>Call (Barcelona), 194–197, 199–202
>Cano y Cueto (Seville), 116
>Cervantes, *see* Miguel de Cervantes
>>Saavedra, Cervantes
>Cipriano (Zamora), 22

Compañía (Lérida), 204
Conde de Ibarra (Seville), 121, 122, 133
Condesa Carmen Pizarro (Luceno), 157
Corral del Rey (Seville), 117
Coso (Zaragoza), 208, 209
Don Jaime de Aragón (Zaragoza), 208,
>209
Esteban Domingo (Avila), 37, 39
Fe (Madrid), 41–43
Fermín González (Burgos), 181
Fernández Ruano (Córdoba), 80, 81
Forza (Gerona), 184, 186–191
Fourquet (Madrid), 43
Garcilópez (Ecija), 93, 94
Ignacio Gazapo (Zamora), 18–21
Juan Bravo (Segovia), 49, 54
Judería (Barcelona), 195
Judería (Cazalla de la Sierra), 141
Judería (Madrid), 114
Judería Nueva (Segovia), 54
Judería Vieja (Segovia), 54
López Núñez (Avila), 38, 39
La Vega (Zamora), 24, 26, 27
Leones (Segovia), 54
Levies (Seville), 121, 133
Libreros (Salamanca), 32, 33
Maimonides (Córdoba), 80, 81
Manteca (Zamora), 20, 21
Matías Rodríguez, 10, 11, *see* Calle, del
>Arco (Astorga)
Mateos Gago (Seville), 118, 120, 134
Mayor (Zaragoza), 208, 209
Moneda (Salamanca), 31
Moreno (Zamora), 23
Muerte (Seville), 124, 125
Pimienta (Seville), 117, 123, 124
Ramos Carrión (Zamora), 22, 23
Real (Segovia), 49, 51, 53
Reyes Católicos (Toledo), 61, 65
Ribera del Puente (Salamanca), 33, 34
San Andrés (Lérida), 203, 204
San Bartolomé (Seville), 133
San Blas (Carmona), 97–99
San Clemente (Seville), 131, 132
San Esteban (Seville), 117
San Honoratio (Barcelona), 195–197
San José (Seville), 121, 122, 133
San Lorenzo (Gerona), 190

San Lorenzo (Zaragoza), 209
Santa Agueda (Burgos), 180, 182
Santa Isabel (Plasencia), 43, 169–171
Santa María La Blanca (Seville), 116
Santa Marta (Seville), 120
Santa Teresa (Seville), 128
Santo Domingo del Call (Barcelona),
    195–197, 200–202
Sauco (Segovia), 49
Sierpes (Seville), 157
Sinagoga (Cazalla de la Sierra), 141
Sinagoga (Gerona), 41, 42, 141, 187,
    189, 191, 200, 201
Sinagoga (Madrid), 41
Sinagoga Major (Barcelona), 200, 201
Susona (Seville), 124, 125
Tentenecio (Salamanca), 32–35
Travesía de San Lorenzo (Madrid), 43
Trinidad (Barcelona), 199
Verónica (Zaragoza), 210
Vera Cruz (Salamanca), 32, 33
Verde (Seville), 131, 132
Vida (Seville), 116, 123
Virgen de la Alegría (Seville), 131, 132
Virgen del Monte (Cazalla de la Sierra),
    140, 141
Ximénez (Seville), 128
Zurita (Madrid), 42
Callejón de la, de las; del, de los...
    Agua, 116, 117, 123, 124
    Agua (Seville judería), 116, 117, 123,
    124
    Aragoncillo, 150, 151
    Inquisición, 136, 137, 159
    Judería, 116
Capilla Real, 112
Carmelite Order, 38, 128
Carthusian monastery, 135
Casa de la Panadería, 45
Castile, 8, 16, 24, 37, 47, 49, 59, 68,
    111–114, 154, 159, 179, 181, 185,
    194, 205
Catalonia, 5, 114, 193–195, 203, 205
Celtiberian, 49, 100, 122, 194
Christendom, 77, 123, 149
Comuneros, 170
convents, 50, 51, 128, 133, 217
    Convent of Las Dominicans, 122

Convent of Madre de Dios, 133
Convent of the Incarnation, 38
Convento de Santo Angel, 133
conversion of Jews to Christianity, 100
    Diego de Triana (Seville), 109
    Folktale of pepper tree, 123
    Friar Alonso de Espina (1459 in
        Segovia), 51
    in Barcelona, 199
    in Burgos, 182
    in Carmona, 100
    in Gerona, 188
    in Seville, 136
    in Toledo, 57, 59
    in Zaragoza, 211
    marrano, 45, 94, 100, 114, 124, 136,
        149, 215
    San Vicente Ferrer (Salamanca), 31
    Santa María del Miracle (Lérida), 203
    Santa Teresa of Avila, 39
    Sisebut, Visigoth king (612), 6, 7
    Susona family (Seville), 124
conversion of synagogues into churches
    All Saints (Avila), 39
    Corpus Christi (Segovia), 14, 50–54, 56,
        62, 100
    Espíritu Santo (Cáceres), 162, 164, 165,
        167, 168
    Holy Mary the Virgin, 2
        Seville, 14, 119, 120, 122, 128–130,
        132
        Toledo, 2, 52, 53, 57, 61–66
    La Trinidad (Barcelona), 199
    Nuestra Señora de La Vega (Zamora),
        25, 26
    Our Lady of the Transit (Toledo), 2, 52,
        57, 58, 60, 61, 65–68, 70–74, 85,
        100, 133, 135, 211
    San Blas (Carmona), 96–100
    San Lorenzo (Gerona), 190
    San Miguel (Alcalá de Guardaira), 104,
        105, 107
    San Pedro (Bembibre), 14
    Santa Cruz (Seville), 127
    Santa Isabel (Plasencia), 170
    Santa María del Miracle (Lérida), 203
    Santa María La Blanca, *see* conversion
        of synagogues into churches, Holy

Mary the Virgin
conversos, *see* conversion of Jews to
    Christianity, conversos
Cortijo del Judío (Jew's Ranch or Farm), 112
councils, 6, 57, 144
    City Council of Madrid, 42
    City Council of Vitoria, 183
    Council of Elvira, *see* Council of Illiberis
      (Granada),
    Council of Illiberis, 6, 144
    Council of Nicea, 6
    Eighth Council of Toledo, 59
    Third Council(s) of Toledo, 6
Cross and the Crescent, 8, 149

Day of Atonement, 72, 136
    Kol Nidre prayer, 136, 143
decrees and declarations
    Decree of Expulsion, *see* expulsion,
      Expulsion of 1492
    Fuero de Salamanca, 30
    Generalissimo Francisco Franco's 1949
      decree, 4, 174, 216
    inconspicuous synagogues by decree,
      221
    King Sisebut's evil decree, 6
    Papal Bull (12 May 1415), 189
    Papal Bull, Lyon, France (13 April,
      1250), 89
destruction of
    First Temple of Jerusalem, 5
    Second Temple of Jerusalem, 5, 109
    Spanish Jewry, 92, 94, 186, 198
    synagogues destroyed by Ferrand
      Martínez in
      Alcalá de Guadaira, 92
      Cantillana del Río, 91, 92
      Coria del Río, 92
      Ecija, 92
    Temple of Jerusalem, *see* Tish b'Ab
Disputation of Tortosa in 1414, 211

El Arahal and Puebla de Cazalla, 147
El Cid, 180–182
explorers
    Christopher Columbus, xxxi, 1, 115,
      135, 159, 194, 214
    Francisco Pizarro, 157, 160
    Hernán Cortés, 160

Magellan, 135
    Pedro de Alvarado, 160
expulsion, xxxi, 9, 194
    Expulsion of 1492, xxxi, 3, 5, 19, 25, 33,
      38, 41, 42, 55, 56, 60, 66, 114, 121,
      140, 145, 149, 162, 170, 183, 188,
      209, 213, 215, 218
    pre-, xxxi, 215
extant constructions, 18, 35, 65, 86, 100,
    176, 207, 210

French influence, 7, 128, 181, 185, 194

Germanic hordes, 6, 30, 109
God, 2, 22, 57, 59, 69, 75, 79, 125–127, 136
    Kiddush ha Shem, 57, 107, 125, 132
    Shekhina, 127
Greece, 4, 7, 73, 77, 92, 185

Hebrew inscriptions, 1, 51, 52, 67–72,
    86–88, 111, 125, 133, 184, 185,
    211
history, Jews of Spain in, xxxi, 1, 3, 5, 6, 57,
    77, 134, 156, 162, 207
    Alcalá, 107
    Béjar, 173
    Córdoba, 79
    Gerona, 186
    Granada, 144
    Lucena, 156
    Málaga, 149
    Salamanca, 30
    towns and cities with Jewish names, 173
      Behar, Sephardic family name, 173,
      174
    Zaragoza, 207
Holy Office of the Inquisition, xxxi, 1, 9
    Avila, 38
    Córdoba, 82
    Madrid, 44, 45
    Seville, 114, 125, 136–138
    Torquemada, 1, 136
    Zaragoza, 211

Iberian Peninsula, xxxi, 5, 92, 114, 128, 144,
    181, 207, 215
Instituto Arias Montano, 3
invasions, 127, 128, 149
    Napoleonic, 127, 128

Isaac al-Fasi (Lucena teacher), 156–158
Isaac Makheb (Córdoba Jewish builder), 84,
    87
Islam, 64, 77, 123, 139, 205
    conversion of Jews to, 78
    Giralda of Seville, 123
    in Burgos, 181
    in Gerona, 185
    in Málaga, 149, 155
    in Zaragoza, 208
    mosque of Córdoba, 75, 79
Israel, 33, 53, 56, 57, 63, 69, 70, 79, 84, 111,
    140, 212
Italy, 173, 216

Jesuit, 32, 204, 209, 211
Jesus Christ, 5, 9, 16, 22, 50, 51, 59, 92,
    127, 182, 199
    Host, 2, 50, 51, 53
Jewish cemeteries, 5, 10, 24, 33, 43, 118,
    121, 152, 153, 170, 171, 183–185,
    197, 199
    Judizmendi, 5, 183
    La Cuesta de los Hoyos (Segovia), 55,
        56
    Montjuich, 3, 5, 185, 197, 199
Jewish communities and towns of
    Alcalá de Guadaira, 105, 107
    Astorga, 11
    Avila, 39
    Béjar, 173, 174
    Barcelona, 4, 193, 194, 198, 199, 202
    Bayonne, 183
    Burgos, 182
    Cáceres, 161, 163
    Córdoba, 78, 80
    Carmona, 95, 96, 100
    Cazalla de la Sierra, 140, 141
    Ecija, 92, 93, 95, 100
    Gerona, 185, 188–190
    Gibraltar, 4, 213, 215, 216, 218, 220,
        222
    Granada, 143, 145, 147, 149
    Jerez de la Frontera, 140
    Lérida, 203
    León, 2
    Lucena, 154–156
    Madrid, 3, 42

Paterna area, 111, 140
Plasencia, 170
Salamanca, 30, 32, 36
Segovia, 49, 54, 56
Seville, 4, 93, 109, 111, 113, 114, 119,
    123, 128, 133
Spain, 5, 140
Toledo, 8, 57, 59, 60
Vitoria, 183
Zaragoza, 207, 211, 212
Jewish ghettos, 2, 23, 60, 145
Jewish spoors, 1, 5, 43, 111, 140, 143, 144,
    157, 171
Jews
    Ashkenazic, 4, 199, 214, 220
        Ashkenazim, 4
    notables, 137, 188, 199
    Sephardic, 3, 4, 173, 199
        law promulgated by Primo de Rivera,
            4
        Sephardim, 3, 4, 214

Kaddish, 79, 83
kahal (community), 194, 195, 197, 220, 221
Kahal Kadosh Nefutsot Yehudah (Holy
        Congregation of dispersed of
        Judah), 194, 195, 197, 220, 221
khevra (Zaragoza), 209
Kiddush, 57, 107, 125, 132
kings, warriors, and rulers, 6, 8, 59, 60, 74,
        75, 92, 109, 111, 113, 143, 149,
        181, 182, 188, 194
    Alfonso I, 211
    Alfonso III, 24, 181
    Alfonso IX, 161
    Alfonso VI, 8, 41, 59
    Alfonso VII, 59
    Alfonso X, 8, 60, 65, 111, 140
    Catholic Kings, Ferdinand and Isabella,
        xxxi, 49, 115, 143–145, 149, 159,
        161, 183, 194
    and Columbus voyage of 1492, xxxi
    and Decree of Expulsion of 1492,
        xxxi, 143–145, 183
    and the Expulsion, *see* expulsion, of
        1492
    Charlemagne, 185, 188, 207
    Counts of Barcelona, 185

Emperor Augustus, 5, 207
Emperor Trajan (Roman Empire), 160
Felipe II, 41, 42, 59
Ferdinand I, 194
Ferdinand III, 8, 96
Fernando II, 30
Fernando III, 78, 81, 89, 92, 93, 111, 112, 119, 127–129, 132
Fernando IV, 41
Leovigildo (Cáceres), 161
Musa (Seville), 109, 215
Pedro el Cruel (Toledo), 60, 66, 69, 70, 73, 122, 135
Reccared (Visigoth), 6
Recesvinto (Visigoth), 59

La Costa Brava, 193
La Costa del Sol (Sun Coast), 147, 151
Luis de Santangel (Seville), 115, 137

Maimonides of Córdoba (1135-1204), 7, 75, 77, 78, 80–83, 88, 89, 181
Guide for the Perplexed (Dux Dubitans in Latin and Moreh Nebukhim in Hebrew), 75
Martínez, Ferrand, 92, 105, 113, 114, 119, 120, 186
massacre of, 7, 9, 60, 61, 94, 100, 113, 120, 136, 145, 161, 180, 182, 202, 203, 211
1391 (Alcalá de Guadaira), 107
1391 (Barcelona), 202, 211
1391 (Burgos), 180, 182
1391 (Seville), 120
1391 (Zaragoza), 202, 211
1474 (Carmona), 100
August 13, 1391 (Lérida), 203
by Ferrand Martínez, 113
December 20, 1066 (Córdoba), 145
Ferrand Martínez, *see* Martínez, Ferrand
June 20, 1391 (Carmona), 100
June 20, 1391 (Ecija), 94
June 20, 1391 (Toledo), 61
May 7, 1355 (Toledo), 60
Moorish constructions
Alcazaba, 148, 150–153, 155
Alhambra, 1, 79, 143, 145, 194
Boabdil el Chico, 143

Hall of the Ambassadors, 143, 145
Gibralfaro, 150, 152, 153
Moors and, 89, 214
Jews, 207
recapture of holdings, 215
relinquishing holdings, 89, 92, 161, 207, 211
mountains, 2, 13, 16, 35, 47, 48, 144, 148, 152, 153, 155, 160, 169, 177, 185, 193, 197, 213
Gredos, 169, 177
Jebel al Tarik, 215
Jebel Musa, 215
Pyrenees, 2, 149, 181
Sierra de Guadarrama, 47
Sierra de las Cabras, 148
Sierra Morena, 77
Sierra Nevada, 142, 143

North Africa, 7, 78, 109, 149, 181, 205, 213, 218, 221
Berbers, 7, 78
Moslems, 109

Oriental, 67, 68, 77, 78, 103, 130, 149, 160

pagans, 6
painters
El Greco, 73, 74
Murillo, 116, 127, 128
Valdés Leal, 125–127
Paseo de los Cubos (Burgos), 182
Passover, 59, 147, 177
Patio de las Banderas, 113–116, 118, 123
persecutions, 7, 8, 33, 60, 78, 123, 136, 140, 145, 161, 209
Phoenicians, 5, 77, 78, 149
plagues, 183, 211
Plaza de la, de las; del, de los...
Aguila (Alcalá de Guadaira), 104, 108
Alfaro (Seville), 116
Azoguejo (Segovia), 49
Bulas (Córdoba), 88
Curtidores (Seville), 119
Doña Elvira (Seville), 116
Judería, *see* Calle, de Ignacio Gazapo
Lavapies (Madrid), 41, 42
Manuel Ribé (Barcelona), 196, 200–202
Mayor (Madrid), 42, 44, 45

Mayor (Segovia), 49, 51
Mayor (Zamora), 22
Merced (Salamanca), 30, 31, 54, 55
Merced (Segovia), 30, 31, 54, 55
Mercenarias (Seville), 133
Río (Segovia), 34, 35
Refinadores (Seville), 116
San Jaime (Barcelona), 195–197
Santa Cruz (Seville), 122, 126–128
Santa Lucía (Zamora), 21, 22
Santa María La Blanca (Seville), 128
Santa Marta (Seville), 118, 134
Toros (Málaga), 150
Triunfo (Seville), 113, 114, 116, 118, 122
Verónica (Zaragoza), 209
Victoria (Málaga), 148
Vida (Seville), 123
Virgen de los Reyes (Seville), 118, 120, 134
poets
Judah ha Levi (Toledo), 89, 156–158
Manolo Machado (Andalusian), 78
Moses Ibn Ezra (Granada), 146
Solomon Ibn Gabirol (Granada), 146
pogroms in, 9, 66, 100
Burgos, 182
Cáceres, 163, 165
Carmona, 100
Ecija, 94, 100
Gerona, 185, 186
Seville, 119, 127
Toledo, 61
Pope Innocent IV, 89
Province of Betis, 144
Psalms, 64, 68–72, 79, 85
Puerta de la, de las; del, de los...
Almodóvar, 79, 81
Almohade, 106
Almohade (Alcalá de Guadaira), 106
Carmona, 117
Carne, *see* Puerta, de la Judería
Judíos, 79, 81
Judería, 116, 118, 121, 132
San Vicente, 38, 39
Sevilla, 96
Puerto de la, de las; del, de los..., 47, 135, 148, 155
León, 148, 155

Mulas, 135
Navacerrada, 47

rabbis, 51, 84, 87, 198, 218, 220, 222
racial issues, 9, 207, 211, 215
Rambam (Rav Moshe ben Maimon), *see* Maimonides of Córdoba (1135–1204)
Reconquest of Spain from Moslem domination (13th century), 7–9, 42, 61, 79, 96, 103, 114, 115, 123, 144, 162, 173, 207, 211
Effect on Jewish population, 7–9, 42, 211
regions of Spain
Andalucía, 7, 77, 78, 92, 114, 139–141, 153, 157–159, 161, 165, 173, 181, 195, 214
Jerez de la Frontera, 140, 141, 159, 160, 214
Sanlúcar de Barrameda, 159, 214
Basque, 5, 159, 183
Castile, 8, 16, 37, 47, 59, 68, 113, 114, 159, 179, 181, 194, 205
El Aljarafe, 111, 159, 160
Extremadura, 159–161
Los Monegros, 205
rivers, 13–15, 18–22, 30, 33–36, 49, 56, 92, 99, 104, 135–138, 142, 159, 161, 184, 185, 188, 191, 204, 205, 208
Acera del Darro (Granada), 142, 145
Adaja (Avila), 37
Arlazón (Burgos), 179
Cinca (Zaragoza), 205
Clamores (Segovia), 49, 55, 56
Duero (Zamora), 19, 21
Ebro (Zaragoza), 206, 207
Esla (Zamora), 16
Genil (Ecija), 91, 94
Guadaira (Alcalá de Guadaira), 103–106
Guadalhorce (Lucena), 155
Guadalquivir (Córdoba), 75
Guadalquivir (Seville), 111, 135, 138
villages along Guadalquivir River, 91, 92
Guadiana (Cáceres), 160
Jerte (Plasencia), 169
Manzanares (Madrid), 42

Odiel, 159
Onyar (Gerona), 184, 188, 191
Segre (Lérida), 203
Tagus (Toledo), 61, 65
Tinto, 159
Tormes (Salamanca), 29, 34
Roman, 5, 6, 25, 104, 123, 160
   aqueducts, 49
   Barcelona, 194
   bridges, 29, 33, 34, 36, 106
   Cáceres, 161
   Córdoba, 78
   Catholicism, 6, 78
   domination of the Iberian Peninsula, 5
   Empire, 6, 160
   fortresses, 104
   Gerona, 185
   Granada, 144
   Lucena, 155, 158
   Málaga, 149
   Province of Lusitania, 160
     Emerita Augusta (Mérida), 160, 161
   settlements with possible Jewish
     connection
     Córdoba, 78
     Ecija, 92
     Elche, 5
     Granada, 144
     in Toletum, 57
     Lucena, 155, 158
     Salamantica, 29
     Seville, 109
     Zaragoza, 207
   Seville, 96, 109, 113, 155
   walls, 11, 23, 24, 96, 161, 207, 208
   Zaragoza, 207, 208
Rome, 30, 77, 149
Rosh ha Shonah, 72

Sabbath, 21, 31, 36, 57, 59, 195, 198, 218,
   219, 222
sacristan, 15
Sagrado Corazón de Jesús, 15, 16
Salón Tinell, 193–195
Samuel ha Levi Abulafia
   and Palace of Samuel ha Levi, 58, 73,
   74

   and Pedro el Cruel, 61, 65, 66, 69, 70,
     73, 74, 135
   as builder of Synagogue of El Tránsito,
     9, 68, 73
   reorganized the tax-collecting system,
     74
School of the True Cross, 31
shamas, 15, 16
Shar Hashamayim, 219, 220
Star of David, 133
Straits of Gibraltar, 214
Subida de la Coracha, 150–153

Talmud, 60, 156, 158, 186, 209
Tarifa, 214, 215
Tetragrammaton, 126
Thirty-sixth International Congress of
   Americanists, 193
Tish b'Ab, 114
towers of
   Alcalá de Guadaira, 104
   Avila, 37
   Córdoba, 80
   Carmona, 95, 97
   Ecija, 61, 91, 92
   Gerona, 185, 188
   Salamanca, 31, 32, 34–36
   Segovia, 55
   Seville, 109, 114, 122, 123, 135
     Church of San Bartolomé, 11, 119,
      131, 132
     Giralda, 91, 109, 112, 114, 118, 122,
      123, 127, 134, 135
     Torre del Oro, 74, 135, 137
   Toledo, 68
   Zamora, 16
   Zaragoza, 207, 208
traditional synagogue functions
   beth ha knesseth (house of assembly),
     107
   beth ha midrash (house of study), 107
   beth ha tefillah (house of prayer), 107

Visigoth, xxxi, 2, 6, 7, 25, 30, 57, 59, 60, 78,
   92, 109, 113, 122, 123, 128, 130,
   144, 149, 161, 185, 194, 207
   Lex Romana Visgothorum (Roman Law
     of the Visigoths), 6

war, 4, 11, 14, 16, 77, 112, 149, 161, 213, 215, 216

writers, philosophers, and historians

    Américo Castro, 3

    Angel Pulido, 3

    Fidel Fita, 3

    Francisco Cantera Burgos, 2, 3

    Gil González Dávila, 31

    José Amador de los Ríos, 3

    José María Vallicrosa, 3

    Julio Caro Baroja, 3, 38

Maimonides, Rambam (Rav Moshe ben Maimon), *see* Maimonides of Córdoba (1135–1204)

Miguel de Cervantes Saavedra (writer), 157, 186, 187, 189–191

    Calle de Cervantes, 186, 187, 190, 191

    Traversía de Cervantes, 190, 191

Salo Baron, 2

Ytzhak Baer, 2

Yom Kippur, *see* Day of Atonement